The Unofficial Trollope

BILL OVERTON

Lecturer in English, Loughborough University

THE HARVESTER PRESS · SUSSEX

BARNES & NOBLE BOOKS · NEW JERSEY

First published in Great Britain in 1982 by
THE HARVESTER PRESS LIMITED
Publisher: John Spiers
16 Ship Street, Brighton, Sussex

and in the USA by
BARNES & NOBLE BOOKS
81 Adams Drive, Totowa, New Jersey 07512

British Library Cataloguing in Publication Data

Overton, Bill
   The unofficial Trollope.
   1. Trollope, Anthony – Criticism and interpretation
   I. Title
   823'.8   PR5687

   ISBN 0-7108-0455-5

Library of Congress Cataloging in Publication Data

Overton, Bill.
   The unofficial Trollope.

   Includes bibliographical references and index.
   1. Trollope, Anthony, 1815-1882. 2. Novelists,
English – 19th century – Biography. I. Title.
PR5686.O9 1982   823'.8 [B]   82-4288
ISBN 0-389-20302-5   AACR2

Typeset in 11 point AM Baskerville
and printed in Great Britain by
Photobooks (Bristol) Ltd
Barton Manor, St Philips, Bristol

Contents

Texts cited

As there is no standard edition of Trollope, I refer to the Oxford University Press' World's Classics series as being the most complete and most accessible edition available; and to Trollope's *An Autobiography*, in the same series, revised by Frederick Page. Where no World's Classics edition exists, I refer to the first edition. All quotations are identified by page numbers, with volume numbers where necessary, in parentheses immediately after the reference. Quotations from *The Letters of Anthony Trollope*, edited by Bradford Allen Booth (London and New York, Oxford University Press, 1951), are identified in the same way. N. John Hall's new edition of the *Letters* had not been published when I completed this book, so I have included dates to aid reference to it.

Trollope wrote so many novels that a chronological list is a help. The one below is in order of book publication, and includes dates of composition. It is based on similar lists in Michael Sadleir (1927), *Trollope: A Commentary*, London, Constable, (revised 1945); reprinted London and New York, Oxford University Press, 1961, and in P. D. Edwards (1977), *Anthony Trollope: His Art and Scope*, St. Lucia, Queensland, Queensland University Press; Hassocks, Sussex, Harvester Press; and New York, St Martin's Press, 1978.

Chronology of Trollope's Novels

The Macdermots of Ballycloran, 3 vols., London: Newby, 1847. Written 1843-5.
The Kellys and the O'Kellys, 3 vols., 1848. Written 1847. WC,*
1929.
* WC=World's Classics edition.

La Vendée, 3 vols., London, Colburn, 1850. Written 1849.

The Warden, 1 vol., 1855. Written 1852-4? (see Chapter 2, below). WC (1918), 1969.

Barchester Towers, 3 vols., 1857. Written 1855-6. WC (1925), 1966.

The Three Clerks, 3 vols., 1858. Written 1857. WC (1907), 1952.

Doctor Thorne, 3 vols., 1858. Written 1857-8. WC (1926), 1963.

The Bertrams, 3 vols., London: Chapman & Hall, 1859. Written 1858.

Castle Richmond, 3 vols., London: Chapman & Hall, 1860. Written 1859-60.

Framley Parsonage, 3 vols., 1861. Written 1859-60. WC (1926), 1961.

Orley Farm, 2 vols., 1862. Written 1860-1. WC (1935), 1970.

Rachel Ray, 2 vols., 1863. Written 1863. WC 1924.

The Small House at Allington, 2 vols., 1864, Written 1862-3. WC (1939), 1963.

Can You Forgive Her?, 2 vols., 1864. Written 1863-4. WC (1938), 1968.

Miss Mackenzie, 2 vols., 1865. Written 1864. WC, 1924.

The Belton Estate, 3 vols., 1866. Written 1865. WC (1923), 1969.

Nina Balatka, 2 vols., 1867. Written 1865. WC with *Linda Tressel* (1946), 1951.

The Last Chronicle of Barset, 2 vols., 1867. Written 1866. WC (1932), 1967.

The Claverings, 2 vols., 1867. Written 1864. WC (1924), 1951.

Linda Tressel, 2 vols., 1868. Written 1867. WC with *Nina Balatka* (1946), 1951.

Phineas Finn, 2 vols., 1869. Written 1866-7. WC (1937), 1969.

He Knew He Was Right, 2 vols., 1869. Written 1867-8. WC (1948), 1963.

The Vicar of Bullhampton, 1 vol., 1870. Written 1868. WC (1924), 1963.

The Struggles of Brown, Jones and Robinson, 1 vol., London, Smith, Elder, 1870. Written 1857, 1861.

Sir Harry Hotspur of Humblethwaite, 1 vol., 1871. Written 1868-9. WC, 1928.

Ralph the Heir, 3 vols., 1871. Written 1869. WC, 1939.

The Golden Lion of Granpère, 1 vol., 1872. Written 1867. WC, 1946.

The Eustace Diamonds, 3 vols., 1873. Written 1869–70. WC (1930), 1968.

Phineas Redux, 2 vols., 1874. Written 1870–1. WC (1937), 1964.

Lady Anna, 2 vols., 1874. Written 1871. WC (1936), 1950.

Harry Heathcote of Gangoil, 1 vol., London, Sampson, Low, 1874. Written 1873.

The Way We Live Now, 2 vols., 1875. Written 1873. WC (1941), 1968.

The Prime Minister, 4 vols., 1876. Written 1874. WC (1938), 1968.

The American Senator, 3 vols., 1877. Written 1875. WC (1931), 1962.

Is He Popenjoy?, 3 vols., 1878. Written 1874–5. WC (1944), 1965.

An Eye for an Eye, 2 vols., London: Chapman & Hall, 1879. Written 1870.

John Caldigate, 3 vols., 1879. Written 1877. WC (1946), 1952.

Cousin Henry, 2 vols., 1879. Written 1878. WC, 1929.

The Duke's Children, 3 vols., 1880. Written 1876, revised 1878 (see Chapter 3, below). WC (1938), 1963.

Dr. Wortle's School, 2 vols., 1881. Written 1879. WC (1928), 1951.

Ayala's Angel, 3 vols., 1881. Written 1878. WC (1929), 1968.

Kept in the Dark, 2 vols., London, Chatto & Windus, 1882. Written 1880.

Marion Fay, 3 vols., London, Chapman & Hall, 1882. Written 1878–9.

The Fixed Period, 2 vols., Edinburgh and London, Blackwood, 1882. Written 1880–1.

Mr. Scarborough's Family, 3 vols., 1883. Written 1881. WC, 1946.

The Landleaguers, 3 vols., London, Chatto & Windus, 1883. Written 1882 but unfinished.

An Autobiography, 2 vols., 1883. Written 1876. WC (1923); revised edition (1953), 1968.

An Old Man's Love, 2 vols., 1884. Written 1882. WC (1936), 1951.

Preface

The purpose of this book is to take stock of Trollope's work one hundred years after his death. Briefly, I shall argue for the value of an unofficial side to his fiction, working beneath and at times contradicting the beliefs he maintained explicitly. And, taking seriously the word 'chronicles' which he often applied to his novels, I shall try to show what they have to tell both officially and unofficially about Victorian Britain.

The book is organised simply. First comes a short introduction to the idea of an unofficial Trollope, followed by two chapters describing in detail how the kind of fiction he wrote was shaped by the expedients he adopted and developed in order to become a successful writer. These chapters include an examination of his methods of composing and revising, showing how they bear on the relation in him between businessman and novelist as well as how the unofficial element in his fiction was released. Chapters 4 and 5 present two of the main channels through which the unofficial Trollope found expression. They pursue from opposite angles an imaginative pattern that runs throughout his work, first by surveying the whole body of his fiction, then by concentrating on a single passage. By 'pattern' I don't mean something abstract, so the chapters also explore what it adds up to as a response to the history, social as well as personal, that Trollope lived; and they offer comparisons with other Victorian novelists. The last two chapters discuss Trollope's more direct and explicit representations of his world. Chapter 6 is about the official view reflected in novels which tie themselves to ideology. Chapter 7 considers Trollope's unofficial challenges to conventional thinking, and argues that it is in its relation to ideology that his special kind of realism has to be seen. The limitations as well as the successes of that realism provide a final pointer to Trollope's value as a novelist, a question each chapter puts in a different way. To this I hope the whole book contributes a coherent answer.

I wish to thank Sidney Sussex College, Cambridge for the research fellowship which helped me to consolidate and advance previous work I had done on Trollope; and the British Academy and its Small Grants Research Fund in the Humanities for an award which enabled me to study Trollope's manuscripts at Princeton University, New York, and at Oxford. I also wish to record my gratitude to Mr. Robert H. Taylor of Princeton, to the Carl and Lily Pforzheimer Foundation, Inc., in respect of the Carl H. Pforzheimer Library in New York, to the Beinecke Rare Book and Manuscript Library, Yale University, and to the Bodleian Library. This is not only for permission to study Trollope manuscripts but to publish some of my findings. In addition I have been greatly helped by the staff of the institutions I have named and of the following: the Taylor and Parrish Collections at Princeton University, Cambridge University Library, the Pilkington Library of Loughborough University (especially its Inter-Library Loan Department), and the Berg Collection of the New York Public Library, where I was allowed to examine the manuscript of Trollope's *Miss Mackenzie*.

Earlier versions of Chapters 4 and 5 and of part of Chapter 2 have appeared elsewhere, respectively as 'Self and Society in Trollope', in *ELH: A Journal of English Literary History*, **45**, 1978, 285–302; as 'Trollope: An Interior View', in *Modern Language Review*, **71**, 1976, 489–99; and as 'Trollope's Irish Fiction', in *1837–1901: Journal of the Loughborough Victorian Studies Group*, **2**, 1977, 1–7. This material is included here by kind permission of the editors and, in the first case, of the Johns Hopkins University Press.

I could not have completed this book without much help and support from my wife Susan, and to her it is dedicated.

1 Introduction: The Unofficial Trollope

Trollope Redux has been the unspoken subtitle of most critical writing on Trollope since at least Michael Sadleir's *Commentary*. No Victorian author can have enjoyed such frequent attempts at rehabilitation – or is in so much need of it, as each new try effectively witnesses. There is, then, a 'Trollope problem', and it looks like a problem of evaluation. Most recent writers on Trollope assume or claim outright that he is a major Victorian novelist.[1] Yet at the same time, for apparently the strongest of reasons, other critics enter severe reservations. To take only one example, Terry Eagleton declares that Trollope's work 'bathes in a self-consistent, blandly undifferentiated ideological space', whose aesthetic is 'an anaemic, naïvely representational "realism" which is merely a reflex of common-place bourgeois empiricism'.[2] Even without benefit of translation, this doesn't sound too flattering. Yet the nub of Eagleton's charge is in keeping with a repeated criticism from Trollope's own time to the present: that he takes too much for granted to challenge imagination as a major writer should.[3]

What is extraordinary about Trollope's reputation is this gap between confident, wholehearted acceptance and downright contemptuous rejection. Nothing like it occurs with any other Victorian novelist, and for this reason it isn't to be explained simply by the various biases of profession, culture, or politics maintained by each critic. But the problem, I suggest, isn't at root one of evaluation. Its source is rather a division within Trollope as novelist. This division is between two separate and distinct kinds of consciousness. On the one side there is what Trollope said either in his own person or in his conventional role as narrator and commentator in his fiction. On the other side is what emerges from the structure of individual novels, and of his

1

fiction as a whole. Peter K. Garrett expresses the distinction concisely when he remarks that in *Can You Forgive Her?* the complexity of presentation 'far exceeds the narrator's powers of summary generalization'.[4] By and large, Trollope's recent supporters respond to the complexity, his detractors to the conventional mode and surface statements. But a proper assessment of Trollope needs to take into account both elements, and especially their relationship. Separate and distinct as they may be, they stemmed nevertheless from one man and from the sum of his imaginative and other experience. I shall be arguing for the importance and value of the unofficial Trollope, who finds expression indirectly and in part through what Garrett calls the 'complexity of presentation' in the fiction. This unofficial element I define as that level of awareness implied in the novels which reaches beyond their writer's ordinary thinking. But the unofficial can be understood only in relation to the official, and the coexistence of both elements has to play a major part in determining Trollope's value.

Trust the tale not the teller, then. But Lawrence's familiar dictum applies with special force to a novelist whose erratic judgment of his own work often displays a striking dissociation between what he could imagine and what he could formulate and discuss. If Trollope's critics have had trouble telling where his achievement consists, the writer had still more. In his *Autobiography* he obstinately defended two of his worst novels, *La Vendée* and *The Struggles of Brown, Jones and Robinson* (69–70, 138). He preferred *The Three Clerks* to *The Warden* and *Barchester Towers* (96), *Nina Balatka* to *The Eustace Diamonds* (296). It can only be hoped that he wrote with tongue in cheek when he wondered whether the cardboard scenes of his play *The Noble Jilt* might not be 'the brightest and best work' he had ever done (75). Certainly he hedged his bets on that score. In one place he declares that one of his travel works, *The West Indies and the Spanish Main*, was 'the best book that has come from my pen' (111). Elsewhere, however, he calls *The Last Chronicle of Barset* 'the best novel I have written' (236). Perhaps there's a distinction between 'book' and 'novel', as he repeated his opinion of *The Last Chronicle* to a friend (*Letters*, p. 317, 1 May 1874), but if so he didn't explore it. Instead he complicated the issue further by saying that his development of characters in the

Palliser series was 'the best work of my life' (159). This suggests
at least a view expressed by most of his supporters – that his
special skill lay in characterisation. Trollope tells how he
recognised this from his success with *The Warden* (85), and it
governs his idea of what, if anything, he might be remembered
by (310). Characterisation is, too, the quality he always
emphasises in discussing novel-writing. Yet for all its importance it's a limited and in some ways a misleading criterion. It
was on this ground that Trollope dismissed Dickens, and over-
rated Thackeray's *Henry Esmond*.

One reason why Trollope was wrong about his failures is that
in discussing his novels he couldn't stand outside his official self.
What his inferior works have in common is their expression of
raw ideology. *La Vendée* idealises the landed estate, and
recommends, sixty years on, a restored French monarchy.
Brown, Jones and Robinson is an attempt at a humorous satire on
commercial dishonesty. The theme is central to *The New
Zealander*, Trollope's neglected tract for his times which first saw
print only recently,[5] and also to his official message in other
works, particularly at the same period: *The Three Clerks, Doctor
Thorne, The Bertrams, Orley Farm*, and later *The Way We Live Now*.
But the satire is only too obvious; the moral message too often
trite. Trollope had little capacity for dramatising ideas, though
the ideas his work suggests are frequently subtle and fertile. *The
Fixed Period*, a late work about compulsory euthanasia, and the
unfinished *Landleaguers*, about English policy in Ireland, are
further examples. Also, perversely to his credit, Trollope was
notably bad at adapting his work to what he thought was the
market. *Marion Fay* was an attempt to re-establish himself in
another vein after it had become clear that *The Prime Minister*
had failed. Trollope's working plan for the novel suggests it was
meant to differ from his usual work because, uniquely, it
emphasises plot rather than character.[6] Untypically sentimental
and melodramatic, the novel points to a difference between the
official self who drew up the plan and the imagination which
could only fleetingly realise it.

It is in his practical criticism that Trollope seems least in
touch with his own writing. The fault of *The Claverings*, he
bluntly charges, is the weakness of its hero (*Autobiography*, 169).
Yet this is to accept the same trite assumptions about conven-

tional heroes that he had repudiated in the novel itself (295–6) and elsewhere (e.g. in *The Eustace Diamonds*, 313–17). His discussion of *Phineas Finn* is disarmingly obtuse on two major points. He says it was a blunder to take his hero from Ireland because it was difficult to obtain sympathy 'for a politician belonging to a nationality whose politics are not respected in England' (*Autobiography*, 272). Perhaps this hindered the character's popularity with English readers, but the same argument shows why for the novel Trollope's instinct was right. Phineas Finn's interest stems largely from the insecurity of his political life, and one reason for that insecurity is that he is Irish. Again, Trollope says he botched the novel's ending by having Phineas marry his Irish fiancée. But the point of the ending is that Phineas reaffirms his integrity which he has all but compromised. This he does through his marriage as well as through resigning on an Irish issue and returning to Ireland. Trollope's eye to popularity in the first of these criticisms on *Phineas Finn* helps explain his readiness to condemn *He Knew He Was Right*. Here he observes: 'It was my purpose to create sympathy for the unfortunate man who, while endeavouring to do his duty to all around him, should be led constantly astray by his unwillingness to submit his own judgement to the opinion of others' (*Autobiography*, 276). This is fair enough for a capsule summary, though the novel's title does almost as well, but the extraordinary thing is that Trollope rejected the book because his readers found little with which to sympathise. With a criterion as woolly and spineless as this he wrote off all his psychological insight. Henry James, in a fine tribute, was to recognise the novel as one of Trollope's best:[7] its author panned it in half a paragraph.

Some of Trollope's statements about his own work are almost inexplicable. Of *Orley Farm*, for instance, he observes that the plot is probably his best but that 'it has the fault of declaring itself, and thus coming to an end too early in the book' (*Autobiography*, 143). Yet the reader knows very well that Lady Mason forged her husband's Will long before Trollope confirms this, as the narrator recognises in his commentary (*Orley Farm*, II, 42). P. D. Edwards has claimed that Trollope leaves the issue marginally in doubt for a tiny gain in suspense.[8] But this is very unlikely, since as Edwards says Trollope's opening description of Lady Mason drops several hints, and it isn't long before her own lawyer suspects the truth. Where suspense comes into play in *Orley Farm* is in questions of finer interest than the bare fact of guilt. The reader wants to know whether Lady Mason will confess, and if so how, and then how others will respond to her. These questions the narrative encompasses, but the author in his summary comments couldn't appreciate the subtlety of his achievement. Further examples of the same kind could be added, and they can't all be put down to carelessness, a bad memory, diffidence or its twin, bravado. Not all writers are perceptive critics of their own work, nor should this be surprising. Criticism is as different an activity from writing as playing a game is from talking about it, and it isn't very often that the two skills are developed equally. Trollope can offer good practical advice on writing, for instance on how to manage dialogue;[9] and his comments on how he saw his characters are usually astute, as when he sketches his idea of Plantagenet Palliser (*Autobiography*, 307–09). But the opinions he has to contribute on his own work demonstrate again and again that he had unusually little articulate sense of its qualities and value.

An equally sharp discrepancy shows up between some of Trollope's official beliefs and what is witnessed to by his writing. The clearest example is what he thought about the role of women. Here his convictions remained aggressively conventional throughout his life. They are adequately represented by a lecture on 'The Higher Education of Women' which he produced at the height of the emancipation debate in the late 1860s. The lecture belies its title; as Trollope recognises in his closing remarks, he has little to say about education. What he does say is confined to education for ornament, charity and household management – in that order. The lecture is really a homily on duty, and at the time it was given it could mean only one thing: know your place. That, to Trollope, was God-given, so the emancipation movement could have no other motive than 'a certain noble jealousy and high-minded ambition on the part of a certain class of ladies who grudge the other sex the superior privileges of manhood'. For the same reason he had already refused, in *North America*, what he allowed was logic 'so conclusive . . . that it admits of no answer' in favour of political rights for women. He would only add that 'the mutual good relations between men and women, which are so indispensable

to our happiness, require that men and women should not take
to voting at the same time and on the same result'.[10] He was
writing nearly a decade before the introduction of secret voting
– which he opposed. Even so, his main motive for denying
political rights to women was his conviction in the supremacy of
men, which he said was as certain to him 'as the eternity of the
soul' (*Letters*, p. 418, 4 April 1879). A woman had therefore to
submit herself in marriage, as he did not hesitate to argue with
Kate Field, the young American feminist who was so dear to
him. He closed his chapter in *North America* on 'The Rights of
Women' with a characteristically blunt epigram: 'The best right
a woman has is the right to a husband.'[11]

These forthright pronouncements of Trollope the man find
echoes in much of his fiction. Alice Vavasor, in *Can You Forgive
Her?*, is stated to hold 'some undefined idea of the importance to
her of her own life' (I, 134). To this the narrator has a pat
answer: 'Fall in love, marry the man, have two children, and
live happy ever afterwards.' Miss Mackenzie, in the novel
named after her that Trollope wrote next, isn't even allowed to
live as a spinster. His ingenuous plot first makes her an heiress,
then takes all her money away so that she has to depend on the
chivalry of the man who had earlier proposed to her. It's hard to
believe Trollope's profession in the *Autobiography* (162) that he
was trying to write a novel without love. Ten years on, in *Is He
Popenjoy?*, he mounted his crudest attack on women's emancipation, with cartoon cut-outs in Baroness Bannman and Olivia Q.
Fleabody and an institution called the Female Disabilities. The
message, as so often in his fiction, is that a woman accepting her
place has her proper influence through home and husband.

Trollope's official view is then reinforced both by his design
in his novels and by explicit remarks in their telling. Yet the
pattern to emerge from what his female characters experience is
quite different. One common factor is their powerlessness: Linda
Tressel, who 'had not learned to recognise the fact of her own
individuality' (*Linda Tressel*, 297), never has a chance. She is
stifled to death not just by the intransigence of her aunt and the
insensitivity of the husband arranged for her, but by her lover's
masterful arrogance and the indifference of all around. This
extreme example is echoed in Lucinda Roanoke's breakdown,
caused by her forced engagement (in *The Eustace Diamonds*), and

by the literal imprisonment of John Caldigate's wife (in *John Caldigate*). What sharpens the point in each case is that a woman is actually the tyrant, even as both she and her victim suffer from the ideology she enforces: Trollope knew the psychological compensations a sense of inferiority would supply. Lily Dale vows, once jilted, to stay an old maid; Emily Wharton, in *The Prime Minister*, clings to her self-mortification for having married the wrong man. Even *Miss Mackenzie*, for all its inadequacies, communicates a sense of the heroine's isolation and lack of practical knowledge – a condition shared by that very different person Lizzie Eustace in *The Eustace Diamonds*. Trollope shows no signs whatever of respecting the arguments advanced by J. S. Mill in *On The Subjection of Women* in 1869. Yet, as Juliet McMaster has pointed out, *He Knew He Was Right* illustrates in the same year the legal prejudice by which a husband's rights greatly outweighed his wife's regarding custody of a child.[12]

These are female disabilities of a different order from those mocked by the same phrase in *Is He Popenjoy?* Trollope didn't abandon his opinions, he simply failed to attend to the lessons his own work might have taught him. Again and again his fiction reaches beyond its conventional premises. He will start out from a bland moralism – that a woman's place is in marriage, or that marriage for ambition is wrong – but these simplifications the novels soon disarm. Despite Trollope's no-nonsense rebuke to Alice Vavasor, the reader of *Can You Forgive Her?* soon wonders why forgiveness is a problem. It's the novelist, contradicting his spokesman, who has shown that her fiancé's torpid dominance, his refusal to see her point of view, is intolerable. In *The Claverings* Trollope spares no rhetoric when Lady Ongar tries to enjoy the fruits of having sold herself into marriage. He can't, however, neutralise the strongest and most admirable character of his novel, any more than he can help showing how shabbily she is punished.[13] Similarly, Lady Laura Kennedy comes to grief by marrying in order to gain political influence a man she doesn't love. John Sutherland has noted the link here with Mill;[14] the point is that though Trollope disapproved of the act officially, he sympathetically presented its motive. Lady Laura's need for independence, her muted rebellion against constraints, form only the principal statement of a theme playing throughout the Palliser novels from Alice Vavasor to Lady Glencora,

Violet Effingham to Madame Max Goesler, and finally to Lady Mabel Grex.[15] It's hard to imagine how so continuously sensitive an account could have cohabited mentally with such raucous prejudice elsewhere. (There's a caricature feminist in *He Knew He Was Right* as well as in *Is He Popenjoy?*) The contradiction proves how remote Trollope was from his unofficial self. He could vividly imagine, and realise in his writing, what the position of a woman entailed, yet he had no ear for the conclusion crying out to be drawn: that women might have abilities which only a career could fulfil.

There are two essential reasons why Trollope stubbornly maintained his prejudices in the face of what his own work should have told him. The first may be expressed as a general law: the messages of fiction differ from those of proposition. A poem, play or novel is formed according to principles quite other than those which govern the expression of an opinion or the construction of an argument. The tale not the teller is to be trusted, because as an imagined whole the tale, if it convinces, brings into activity a field of resources richer than can be mustered by didactic intent or deliberated conviction. This provides a further explanation why writers aren't necessarily reliable guides to their own work. It also helps clarify how, famously, novelists such as Scott, Balzac and Tolstoy contradict in their writing their explicit social and political views.[16]

The second reason is more specific and is bound up with Trollope's own history and personality. One effect of the isolation and exclusion he underwent in early life, recorded in his *Autobiography*, was an impulse to conform. So, despite his pugnacity, his personal style of militant independence, one part of him was always ready to embrace the conventional line, repeat the reach-me-down prejudice – especially when conscious of what his market would expect. In *The Claverings* his hero pronounces: 'No man has a right to be peculiar. Every man is bound to accept such usage as is customary in the world' (232); and though Trollope has acknowledged that the speaker is hardly heroic, it isn't clear that he intends any irony. But at the same time, as *The Claverings* also shows, he could penetrate the deceptions and expose the inequities of conventional thinking.

His presentation of Jewish characters illustrates how he oscillated between prejudice and understanding. For some years an argument has flickered in and out of books and journals as to whether or not Trollope was anti-Semitic. Philip Hobsbaum has led the prosecution,[17] and his anger appears not without cause. Trollope's repeated attacks on Disraeli invariably sound racial overtones, whether the man himself or Daubeny, his surrogate in the Palliser novels, is in question. Then there are the moneylenders of several novels, notably *Mr. Scarborough's Family*, Ferdinand Lopez in *The Prime Minister*, and most of all Joseph Emilius – whom Trollope not only caricatures grossly in *The Eustace Diamonds*, but transforms into an implausible murderer in *Phineas Redux*. Trollope plainly associated Jews with his pet obsession: dishonesty in commerce and politics. But Trollopians have sprung to the defence. They cite a sympathetic presentation of Jews in *Nina Balatka* and in Ezekiel Brehgert of *The Way We Live Now*.[18] Some argue that Lopez is more complex than the stereotype would suggest.[19] And R. C. Terry quotes an approving testimony from the author himself, that he had 'invariably found Jews to be more liberal than other men'.[20] It looks as if the defence has a case worth arguing too.

One way of solving the problem is suggested by Edgar Rosenberg's study of Jewish stereotypes in *From Shylock to Svengali*.[21] It's unfortunate that this excellent book should have figured so little in the debate on Trollope's alleged anti-Semitism, though it has long been available. Rosenberg places Trollope's treatment of Jews in its literary and historical context, which casts a much clearer light on how the novelist handled the stereotypes. The conclusion he enables is that Trollope's image of the Jew runs the gamut from prejudice to enlightenment. On the one hand there is what he says of Disraeli ('People cannot suddenly be made great and good by the wisdom of a Jew' in *The New Zealander* [27]), or of Emilius in *The Eustace Diamonds* ('a nasty, greasy, lying, squinting Jew preacher' [667]). These are stock figures, set up to be knocked down, and they represent Trollope's readiness to exploit the stereotype at its most strident. On the other hand there are the characters with whom, as he says in his *Autobiography*, he lived and became intimate; and these tell a different story. As Rosenberg indicates, Jewish characters, even at Trollope's most sympathetic in *Nina Balatka* and *The Way We Live Now*, never wholly escape the stereotypes, but they show a level of understanding on Trollope's part that, at least on the evidence of these novels, renders the charge of anti-Semitism difficult to argue. Melmotte in *The Way We Live Now* is a particularly interesting example because there's such a difference between his ideological role – as an 'alien intruder' in Hobsbaum's account – and the effect he has in the story. Rosenberg demonstrates both that Melmotte is scarcely worse than the English cheats and hypocrites who surround him, and that Trollope makes him much more the man than the villain. Both points are confirmed by the fact Rosenberg mentions, that Trollope's working papers for the novel indicate that initially Melmotte's role was to have been minor.[22] In the writing of *The Way We Live Now* Melmotte clearly came to fascinate his creator, who achieves a real complexity and even an inwardness as he describes his character's downfall.[23]

Brehgert, though a more peripheral figure, is also complexly handled. His role is to court the daughter of a proud, prejudiced, but declining Tory squire. Trollope plays on Brehgert's Jewishness to emphasise how unacceptable he is to a true-blue Englishman who opposed admitting Jews to parliament. The daughter thinks poorly of her suitor too, though she's willing to accept him for his wealth, but when she argues over the marriage settlement the tables are suddenly turned. Brehgert politely withdraws, justifying his action with unanswerable temperance. He emerges very much the more honourable party, leaving the squire and his family to stew in their bigotry and, incidentally, exemplifying a type of responsible businessman opposite to Melmotte. Perhaps the only trouble with this neat reversal is the assumption that a man like Brehgert would have put up with the contempt of the girl and her family to marry into the squirearchy. But that was the *donnée* of the satire which, once it has declared its aim, takes Brehgert's part to home in on the Longestaffes. Here at least, contrary to Hobsbaum's argument, Trollope has not appealed to anti-Semitic prejudice but dramatised it. He has reversed an ideological bias which governs him elsewhere. For all his loyalty to the idea of the estate, upheld in *The Way We Live Now* by the unconvincing Roger Carbury, and for all his hostility to speculators and financiers, the novel demonstrates that the real danger to English society is in the ignorance, laziness and incompetence of the ruling class. No wonder it was so badly received. Approval came only from the *Daily Telegraph* and the *Times* – whose editor knew Trollope, and had expressed similar warnings.[24]

The three sets of examples I've given – concerning what Trollope said about his own work, about the woman question, and about Jews – will I hope have illustrated the duality of his mind, its capacity for commitment to conventional beliefs and for entertaining on another level a different order of moral and human perception. To recognise this duality is, on the one side, to become more sharply aware of the novelist as a person in history, holding opinions and presuppositions that conflict with our own. But on the other side it is to grasp why he hasn't stayed embalmed in his period, as the merely conventional writer his harshest critics have found in him.

I have suggested two reasons, one general and one specific, why Trollope's fiction often implies more insight and awareness than his stock attitudes argue. There is a third explanation in his practice of writing. What is unusual and characteristic about how Trollope worked is that he deliberately insulated his writing from his ordinary life. Probably he took the example from his mother. In his *Autobiography* he describes how during the terminal illnesses of his father and brother, and later also of his sister, medicine bottles and ink bottles held equal place in the household (24). While Mrs. Trollope nursed the sick, and looked after the other members of the family, she was supporting them all by her writing. Trollope comments: 'Her power of dividing herself into two parts, and keeping her intellect by itself clear from the troubles of the world, and fit for the duty it had to do, I never saw equalled' (25). Yet he was later to furnish a similar if not equal example himself, often writing in railway carriages and finishing more than one entire novel at sea. And he followed his mother in another way: his famous habit of writing before breakfast was taken from Mrs. Trollope who he says, 'was at her table at four in the morning, and had finished her work before the world had begun to be amused' (21). Strict self-discipline was essential for this on the part of both writers, but with Trollope a further habit was still more important. Long before he ever wrote a novel, in his loneliness as a child, he had begun to tell himself stories. These weren't ordinary daydreams because they were carried on for long periods, and in accordance with self-imposed laws. This is how Trollope sums up his account of the habit in his *Autobiography*: 'I learned in this way to maintain an interest in a fictitious story, to dwell on a work created by my own imagination, and to live in a world altogether outside the world of my own material life' (37). Writing novels was, with a few changes, an extension of the same habit. So Trollope, like his mother, divided himself into two parts. The official, everyday self worked at the Post Office or, following retirement, carried on a variety of literary work. He played Whist at his club, dined and talked; he hunted, and he banged about the world. All the while, in that compartment of time and place reserved for his writing, there was quietly unfolding the expression of an unofficial self.

But if Trollope, like his mother, divided himself into a writing and an everyday self, he also went one better. He widened that division by developing a rigid schedule of composition. His working methods, which I shall describe in Chapter 3, bureau-cratised what his imagination offered. They submitted to strict routine the continuation in writing of the 'castle-building' as he called it (*Autobiography*, 37) which had gone on in his head since childhood. Yet such a discipline enabled a paradoxical freedom, for by concentrating his attention on the mechanics of quotas and timetables it provided a channel for imaginative release. All the better if the release were profitable – Trollope often insisted, as roundly as Samuel Johnson, that there was nothing wrong with writing for money.[25] But that was the voice, impatient with humbug, of his official self. Late in his career a friend said Trollope wouldn't write novels if he weren't paid. The reply was categorical: 'Most certainly I would; – much rather than not write them at all' (*Letters*, p. 394, 18 April 1878). For all his loud defences of writing for money, and his naïve satisfaction in how much he had written and how much he had made, Trollope couldn't escape his need to create fictions. The apparent contradiction illustrates once more the gap between the role he played as a man and the self he had to inhabit as a writer. The trouble was that the one was so rarely within shouting or whispering distance of the other. Again and again Trollope's public self recalls the figure who roared out at a meeting: 'I differ from you entirely!', and then asked: 'What was it you said?'[26]

As he testified in his *Autobiography*, Trollope's sense of having been a pariah at school and a failure in his early career at the Post Office infected him with a deep need for acceptance and approval. His peculiar suffering at school consisted in exclusion from within the privileged gentlemanly world to which, thanks to his father's insolvency, he could only belong through charity. The result was that the aim of his life, frankly admitted in the *Autobiography* (146), was to join 'the society of the well-born and of the wealthy' in which he hadn't been able to share, though living within it. His official self, with its combination of an aggressive, opinionated manner and a willingness to defer to accepted wisdom, was the product of that aim. At the same time, however, he kept within him all his life an inner detachment born of his experience as an outsider inside the community he belonged to. His novels repeatedly show an instinctive, though often ambivalent, sympathy for the exposed or isolated person. His narrative voice, with its amused and apparently tolerant worldly wisdom, can shift almost imperceptibly into a criticism of established assumptions much sharper than its tone would seem to allow. Most of all, the organisation of his stories, the way they are made to work out, can at their best imply a far more telling vision and perception than their conventional surface proposes. It is through these three principal routes that the unofficial Trollope finds his way out, and later chapters of this book will illustrate each one of them.

There is, though, no reason to privilege the unofficial Trollope. Those perceptions that emerge from his work which he didn't consciously appropriate, or articulate discursively, are still open to question and criticism. I have quoted Eagleton's statement that Trollope's work 'bathes in a self-consistent, blandly undifferentiated ideological space' (see p. 1). If this is some way from the truth, as I shall argue especially for the unofficial element in the novels, then it isn't true either there or anywhere else that Trollope establishes a deliberately and continuously critical relation to ideology. Instead, the unofficial Trollope produces a version of ideology under pressure, in which inconsistencies break the surface and the bland message of conventionality gets checked or disrupted. Trollope was indeed, as Eagleton suggests, saturated in the rules and assumptions of his class, but in his best work he develops what they entail with the effect of revealing their inequity or arbitrariness. This kind of pressure, however, always stays hesitant. That is why Trollope's achievement has its limits, even if they're not so slender as Eagleton claims.

One example of the unofficial Trollope's limitations is an underlying movement in his work. His novels often end in resignation or disengagement. The two works that start and finish the Barsetshire series are type cases: Harding resigns his wardenship, Crawley his curacy. But in both cases it's resignation with credit, and finally to a comfortable place. The whole series, P. D. Edwards has argued, presents the creation of an increasingly secure, self-sufficient enclave[27] – a myth which helps explain why the series has been so popular, especially when nostalgia becomes once more what it used to be, as in wartime: similarly with Trollope's two main political characters, and with the Palliser series. The central acts of both Phineas Finn and Plantagenet Palliser are resignations, and the underlying myth of the Palliser novels is that politics is a dirty game from which it may be appropriate for an honourable man to withdraw. Not that Trollope allows such a verdict to pass unchecked – he makes it clear that both characters are to return to parliament. Yet virtuous withdrawal is the conclusion implied by the shape of the series, and by the tone of its ending. Trollope's official self was right to resist such a message, with its inner self-pity and its effective admission that politics achieves little of worth, but he couldn't wholly censor it out. It had been built too deeply into the whole structure of his work.

So Trollope's unofficial side can't be identified in any simple way with what is best in his writing. Part of his achievement is the result of conscious artistry, though often enough in his *Autobiography* he seems to scout the idea. Much as he valued spontaneity in writing, he wasn't an unconscious artist. Equally, however, his comments on his work and their own inner contradictions don't suggest that he possessed the degree of formal control and awareness with which some of his recent critics have credited him.[28] He wasn't a typical Victorian bourgeois, accepting complacently the prejudices of his world. But neither was he a Victorian Borges, insidiously turning fictional conventions inside out. He had decided views on a range of topics: some went against the grain of what people in his class ordinarily thought, some against the grain of what he ordinarily thought himself. And he was in some respects a deliberate craftsman, tailoring volumes and serials carefully, juxtaposing plots and sub-plots, characters and circumstances, with predictably complex results. But the nature and quality of his fiction can't be defined from the exclusive standpoint either of a political or of a formal critique. The two must be brought together, and they must be related among other factors to the publishing conditions to which all Victorian novelists had to adapt. It's necessary to explore how far what Trollope wrote depended on what he experienced in his society, and on what forms were available in which to express himself. In order to show how the unofficial Trollope developed, an account of how he produced himself as a writer must come first.

2 *The Novelist Produces Himself (1)*

Unusually among the major Victorian novelists, Trollope took a long time to establish himself. Perhaps only Meredith's success arrived comparably late, and then mainly because the ban by Mudie's Lending Library on *The Ordeal of Richard Feverel* severely hampered the sales of his best early work. Dickens, Thackeray, Charlotte Brontë, Mrs. Gaskell, George Eliot, even Hardy – none, though some had their troubles, had to wait as long as Trollope to find a welcoming, paying audience. Trollope's wait lasted for nearly seventeen years, starting in September 1843 when he began *The Macdermots of Ballycloran*, and ending only in 1860 when *Framley Parsonage* – his tenth novel – finally made his own name and helped make that of the newly founded *Cornhill Magazine*. The story of the wait has been well told by John Sutherland, who emphasises Trollope's bad luck with most of his publishers and his difficulties in finding a subject that would sell.[1] But really the problem was wider. It was not simply as a novelist that Trollope wanted to succeed, but as an author. His early efforts at writing show him experimenting not only in choice of subject but in form and genre. And the time he had to wait for success was to colour the attitude he formed to his career.

In his *Autobiography* Trollope tells how from the time he left school he wanted to be an author. His motive, I have said, came from the 'castle-building' of his youth and his need to achieve a success and acceptance which school and early manhood had denied him. His mother's career as an author set an encouraging example. The question was how to get started. While a clerk in London, he was on his own account almost permanently in debt and demoralised. Transferred to Ireland, to take up a job no one else wanted, he gained independence and self-discipline for the

16

first time. More important for his ambition, he also found a subject for writing, seen and realised at first hand in the close knowledge of the country he obtained as a surveyor's clerk. According to the *Autobiography*, it was from a sense of the place that the story of his first novel came to him (60). Walking with a friend, he came on a ruined country house and tried to account imaginatively for its condition. Such a sight cannot have been uncommon, as Ireland was entering the throes of the economic disaster which was to culminate in the loss of over two million people from famine, disease, and emigration.[2] What Trollope does in his novel is to represent, through the fate of the Macdermot family, the plight of the whole country.

The Macdermots of Ballycloran is interesting not just as Trollope's first novel, and as a strikingly good one; it is also an account, with its own power, of Ireland on the edge of catastrophe, and an account produced by an Englishman for English readers. Trollope took conscientious steps to make his Irish experience available to his countrymen. He did his best to convey what Irish speech sounded like, avoiding on the whole stage-Irish mannerisms,[3] and he attempted, by description and comment- ary, to create a sense of Irish life and problems. In one respect he went too far, including two humorous chapters much in the style of the Irish comic writer Charles Lever. Both disrupt not only the narrative line but its tone, and Trollope deleted them when he revised the novel for the later editions made possible by his popularity after 1860.[4] Much better judged was his invention of a plot which, conventional in itself, might interest his readers and at the same time assist him in dramatising his sense of Ireland's tragic condition. The downfall of the Macdermots begins in a debt incurred for the building of a showy house during the prosperous years of the beginning of the century. As the agricultural crisis advances, they become unable to extract from their tenants the inflated rents they need to survive, and must inevitably be crushed by their creditors. This process Trollope's plot accelerates. Feemy Macdermot, the daughter of the family, has a love affair with a revenue officer, Captain Ussher, whom her brother Thady kills believing he is trying to abduct her. Thady is charged with murder, and, as his sister dies in childbirth before she can give the evidence that might save him, he is executed and the family meets its destruction. The achievement of Trollope's plot is to demonstrate the link between landlord and tenant by implicating Ussher in the troubles of both. If the Macdermots had not been brought low by debt, Ussher would have had no chance of dishonouring Feemy, and Thady would never have leagued himself with his tenants by taking the secret oath which tells so dangerously against him at his trial. Similarly, the peasants would not have been impoverished by high rents if their landlords did not need money so desperately, and they might therefore have kept freer from crime and Ussher's clutches. But even the peasants' loyalty to Thady only makes things worse for him. Three of them try to avenge their master by attacking his most rapacious creditor, but the outrage only makes the government more determined on Thady's exemplary punishment.

Sutherland has claimed that in writing his first three novels Trollope 'was aiming at a large market by exploiting cataclysmic current events'.[5] Though this does no injustice to *La Vendée*, I don't think it can be true of *The Macdermots*. Trollope began his first novel in 1843, completed it in 1845, and sent it to the publishers in July of that year (*Autobiography*, 61-3). This was certainly before Irish distress had become 'cataclysmic' (Sutherland assumes it was written after the Famine). Besides, Trollope must have known that an Irish subject wouldn't of itself necessarily find popularity. The English public took little interest in Ireland, except as a source of high-jink humour and comic anecdote. Caricatures of Irish people in, for example, *Punch*, illustrate the extent of prejudice against them.[6] It isn't by accident that references to Ireland are conspicuously few, even in the writings of novelists who concerned themselves with social problems, such as Dickens, Mrs. Gaskell, Charles Kingsley, and George Eliot (Disraeli is one exception). Trollope wrote his first novel about Ireland because it was in his immediate experience. He was writing about what he knew, if only as an outsider; and he may also, obscurely, have identified the Macdermots' downfall with the collapse ten years before of his own family.

In several ways Trollope's diagnosis of what had gone wrong with Ireland ought to have proved acceptable to English readers. He was writing, probably deliberately, in the tradition of Maria Edgeworth and Sir Walter Scott. His theme is the downfall of a family and an estate (compare *Castle Rackrent*, the

best and most famous of Edgeworth's novels), the novel climaxes
with escape, pursuit and trial (a mixture frequent in Scott), and
there is a wealth of vigorous idiom in the customs and speech of
his characters. Similarly, the novel's thinking isn't exactly
unorthodox. It seems to place responsibility for Irish distress not
where it belongs, with English colonialism, but with Irish
extravagance and weakness. The disaster comes, on this view,
from the breakdown of an institution good in itself, that of the
landed estate. Yet the novel also shows signs of a deeper insight
and especially understanding. It includes an attack (I,200) on a
non-resident English landlord, whose only interest in his estate is
to milk it for what little it's worth, never mind the consequences.
And it creates a feeling of tragic inevitability, strong especially
in the treatment of the central character Thady. Imagery and
action alike suggest that the Macdermots are doomed through
causes not of their own making. Trollope's sympathy for Thady
and his family outstrips his conventional economic analysis, and
for this reason the story might have been more uncomfortable to
a contemporary English reader than he probably meant. The
Spectator observed that 'the subject is not well chosen, and is too
elongated'; while the tone of the *Athenaeum* was equally discouraging: 'Clever as this tale is, however, it does not produce a
pleasant impression.' Reviewers from less exalted periodicals,
such as *John Bull* and *Howitt's Journal*, were more enthusiastic,[7]
but they didn't help sell the novel.

In his second novel, Trollope markedly changed his approach.
He would still write about Ireland, because he knew and cared
about the country, but if tragedy wouldn't suit, then perhaps
comedy might. *The Kellys and the O'Kellys* was written in 1847
and published in 1848. In form it combines a conventional love
and property plot with a succession of Irish genre scenes
probably influenced by the Banim brothers, William Carleton,
and Gerald Griffin, as well as by Charles Lever.[8] That Trollope
partly achieved his aim is confirmed not so much by the *Times*
review which he ruefully cites in his *Autobiography* ('substantial,
but a little coarse', 66–7), as by the *Athenaeum*'s preference for this
novel over *The Macdermots*, 'because though not more powerful,
it is less painful'.[9] Plainly anodynes about Ireland were what
most critics wanted, and in *The Kellys* Trollope met them
halfway. E. W. Wittig has argued justly that the novel fails

because it represents 'an inadequate reaction to the Irish situation'.[10] This failure results in part from Trollope's readiness to compromise his idea of Ireland, as expressed in *The Macdermots*, in order to produce a saleable fiction. Yet there's more to be said for the novel than Wittig allows. Underneath the comedy runs an appraisal of Ireland's condition which is at least serious, and consistent both with itself and with Trollope's thinking elsewhere.

The focus of that appraisal is indicated by the novel's subtitle, *Landlords and Tenants*. Its seriousness is suggested by the fact that Trollope set his story in one of the poorest parts of Ireland, the West. The landlord, Francis O'Kelly, has succeeded to a title, an estate, and a large debt. The estate is no longer prosperous because after the family had been raised to the peerage in 1800 O'Kelly's grandfather had devoted himself to the English court. No doubt the peerage was one of the sweeteners by which the English ensured Irish compliance with the Union, but it did no good either for the O'Kellys or their dependants. While the absentee viscount consumed his rents in fashionable style at Court, his agent was systematically converting much of the property to his own uses. As in *The Macdermots*, it's the middleman who prospers. In this case, though, both landlord and tenant look after themselves better. Just as O'Kelly restores his family's position by means of a rich marriage, so Martin Kelly, his tenant and distant relative, improves his prospects by marrying the daughter of the offending agent. In this way, part of the O'Kelly property taken over previously by the agent goes to establish on a sounder footing a tenant who shares the landlord's interests. The chief merit of Trollope's plot is its firm basis in what had happened in Ireland since the Union. Though the story is comic in treatment, that isn't wholly a limit because it has first been grasped historically. That Trollope's aim wasn't at root conventional is indicated by a complaint from one critic that hero and heroine never meet till the end, when their sole conversation consists of a sentimental ejaculation from the one, duly echoed by the other.[11] Though prepared to nod towards romantic expectations, Trollope was more interested in economics, but his diagnosis is tendentious: Ireland's problems are to be solved by reinvestment. The novel is a comic blueprint for social and economic recovery, which is to be effected by injecting fresh capital and renewing the partnership between landlord and tenant.

What *The Kellys* deliberately suppresses is the case for political change. It begins in Dublin, with the trial of Daniel O'Connell. But the object of Kelly's visit has nothing to do with O'Connell – it's to ask his landlord's advice about his proposed elopement. This conversion of the social problem into a plot about marriage doesn't go undefended. Trollope emphasises that for all the feeling over the trial while it was in progress, interest quickly died away once it had ended; and he implies as the novel goes on that it was, after all, irrelevant. A modern Irish historian has summarised the period after the trial in these words: 'Social issues, especially the relations between landlord and tenant, rather than the old demand for repeal, were to determine much of the character of Irish politics from the autumn of 1848 onwards until late in the eighteen-fifties.'[12] This makes Trollope's reading of the period look pretty convincing. He suggests that nationalism went only skin deep. Kelly may pay an advance subscription to the *Nation* before he leaves, and O'Kelly may name his racehorses after the heroes of old Ireland, but finally both express their patriotism most effectively through cash. This, however, is an Establishment view, one an Englishman would want to believe in, There were other reasons than Trollope admits for Repeal agitation collapsing – among them English repression, O'Connell's age and personality, the influence of ideas like Trollope's, and above all the utterly demoralising effects of the Famine. Trollope refused to draw a conclusion which his own story might have prompted. It wasn't just the plight of the O'Kelly estate that grew from the Union.

Three ways of apprehending the Irish problem may be distinguished from Trollope's first two novels. To begin with there is the ideological view I've discussed, centring on the idea of the estate and on unquestioned loyalty to British supremacy. Then there are Trollope's attempts to mediate his sense of Ireland's condition to an English readership, initially through a tragic novel recalling Edgeworth and Scott, then through a genre-scene comedy. The third way is the most interesting, because here Trollope moves beyond fictional convention and ideology. He admits factors which threaten to contradict his analysis, like the problem of absentee landlords which is more than a feature in both novels. And, especially in *The Macdermots*, he identifies more strongly than he perhaps realised with the victims of bankruptcy and repression. But Trollope wasn't only, or even primarily, a novelist. He was also a servant of the Crown, and, in contrast to his reception as an author, an increasingly successful one. *The Kellys* sold no better than *The Macdermots*. As its publisher bluntly put it, 'readers do not like novels on Irish subjects as well as on others' (*Autobiography* 67). So Trollope temporarily shelved the fiction, especially at its more unofficial. When he next wrote on Ireland it would be with the consciousness not of a novelist, but of a servant of government.

In 1849 Sidney Godolphin Osborne contributed a series of letters to the *Times* attacking the government's relief measures during and after the Famine. Trollope replied with seven letters to the *Examiner* published, with one exception, about a year later.[13] He had not in any way taken part in the official relief efforts, but in his work as a postal surveyor he had at first hand observed them and the terrible effects of the Famine. His letters defended government policy against what he saw as ill-informed punditry. He claimed to present 'facts' rather than the 'novels' which had got into print on the issue more easily (83) – an interesting distinction from someone whose previous writings on Ireland had taken the form, precisely, of novels. He argued with vigour a bureaucrat's case almost wholly sympathetic to the administration. The letters to the *Examiner* are early specimens of what might be called the official Trollope. The sole mode of apprehension they show is the first one distinguished above – the ideological. In such a view the potato blight was a visitation of Providence (e.g. 74, 75, 80, 82). It struck with such devastating force because the country was already nearly bankrupt, thanks to over-mortgaging and extravagance. Trollope summed up this analysis, which is consistent with that implied by his two novels, in the following statement: 'The wealth of Ireland was almost entirely territorial, and the income arising from that wealth had been overdrawn' (79). The solution must accordingly lie in getting rid of the bankrupt. Trollope praised the Encumbered Estates Act of 1849, which was designed to attract new landlords and fresh capital. And with a poor law to provide relief he saw nothing wrong with evictions. The official view also reveals itself in his belief that economic laws forbade distribution of food either free or below market prices. He accepted the argument that the result would be not only to deter ordinary trade but to foster laziness and dependence. For, despite his sympathy for the Irish, he accepted that part of the stereotype which found them lacking in conviction and persistence.

The issue Trollope made central to his defence of government policy he expressed in the following question: 'Could an equal amount of life have been saved at a less expense, and with fewer ill consequences?' (75). His answer, which was 'No', depends on the assumptions described above and on an underestimate of casualties.[14] He doesn't ask whether more lives could have been saved; the need, as far as possible, to save money seems just as strong. This is how he saw the minister's problem: 'He had a balance of seven millions at his banker's, three millions of people to feed, and an account to render at the end of, say twelve months' (82). And his concern for the administrative difficulties is underlined by an intended pleasantry which exposes the institutional blinkers he had put on: 'I have said that no statistical account can be given of the numbers who perished from starvation, but think that a return should be furnished of the clerks who were worried to death at the Dublin office' (85). From a modern point of view it's easy to criticise government policy and the way Trollope endorsed it. What the *Examiner* letters show is the mind-set which held so many Englishmen of the time, and which determined the nature and limits of relief. Trollope's account of the crisis is in keeping with those of other humane, but finally dogmatic, Englishmen. It differs little either in argument or emphasis from the testimony of Charles Trevelyan who was in charge of the relief and was knighted in 1848 in recognition of his services.[15]

Trollope's distinction between 'facts' and 'novels' is worth thinking about. He claimed that his own Irish fiction was authentic – on the whole with some justice. Yet, despite the similarity of the underlying analysis, the fiction shows a different level of consciousness. It isn't just that it's hard to identify the writer of the *Examiner* letters with the author of *The Macdermots*, a comparable division is evident in *Castle Richmond*, written over a decade after the Famine. This presents not only the ideological view, more or less as described above, but also the human response. Trollope states, for instance, the received case against giving charity; then he confesses that it was impossible to avoid giving it (II, 47–8). And, as R. M. Polhemus has pointed out, he created a moving image of suffering, inequity and hopelessness in the scene where one of the principal characters covers the corpse of a baby with a silk handkerchief (III, 78–9).[16] What I'm suggesting is that fiction released Trollope's imaginative sympathy, which was inhibited by his official role. Such a release certainly isn't peculiar among novelists, but it has a special importance in one who was also a government servant. Yet in other ways *Castle Richmond* illustrates again Trollope's preparedness to compromise with his public. Though he says at the end that he might have subtitled the novel 'A Tale of the Famine Year in Ireland' (III, 282), its melodramatic plot is imposed quite artificially on an Irish setting. More even than in *The Kellys*, Trollope's fictional vehicle spoils the social commentary it was designed to carry.

Trollope finally returned to the Irish question in his last novel, which for the sake of completeness I will discuss here briefly. *The Landleaguers*, left unfinished at his death and published in 1883, is a fictional polemic against Gladstone's Irish land policy. The ideology of the estate leads Trollope into special pleading on behalf of those landowners he had himself recommended, in the *Examiner* letters, to invest in Irish properties. He pressed his imagination into the service of his thesis. Even then he couldn't wholly subdue it – his characterisation of the boy Florian shows sensitivity to those caught in the conflict. But the novel's plot, shallow and at times absurd, betrays the strains of the Establishment case to which, by then an outsider to Ireland, he had committed himself totally.[17]

As revealing a failure in its own way is *La Vendée*, Trollope's third attempt to establish himself as a novelist. Written at a time when the revolutions of 1848 were collapsing, and published in 1850, this novel represents Trollope's most ingenuous bid for popularity. Its subject is the counter-revolution of 1793, its bias conservative and traditional. In several respects it was written against the grain. The form Trollope chose was that of the historical romance, still popular but already becoming outmoded. Secondly, he had no direct knowledge of his subject, though he informed himself from such sources as Archibald Alison's *History*

of Europe During the French Revolution and the *Memoirs* (translated
by no less a person than Sir Walter Scott) of Agatha de La Roche-
jacquelein.[18] Worst of all, he was appealing to privileged class
feeling with which he could not wholly identify. This leads to a
crucial contradiction. Trollope tries to demonstrate that the
Royalists are more democratic in a true sense than the so-called
Democrats. They choose as their commander-in-chief Cathelineau, a humble postillion. Cathelineau's acceptance is supposed
to be conclusively sealed when, after he has been killed in the
fighting, the noblewoman he has fallen in love with says she
would have married him. This is historical romance with a
vengeance, not just for the obvious reason, but because Trollope
never faces the fact that Cathelineau couldn't have formed a
relationship with an aristocrat, let alone have thought of
marying one, if there had been no Revolution. It wouldn't be
quite fair to call *La Vendée* right-wing propaganda even though it
ends by looking forward – backwardly – to a restored French
monarchy. The novel attempts to account for a movement that
really took place, and it refuses to type the revolutionaries,
including Robespierre, as inhuman. What distorts the account
is, once more, Trollope's unquestioned loyalty to the values of
the landed estate, and his lapses into sentiment and melodrama.
These were perhaps intended as embellishments to help sell the
novel, but at a deeper level they probably reflect his own
confusions.

For the next four years Trollope wrote no fiction. Threatening
to display 'four 4 vol. novels – all failures!' at the Great
Exhibition (*Letters*, p. 9, undated), he tried several other roles as
a writer. First came the letters to the *Examiner*. Next he
attempted theatre, with a costume drama, *The Noble Jilt*,
written in 1850.[19] This was quickly aborted on the advice of
George Bartley, family friend, actor and former stage manager
(*Autobiography*, 73–4). The play later provided the main plot of
the novel *Can You Forgive Her?*, but this, and a scene in *The
Eustace Diamonds* where Trollope humorously sends a group of
characters to the play's only recorded performance, was about
all the good he got out of it. So again Trollope turned away from
imaginative writing, this time to travel literature. Here his
mother and brother had succeeded, and he was to prove himself
in the same field subsequently. He wrote a sizeable sample of a

handbook on Ireland for John Murray, but when the publisher
failed to reply he abandoned the project in angry frustration
(*Autobiography*, 75). All he did succeed in publishing at this time
was a review of the first two volumes of Charles Merivale's
History of the Romans Under the Empire, in the *Dublin University
Magazine* in 1851, followed by a second review covering the rest
of the work in 1856.[20] No doubt it was satisfying to Trollope to
redeem by scholarship his schoolboy inadequacies. But nothing
else seemed to encourage his writing activities. He appears to
have virtually dropped them from 1851 to 1853 when he was
engaged in the arduous but rewarding task of travelling through
Ireland and part of southern England to survey and reorganise
the system of postal deliveries.

The story of how, on his travels, Trollope formed the idea for
The Warden while wandering around Salisbury cathedral is well
known. Less often noticed are other, perhaps more important,
circumstances surrounding the novel's making. Sutherland has
commented on Trollope's 'notable artistic restlessness' at this
period. He points out that by 1859, having written *The West
Indies and the Spanish Main*, *The New Zealander*, and four further
novels, Trollope would have 'tried his hand at Irish, historical,
English rural, institutional and metropolitan settings. He had
written thesis novels, comedies, romances, satires and, on the
side, travel journals and guide books, a play and a novel-length
critique of English society'.[21] The range is wider still if we
include the letters to the *Examiner* and the contributions to the
Dublin University Magazine, which also included an anonymous
article published in 1855 criticising a report on the reorganisation
of the Civil Service.[22] It's important to record the non-fictional
output, for this breadth of activity shows Trollope's determination to establish himself in a variety of possible roles as an
author. Though he thought his best chance of success lay in the
novel, he repeatedly tried other kinds of writing. His ambition
must have been extraordinarily persistent for him to continue
and break new ground in the face of failure and what would for
most people have been decisive hindrances. His official work
entailed much travelling at a time when Ireland still lacked
railways, he had a young family, and he hunted regularly. *The
Warden* was a fresh start, enabled in exactly the same way as his

Irish fiction, through the close familiarity with its setting which he gained as a postal surveyor. Though the year 1860 was to mark the point when Trollope's career took off with the serialisation of *Framley Parsonage* in the *Cornhill*, the years which saw the gestation of *The Warden* were hardly less critical. It was this novel which first got him talked about and which began the series on which his reputation was to be founded. After the qualified success of its sequel, *Barchester Towers* in 1857, Trollope was able to concentrate on fiction.

What gives *The Warden* further importance is that in it Trollope developed a point of view he would often exploit later. So much is obvious, but the role he took on has an extra interest in that it brought into play a tension between what I have called the official and unofficial sides of his imagination. On the one hand, his work as a government servant helped shape his perceptions, for his insight into the Church as an institution probably came in part from his shrewd insider's knowledge of how the Civil Service operated. On the other hand, and more immediately relevant to *The Warden*, there was his earlier defence of official policy against what he had seen as unfair criticism. For the novel's sharpest imaginative irritant was a series of attacks in the press on how a number of ancient charities were being administered. In order to understand and assess the novel properly some knowledge of these controversies is essential.

The first of the scandals that lie behind *The Warden* became known as 'the Whiston matter'.[23] Robert Whiston, Headmaster of the cathedral school in Rochester, came into dispute with the Dean and Chapter because he was able to prove that the terms of his school's foundation had fallen into abuse. Money which should have gone towards the support of students at the school and at the universities had become diverted by custom to the canons of the cathedral. The canons were pluralists all, only one out of five residing in Rochester for more than two months a year. Yet each thought himself fully entitled to what he received. It was his function as a holder of ecclesiastical office to live well, maintain the cathedral, and dispense charity. Not only had the Dean and Chapter at Rochester spent over £28,000 on the fabric of the cathedral in the twenty-eight years before Whiston began his attack, but they had even restored the school of which he had become the new Head. So they felt they had reason to defend their privileges. But there are two other points for comparison with *The Warden*. Where Whiston was really dangerous was in his insistence on returning to the old statutes. As he knew, his discoveries pointed beyond Rochester to the other cathedrals refounded at the same date, and to other ancient foundations. Secondly, although Whiston won his battle after much expenditure of sweat, tears and ink, he did so at the cost of embittering his relations with the Church at Rochester for the rest of his life. He was a litigious man, and he wasn't allowed to forget it.

As well as the Whiston affair, Trollope mentions the scandal of St. Cross several times in *The Warden*.[24] St. Cross was founded as a charity in the twelfth century at Winchester, mainly for the care of the poor and the aged. Francis North, later Earl of Guilford, was appointed Master of the charity in 1808 by his father the Bishop of Winchester. He already held two compound livings worth an estimated £3500 a year between them. St. Cross brought in an average of £2–3000 a year, and after 1828, when North inherited his title, he had an extra £17,000 a year to play with. When he had become Master, his father had tried to forestall charges of pluralism by appointing him on a secular rather than an ecclesiastical basis, yet he took fees for marriages, baptisms, and burials, and seems not to have noticed any inconsistency. Despite these clear abuses, it's as important as in the Whiston matter, and in the question of Famine relief policy, not to leap to self-righteous conclusions. Geoffrey Best goes so far as to say that 'the notoriety of the case rested on . . . the bourgeois and radical public's delight in seeing a clerical peer in the box'.[25] Both he and Robert Martin acknowledge that the Earl carried out his stated duties conscientiously, erring on the side of generosity if anything. The trouble was his comfortable acceptance of those duties as stated. They weren't the ones laid down by the foundation, but later revisions which had greatly increased the Master's privileges. Habit-blindness probably figures strongest in the sum of the Earl's guilt. As Martin says, what shows best his lack of imagination is his inability to see that his resignation could solve nothing. The whole charity had to be reformed – which parliament managed quite quickly once judgment had gone against him. This is another point to be remembered in approaching *The Warden*, along with something that may come as a surprise. Perhaps the oddest yet most characteristic fact about the St. Cross case is that the man who drew attention to the abuses was a clergyman, who before his retirement to Winchester had himself been a pluralist.

Several other examples demonstrate the topicality of Trollope's subject. One which he also mentions in the novel is the case of Dulwich College. Here again was a foundation which had grown very prosperous, especially with the development of the Crystal Palace close by. Once more the administrators had allowed their own income to increase while leaving the charity on short commons. Dulwich had been the object of more than one previous inquiry, but in 1856 it was finally reformed after a campaign by two of the local churchwardens. What enabled this last inquiry to succeed was the Charitable Trusts Act. This piece of legislation was finally passed in 1853, nearly forty years after it was first mooted, by Lord John Russell – whose activities Archdeacon Grantly finds so sacrilegious in the novel (20). Its passage was another of the events which Trollope had in mind as he wrote this novel.

A final example concerns the mismanagement of a hospital for aged gentlemen connected with the Charterhouse. Lionel Stevenson has argued that an article on this subject in Dickens' magazine *Household Words* gave rise to Trollope's parody of Dickens in *The Warden*.[26] This seems possible, though the circumstances of the affair don't make it a source for the novel in any more particular sense.[27]

All this shows how up-to-date *The Warden* was. But, as I've suggested, Trollope's own attitude to articles and correspondence in the press about these scandals is likely to have been shaped by the parallel with Sidney Godolphin Osborne's letters on Irish relief. The link isn't at all improbable because, as Carol Ganzel has pointed out, in 1853 Osborne sent six letters to the *Times* about an absentee clergyman who turned out to be incapable of undertaking his duties because he was dying:[28] perhaps other holders of office were being attacked unjustly. Since 1835 the Ecclesiastical Commission had been hard at work. This, as Owen Chadwick has put it, was 'an instrument for adjusting ancient endowments to new needs'.[29] If its reforms failed to go far enough, the reason was partly that it was an Establishment body and partly that even moderate steps met clerical hostility. Nevertheless, according to Best, the Commission had achieved enough by the 1850s to oblige reformers to go for smaller game.[30] There remained such out-of-the-way cobwebs as Rochester and St. Cross, and these were calling out a more indignant shaking of brooms than seemed warranted. The clean-up was half-finished, but reformers were still baying for dust. That was the way Trollope saw it, and Best supports him. But there is another element to the issue which neither mentions: the census of 1851 included, uniquely, a questionnaire about church attendance.[31] On 3 January 1854 the report of this religious census was published. Its compiler, Horace Mann, was disturbed that his figures showed about five and a quarter million people failing to perform their Sabbath duty. Even among churchgoers, the established Church enjoyed the loyalty of only just over half of the combined English and Welsh population:[32] there were more dissenters than had been appreciated. Worse, attendance was very low among the working people of London and the new industrial cities, even where the provision of places of worship wasn't totally inadequate. Mann commented: 'It is sadly certain that this vast, intelligent, and growingly important section of our own countrymen is thoroughly estranged from our religious institutions in their present aspect.'[33] So the census, Chadwick concludes, 'finally established the impossibility of treating the establishment as privileged on the ground that it was the church of the immense majority of the country'.[34]

Whether or not the census findings could have been in Trollope's mind as he wrote his novel depends on when *The Warden* was actually written. By his own account in the *Autobiography*, the novel was finished 'in the autumn of 1853' (84). Yet, according to his correspondence with Longman, he only submitted his manuscript, at that time called *The Precentor*, on 8 October 1854.[35] The missing year is difficult to explain. It was unlike Trollope to wait at all having once completed a project. He was always anxious for a decision, and preferably for firm agreement on terms. Equally, it's unlikely that *The Precentor* would have been going the rounds with other publishers for a whole year. Longman was very quick to accept it, and its topicality demanded early publication (it appeared in January 1855, less than three months after agreement on terms had been reached). Probably Trollope confused the dates of this very busy period of his life, in which he spent two years surveying in England, moved to Belfast as Surveyor for the northern Irish counties, and then after eighteen months moved to Dublin. The writing of *The Precentor* is likely to have extended until autumn 1854 instead of reaching completion a year previously. This possibility is strengthened by Trollope's evident surprise in the *Autobiography* that the novel 'was not published till 1855' (84). His memory probably told him of little delay between completion and publication, though the time taken over writing the novel had become hazy. If *The Precentor* wasn't finished until autumn 1854, he would have known about the findings on church attendance while he was still writing it. The point is important not because he anywhere mentions the religious census, or could be taken to refer to it. He does no such thing. The novel is silent on a matter which called the privilege of the established Church in question. As I shall try to show, it tends to favour the Church, abuses and all. It defends even Archdeacon Grantly, the arch-conservative – who is compared to 'the dead branches of an old oak, now useless, but, ah! still so beautiful' (*The Warden*, 55). Yet neither the defence nor the nostalgic tone of such apologetics would have been needed if no threat to the Church had been perceived. That threat was growing, especially in the industrial cities. It became explicit in the attendance statistics, and also elsewhere. For, according to Chadwick, 'although (or because) this was the clerical age of England, it was also the age of an anti-clericalism not seen since the reign of Queen Anne, perhaps not since the Reformation'.[36] This was the atmosphere in which *The Warden* was written and it's with awareness of that atmosphere that the novel needs to be read.

First, Trollope made a number of changes in *The Warden* from what had happened at Rochester, St. Cross, and at other places. The most important alteration is in the position of the reformer. At Rochester, St. Cross and Dulwich the reformers were all ordained clergymen. Whiston and his counterpart at Winchester were both strong conservatives. They started their actions not in a politically radical spirit but simply in an attempt to restore benefits which each foundation required, but which had been let slip by those in authority. Trollope reverses all this. His reformer, with the only too obvious name of Bold, is from newly

rich stock and lives just outside the town. He is a gentleman, for
though qualified as a doctor he lives in leisure, and he takes on
the role of reformer partly to fill the vacuum. Worse than this,
he's a friend of the man whose position he attacks, and in love
with the man's daughter. Trollope also changes the scale of the
controversy. Harding, the warden of the title, is no Earl of
Guilford with preferment bringing in £6000 or so a year on top
of a private income. He's the most inoffensive of pluralists,
receiving annually £800 from the hospital, £80 from a small
living nearby which he pays to his curate, and another £80 for
the position of precentor in the cathedral. Trollope is admirably
precise about such details, though his arithmetic about the
annual cost of the twopence extra per day which Harding pays
to the bedesmen can only be understood with great ingenuity.[37]
Harding's income, then, is comfortable but not exactly opulent.
He doesn't deprive the pensioners of anything to which they're
entitled, but even allows them a small sum extra. And his
surplus has gone mainly to the publication of a work on church
music – hardly a vicious object.

Given that the novel's most attractive character is the
warden, and that his proifit from the abuse is so guileless, an
exercise in whitewashing might be suspected. This impression
seems to be confirmed by Trollope's explanation in his *Autobiography* of what he set out to do in the novel. The passage needs
quoting at length.

> I had been struck by two opposite evils, – or what seemed to
> me to be evils, – and *with an absence of all art-judgment in such
> matters*, I thought that I might be able to expose them, or
> rather to describe them, both in one and the same tale. The
> first evil was the possession by the Church of certain funds and
> endowments which had been intended for charitable pur-
> poses, but which had been allowed to become incomes for idle
> Church dignitaries. There had been more than one such case
> brought to public notice at the time, in which there seemed to
> have been an egregious malversation of charitable purposes.
> The second evil was its very opposite. Though I had been
> much struck by the injustice above described, I had also often
> been angered by the undeserved severity of the newspapers
> towards the recipients of such incomes, who could hardly be

considered to be the chief sinners in the matter. When a man is appointed to a place, it is natural that he should accept the income allotted to that place without much inquiry. It is seldom that he will be the first to find out that his services are overpaid. Though he be called upon only to look beautiful and to be dignified upon State occasions, he will think £2000 a year little enough for such beauty and dignity as he brings to the task. I felt that there had been some tearing to pieces which might have been spared. But I was altogether wrong in supposing that the two things could be combined. Any writer in advocating a cause must do so after the fashion of an advocate, – or his writing will be ineffective. He should take up one side and cling to that, and then he may be powerful. *There should be no scruples of conscience.* Such scruples make a man impotent for such work. It was open to me to have described a bloated parson, with a red nose and all other iniquities, openly neglecting every duty required from him, and living riotously on funds purloined from the poor, – defying as he did so the moderate remonstrances of a virtuous press. Or I might have painted a man as good, as sweet, and as mild as my warden, who should also have been a hard-working, ill-paid minister of God's word, and might have subjected him to the rancorous venom of some daily Jupiter, who, without a leg to stand on, without any true case, might have been induced, by personal spite, to tear to rags the poor clergyman with poisonous, anonymous, and ferocious leading articles. *But neither of these programmes recommended itself to my honesty.* Satire, though it may exaggerate the vice it lashes, is not justified in creating it in order that it may be lashed. Caricature may too easily become a slander, and satire a libel. I believed in the existence neither of the red-nosed clerical cormorant, nor in that of the venomous assassin of the journals. I did believe that through want of care and the natural tendency of every class to take care of itself, money had slipped into the pockets of certain clergymen which should have gone elsewhere; and I believed also that through the equally natural propensity of men to be as strong as they know how to be, certain writers of the press had allowed themselves to use language which was cruel, though used in a good cause. But the two objects should not have been combined – and I now know myself well enough to be aware that *I was not the man to have carried out either of them.* (81–2)

I have italicised the key statements in this remarkable passage, which is so characteristic of the *Autobiography*. Trollope clearly felt that the novel had failed, but in trying to account for the failure he couldn't help but betray his real intention. On the face of it, he accuses himself of lacking artistic discrimination and skill, and of having been hamstrung by an over-active conscience. Reading between the lines, though, he has put his explanation in such terms that his way of presenting the controversy appears the only one that could be just, humane and fair-minded. He protests his shortcomings, but with the effect of displaying his own assessment of the case as both realistic and artless. This is a view which has recommended itself to critics too easily,[38] but I don't think Trollope meant to be devious. He was trying to explain what was wrong with a novel which hadn't succeeded as he'd intended, and in doing so he couldn't avoid conveying what he felt deep down. His comments on *The Warden* are another example of the gap between his official and his unofficial self.

The question the novel requires is how far Trollope achieved the balanced judgement he suggested he had aimed for. First, against John Bold the reformer should be set the ultra-conservative Archdeacon Grantly. Trollope's description of Grantly explicitly casts him as a personification of the secularised Anglican clergy:

As the archdeacon stood up to make his speech, erect in the middle of that little square, he looked like an ecclesiastical statue placed there, as a fitting impersonation of the church militant here on earth; his shovel hat, large, new, and well-pronounced, a churchman's hat in every inch, declared the profession as plainly as does the Quaker's broad brim; his heavy eyebrows, large open eyes, and full mouth and chin expressed the solidity of his order; the broad chest, amply covered with fine cloth, told how well to do was its estate; one hand ensconced within his pocket, evinced the practical hold which our mother church keeps on her temporal possessions; and the other, loose for action, was ready to fight if need be in

her defence; and, below these, the decorous breeches, and
neat black gaiters showing so admirably that well-turned leg,
betokened the decency, the outward beauty and grace of our
church establishment. (*The Warden*, 60–1)

Grantly is a humour character, boiling over with a comic energy
that can release itself only through the machinery of his
prejudices. His safety-valve exclamation of 'Good heavens!', his
utter inability to see the other side of the question, and above all
the secret sensuality behind his churchman's dignity – all these
make him the most vivid figure in the novel. Trollope is
vigorously alive to the gross inconsistencies in Grantly as a man
of religion. The heavy luxuries of Plumstead Episcopi are
signalled in its name, and the Rabelais exchanged for the
sermon is of a piece with the breakfast that seems capable of
feeding the five thousand with no need for a miracle. Trollope
nails the contradictions at a stroke when he declares that
Grantly 'did not believe in the Gospel with more assurance than
he did in the sacred justice of all ecclesiastical revenues' (52). It's
plain that Grantly commits himself to the Church as an
institution, not as a religion. He's completely unscrupulous in
defending its interests, as he shows in his offensiveness to the
bedesmen, to John Bold, and to Harding himself. Yet Trollope
makes play of the contradictions. Grantly is so gloriously awful a
figure that he generates a magnetism Trollope can't allow to the
colourless Bold. It's the archdeacon who enjoys more of the
novelist's sympathies. The book certainly doesn't need the
apology that Trollope put in for him at the end (248–9).

One major way in which Trollope's own thinking is conveyed
is, then, through characterisation. This is also evident with the
minor figures. Those who most influence the action are simply
cardboard cutouts. Sir Abraham Haphazard, the Attorney-
General who takes on the warden's case at Grantly's instigation,
is another humour character – but this time without any
humour. Trollope's two-dimensional description implicitly
excuses itself by claiming that that's how Haphazard is. He's 'a
machine with a mind' (213), who knows the meaning of the
word 'friend' only in its parliamentary sense (214). Again, the
emblematic name gives away the trick at the same time as it
displays the character's function. An Abraham in law, haphazard

in justice, he's guaranteed to win on technicalities whichever side hires him.

Two further examples of skewed characterisation are the bedesmen at one end of the power scale and a newspaper editor at the other. The episode concerning the bedesmen is the most uncomfortable in the novel. Trollope tries to suggest that they're all too human, that old men in a humble station can't be expected not to show greed when promises of wealth are held out. But it won't wash. His real attitude comes out when he calls them 'well-to-do' (27) on a shilling and sixpence a day, when he questions whether their lot could be improved (41), and especially when, near the end, he repudiates 'their vile cabal' (256) as if they were responsible for driving the warden away. Trollope's failure of imagination here needs no emphasis. The only bedesman to be made humanly attractive is Bunce, who accepts that state to which God has called him and stays loyal to Harding. The warden's real antagonist is the editor of the *Jupiter* (Trollope's name for the *Times*). Tom Towers is a paper tyrant, a press dictator – but as a fictional creation with about as much depth as one of his pages. Again this is deliberate. A *Times* leader is faceless, so, Trollope implies, is the man who writes it. And, since he thought the newspaper was setting itself up as an alternative religion, he draws elaborate parallels between the description of Tom Towers' rooms and those of the Archdeacon. These are nicely balanced, for just as the defence Grantly obtains from Haphazard is morally null, so is the *Jupiter*'s prosecution. Behind the editor's *ex cathedra* pronouncements lie the motives of profit and power.

But Trollope offers only an appearance of impartiality. While Towers and Haphazard cancel each other out, there are the bedesmen to tip the scale; just as Grantly's extravagant offensiveness blots out poor John Bold even when he's in the right. Another central way in which Trollope expresses his attitude is through commentary. Again the balance at first seems finely poised. He doesn't hesitate to say that the wardenship 'had become one of the most coveted of the snug clerical sinecures attached to our church' (5). He makes it clear that the income really is malappropriated, even if from no special guilt on Harding's part. More than this, he gives a splendid thumbnail sketch of sinecurism in Dr. Vesey Stanhope, who collects butterflies in Italy on the strength of benefices with names like Goosegorge and Eiderdown (164). Nor does he allow the kind of person who actually did much of the Church's work to be forgotten: the curate who keeps a wife and six children on £80 a year. Against all this Trollope pleads amused tolerance in mitigation, insinuating that 'old customs need not necessarily be evil, and that changes may possibly be dangerous' (15). The best example of special pleading deserves quotation:

> We believe that Mr. Horseman himself would relent, and the spirit of Sir Benjamin Hall give way, were those great reformers to allow themselves to stroll by moonlight round the towers of some of our ancient churches. Who would not feel charity for a prebendary, when walking the quiet length of that long aisle at Winchester, looking at those decent houses, that trim grassplat, and feeling, as one must, the solemn, orderly comfort of the spot! Who could be hard upon a dean while wandering round the sweet close of Hereford, and owning that in that precinct, tone and colour, design and form, solemn tower and storied window, are all in unison, and all perfect! Who could lie basking in the cloisters of Salisbury, and gaze on Jewel's library and that unequalled spire, without feeling that bishops should sometimes be rich!
>
> The tone of our archdeacon's mind must not astonish us; it has been the growth of centuries of church ascendancy; and though some fungi now disfigure the tree, though there be much dead wood, for how much good fruit have not we to be thankful? Who, without remorse, can batter down the dead branches of an old oak, now useless, but, ah! still so beautiful, or drag out the fragments of the ancient forest, without feeling that they sheltered the younger plants, to which they are now summoned to give way in a tone so peremptory and so harsh? (54–5)

'The sweet mediaeval flavour of old English corruption': this is the phrase into which Trollope later distilled his sense of such ambivalent attractiveness.[39] It's hard to resist the indulgent warmth of his appeal, as he must have felt and probably intended.

One place in the novel where Trollope seeks openly to influence his readers is the chapter in which he satirises Carlyle and Dickens. He charges both with gross exaggeration. Each is made to travesty circumstances at the hospital as he has represented them. In the parody of Carlyle, the warden's 'only occupation is to swallow the bread prepared with so much anxious care for these impoverished carders of wool – that, and to sing indifferently through his nose once in a week some psalm more or less long – the shorter the better, we should be inclined to say' (186). In the parody of Dickens, this is how the warden is described:

> He was a man well stricken in years, but still strong to do evil: he was one who looked cruelly out of a hot, passionate, bloodshot eye; who had a huge red nose with a carbuncle, thick lips, and a great double, flabby chin, which swelled out into solid substance, like a turkey cock's comb, when sudden anger inspired him: he had a hot, furrowed, low brow, from which a few grizzled hairs were not yet rubbed off by the friction of his handkerchief: he wore a loose unstarched white handkerchief, black loose ill-made clothes, and huge loose shoes, adapted to many corns and various bunions: his husky voice told tales of much daily port wine, and his language was not so decorous as became a clergyman. (193)

According to Trollope, there are no such villains – at least, no villain where one might be expected, in the holder of the sinecure. He attacks Carlyle and Dickens alike for shabby rhetoric. Yet what should be plainest of all from this chapter is Trollope's own rhetoric, from the facetious names 'Dr. Pessimist Anticant' and 'Mr. Popular Sentiment' to the misrepresentation especially of Dickens. Trollope claimed in his *Autobiography* that satire and caricature could easily go too far. Yet here he is travestying the very people he accuses of travesty.[40] The chapter's last sentence gives his true position away. He writes that the radical reform which has swept over such establishments as Hiram's Hospital 'has owed more to the twenty numbers of Mr. Sentiment's novel, than to all the true complaints which have escaped from the public for the last half century' (194). It's the radical reform that bothers him, not the neglected evil. His own conservative view is only less obtrusive than the populist propaganda he attributes to Dickens.

Part of the rhetoric of Trollope's novel is a studied trading in

personalities and literariness. With Dr. Pessimist Anticant and
Mr. Popular Sentiment the two are combined in an invitation to
sneer at Carlyle and Dickens and their abuse of language.
Elsewhere each device comes separately. When Trollope
describes Grantly's children, he notes that the two girls take
their names from female relatives of the Archbishops of York
and Canterbury (92). This draws attention to the sons' names,
which he does not comment on, but which would have been
recognisable to any moderately well-informed reader.[41] Each is
a facetious sketch of an Anglican dignitary – Charles James
Blomfield, Bishop of London, Henry Phillpotts, Bishop of Exeter
and Samuel Wilberforce, Bishop of Oxford. Trollope makes it
even worse by using Wilberforce's nickname, 'Soapy', for the
youngest son (94), and by associating the son who stands for
Phillpotts with a watering-can (98). This broad kind of humour
is right in the tradition of caricature which Trollope said he had
repudiated; it goes along with the novel's literary allusiveness.
Hiram's will is not so distant a relative of the one that gets
mangled in Swift's *Tale of a Tub*, and the description of the
warden's party, especially of the card-playing, might be
described as Pope without the rape.

Some of the literary devices work better. One good example is
an allegorical description of the church at Plumstead Episcopi.
Rather as the Archdeacon stands for the Church of England, so
does his house of worship, and its faults are treated with the same
indulgence:

> Few parish churches in England are in better repair, or better
> worth keeping so, than that at Plumstead Episcopi; and yet it
> is built in a faulty style: the body of the church is low – so low,
> that the nearly flat leaden roof would be visible from the
> churchyard, were it not for the carved parapet with which it
> is surrounded. It is cruciform, though the transepts are
> irregular, one being larger than the other; and the tower is
> much too high in proportion to the church. But the colour of
> the building is perfect; it is that rich yellow grey which one
> finds nowhere but in the south and west of England, and
> which is so strong a characteristic of most of our old houses of
> Tudor architecture. The stone work also is beautiful; the
> mullions of the windows and the thick tracery of the Gothic

> workmanship is as rich as fancy can desire; and though in
> gazing on such a structure one knows by rule that the old
> priests who built it, built it wrong, one cannot bring oneself to
> wish that they should have made it other than it is. (150)

The tone here is serious, however playful the allegory. The
description is meant to warm the reader out of too critical an
attitude to a structure so informally put together, its ceremonial
hierarchy so remote from its Low Church body. Sherman
Hawkins, in a very thorough piece of detective work on *The
Warden*, has noticed this and the other examples I've mentioned
of Trollope's artfulness.[42] He suggests that Trollope has created
a kind of low-key religious vision in which the warden
transcends the empty faiths both of institutionalised Anglicanism
and of sanctified press. Harding, argues Hawkins, is truly a
precentor in the sense of a guide to spiritual harmony. Allusions
to the pelican, to God that feeds the young ravens, and to St.
Cecilia, suggest to Hawkins an imitation of Christ. No wonder,
according to this interpretation, that Trollope made it twelve
bedesmen instead of copying the thirteen at St. Cross; the
parallel with the apostles can't be missed. So little can it be
missed that Hawkins also finds a Judas, a Gethsemane, and even
a paradisal Garden – complete with snake in the lawyer Finney.
Such overkill threatens what's valid in his argument, but two of
the points to which he calls attention need emphasis. First, *The
Warden* is for Trollope a very literary novel; and second, as
Henry James pointed out,[43] the character of Harding is central.

Trollope's literariness in *The Warden* was part of his attempt to
establish a readership, after the failure of the first three novels.
He took great care over this short work, over its structure as well
as its style and action.[44] If the literariness wasn't wholly good for
the novel in ways I've tried to indicate, it may have helped
impress readers and reviewers (all the reviews selected in the
Critical Heritage volume use the word 'clever'). But though the
experiment may have helped the novelist's confidence, it is
significant that he didn't repeat it. No other Trollope novel is
literary to anything like the same extent. This element in *The
Warden* supplements Sutherland's suggestion that one reason
why the novel succeeded where its predecessors had failed was
its 'unassuming subject matter'.[45] The literary and other

allusions, it might be argued, were largely there for diversion. But the reason Trollope's Irish novels failed was mainly that they were Irish, not that their subject matter was too strong. And it's worth questioning whether what is at issue in *The Warden* is after all so modest.

There is much to support Sutherland's case. If *The Warden* is a novel about change, it deals with an eddy in a backwater not a rapid in the stream. John Bold may be an outsider, but he's only half one: he's a friend of the warden at the beginning, and his son-in-law at the end. Since Harding is already connected with the Bishop, whose son, the Archdeacon, is his own son-in-law, what the novel ends with is an extended family. Then the whole sub-plot, in which Eleanor Harding pleads with Bold to call off his action at the expense of an offer she can't refuse, romanticises the story even as it shows Harding resisting a false solution. Trollope's novel is perhaps less topical than it looks. Though it's about the kind of event that's in the news, neither the issues nor the way they're handled seem truly representative.

Yet, given the conventionality of *The Warden*, and its sympathy for the Establishment, it's in this novel that the unofficial Trollope makes his first characteristic entrance. The novel introduces three themes which are to run in combination through Trollope's fiction. They are themes which his best novels will develop differently, but in them consists much of the insight those novels enable into Victorian society. The first I shall call institutional thinking, by which I mean those habits of mind which limit understanding within a closed system of assumptions devoted to the institution's well-being. *The Warden* features three main institutions: the Anglican church, the press and the law. Each one is represented by an individual who can't see beyond the scaffolding which each has erected to keep itself standing. Grantly sees everything from the perspective of the Church. A kind of justice that threatens clerical supremacy is, to him, unthinkable. To Sir Abraham Haphazard, justice itself is meaningless. The legal code is a world of its own where technicalities not principles of equity govern. Worse still, Tom Towers, the editor, believes himself above morality. The *Jupiter*, Trollope insists, is devoted not so much to truth as to its own pre-eminence. All these characters are sincere in their own terms. But that isn't saying much for them when it's realised how limited those terms are, and how they are designed to protect vested interests.

In the institutions of Church, law, and press, Trollope pinpoints three areas of specialised ethics, and he demonstrates the gaps in social morality, as well as the gaps in understanding, that they create. But it's through the warden himself that he reveals the kind of conflict caused by institutional thinking. Henry James said that Trollope's novel was 'simply the history of an old man's conscience'[46] – a persuasive half-truth, like much of his essay. *The Warden* is less about its central character's conscience than about his abandonment of a perspective to which he has become naturalised by dwelling within it. Trollope presents Harding's confusion and timidity but also, once he has decided to resign, his courage and principle. Harding himself suggests the contrast when he says: 'I cannot boast of my conscience, when it required the violence of a public newspaper to awaken it; but, now that it is awake, I must obey it' (219). Trollope's special pleading on Harding's behalf, in phrases such as 'our good, kind, loving warden' (33), sometimes interferes with the firmness of his conception. That firmness stands out in Harding's mixed motives – his wish both to do the right thing morally and to escape public blame, his bewilderment, and his inconsistency, for instance in proposing that his own resignation need not prevent someone else from taking his place. Like the Earl of Guilford, Harding can't see that resigning solves little, except perhaps a hurt conscience. But unlike the Earl he acts with some strength and integrity.

What forces Harding outside the charmed circle of institutional thinking is another institution, the press. In his portrayal of the *Jupiter*, Trollope raises the question of the extent to which in a developed society people have to rely for their judgements as well as their information on centralised and apparently objective sources. This is a familiar problem in our day, but Trollope saw the dangers in his – though he was unfair to the *Times* in the process. Another danger which he feared from mass circulation newspapers goes deeper. This, the second characteristic theme to be introduced to his fiction by *The Warden*, is the theme of social pressure. As I shall show in Chapter 4, people in Trollope depend to an unusual degree on confirmation from those around them. When this is withheld, or worse when they are censured publicly, their sense of identity falls into danger. This is what happens to Harding when the *Jupiter* accuses him. Harding isn't the man to stay sure of himself when his own unexamined assumptions come under aggressive scrutiny. The old supports to his way of life have crumbled without his knowing it. The new ones, in the shape of Grantly's and Haphazard's professionalism, are unacceptable. Trollope presents the impact of change on and within a slight but in several ways admirable figure. Grantly, Haphazard and Towers are each representative in that they stand for Church, law, and press respectively. Harding is representative in his vulnerability to social pressure.

The third major theme to emerge from *The Warden* is that of insolubility. Any action that Harding can take will entail loss and suffering. If he stays put, he'll be subject to the double penalty of knowing that he's in the wrong and of public shame. He has to deny the easy solutions offered by Sir Abraham's legal niceties and John Bold's capitulation. But hardly any better are the effects of resigning. Indeed, they are actually worse for the bedesmen who are the objects of the charity. The Bishop rightly refuses to replace his friend. Preferment resigned on such grounds shouldn't be offered again. But the Bishop can't bring himself to do anything else. He's from a different age, out of touch, puzzled and incapable. The charity has to wait for its reform till his death some years later. With no warden in residence, the bedesmen die off one by one and the hospital slowly decays. This perhaps is part of Trollope's conservative rhetoric – it might have been better to leave the charity alone, despite the inequity. Yet in another way the ending stands up as authentic. Trollope may link most of his characters in a single family at the end, whereas Whiston made lifelong enemies at Rochester. But in its account of the hospital declining the novel doesn't neglect the painful attrition of change. Reform must come sooner or later, and there are human prices to be paid.

Two further themes of *The Warden* recur significantly in Trollope's later fiction. Trollope had a combative interest in lawyers, and one of his novel's important perceptions is their increasing power at this period.[47] Symptomatic of this is the fact that the case against Harding begins not with John Bold but with his lawyer, Finney. Similarly, Sir Abraham Haphazard doesn't just appear in the novel as a legal robot who can always get a judgment on technicalities. He's also shown in parliament speaking in favour of a Bill which, Robert Martin points out, is a far from extreme parody of a piece of legislation which was actually debated, and with effects similar to those in the novel, in 1853.[48] Here Trollope puts his finger both on the growing importance of lawyers, and, not for the last time, on the artificiality of parliamentary practice – the debate hinges on a clause inserted simply for tactical reasons (198–9). Trollope's experience of marginality helped allow him to put such manoeuvres in parentheses and see them as games. That, and his membership of the Civil Service, is the source of an insight into institutional thinking which extends, later in his career, into more general fields of social behaviour. But there are only two pointers towards this in *The Warden*: the description of the tea party, which is mannered and heavy, and the account of Eleanor Harding's dilemma, which is more interesting. Modesty demands of Eleanor that she renounce her lover, since her plea to Bold to spare her father makes it look as if she's inviting him to propose. The confusion isn't in her so much as in the assumption that's taken for granted, that in courtship the woman must stay passive. This is a slight example of those incongruous problems produced by the rules of ordinary behaviour which Trollope was to explore more fully as he developed. But two limitations to his insight should be noted. The general tenor of *The Warden* suggests that he wasn't sufficiently prepared to step outside the network of presuppositions within which he operated, though he could demonstrate their inconsistencies. Secondly, the idea that organised human activity is like a game can weaken the will for positive change. Someone who accepts that everything runs according to arbitrary rules is likely to put up with them. The alternatives may not seem any better.

Finally, there is the theme of resignation. As I've pointed out in Chapter 1, this runs through Trollope's fiction, and it is central to *The Warden*. Harding resigns his position, Eleanor tries to resign her lover, Bold gives up his case. From one point of view, resignation means affirmation. Self-denial becomes proof of integrity. But there's another viewpoint which the language of *The Warden* conveys. Anyone who reads the novel with some attention must notice the repetition of words like 'comfort', 'content', and their cognates. Often language like this occurs in passages of moral analysis. The sense one gets is that bedrock moral decisions in Trollope are based less on codes of right and wrong than on how far individuals feel happy within them. Sherman Hawkins calls this 'Trollope's moral hedonism',[49] but the explanation is too simple for a novelist who took moral questions seriously. What Trollope has identified is the rule-of-thumb, unthought-out morality on which most people who follow the ordinary codes base their decisions. If it feels right, it is right, and there's no need to go further. But what he has also identified is a habit of mind typical of a society that has undergone little change. That was the condition of the people Trollope was writing about, and resignation while feeling good was one solution to the necessity for those in established positions of accepting change.

I've suggested that both an official and an unofficial Trollope may be distinguished in the novelist's writings on Ireland. The *Examiner* letters express the official self at its most unequivocal, while its counterpart finds a voice, increasingly muffled, in the fiction. These different kinds of consciousness, of response, stem from Trollope's double role as civil servant and novelist, from his bid to produce himself as a writer, and from his early experience of marginality. In *The Warden* they appear for the first time in the form that is later to characterise his work. This double perspective is the source of *The Warden*'s confusions, but also in part of its strength. It isn't, as Trollope claimed in his *Autobiography*, that he had tried to present two equal but opposite cases and found himself in contradiction. Rather, much of the novel consists of special pleading for an established order whose faults are admitted only to be tolerated. Yet the perceptions about institutional thinking, about the stresses of change, cut the other way – and so does the focus on an isolated figure at the centre. The novel is sometimes mistaken, even irritating, certainly not great. But Trollope achieves a subtlety and penetration of insight in areas where his rhetorical intent isn't directly engaged. According to his account in the *Autobiography*, he was aiming at 'balance' almost in the cant sense of today's practice in the media. He shows that there are things to be said for and against Church reform, but weights the scale towards the safest interpretation. Yet making Harding's experience central released a deeper source in his imagination. He saw

the individual caught between institutions that were expoiting
him for their own interest, and this opened his mind to the
distortions and dangers of institutional thinking. Perhaps the
unofficial Trollope depended on the official. Only by working in
an institution, by dwelling within a code, can its workings be
seen – so long as enough detachment is preserved to pursue their
implications. That detachment came from Trollope's impulse to
identify with the person exposed unfairly to public shame. His
unofficial side developed a much fuller awareness in the novel
than its rhetorical bias promises.

Trollope's next work was a product almost entirely of his official
self, built out of his ambition to establish himself as a writer. For
the sequence of events after publication of *The Warden* there is
only Michael Sadleir's account, as the documents he based it on
were destroyed.[50] Evidently Trollope had confidence in his
novel. He must have expected it to sell, for it was topical but not
too topical, and much better suited than his previous works to
the taste of a middle-class audience. He recalled in his
Autobiography: 'Certainly no other work that I ever did took up so
much of my thoughts' (83). All this gave him reason to feel
justified in starting a sequel, as he had planned. But when on 17
February 1855, only a matter of weeks after publication, he
wrote to Longman to ask about *The Warden*'s sales the reply was
discouraging. What is striking is that he then immediately
abandoned *Barchester Towers*, at which he had already made a
promising start, for an entirely different project – most of which
he must have written already. Six weeks later, on 27 March, he
was able to forward to Longman the manuscript of *The New
Zealander*. This shows an almost desperate determination. If *The
Warden* really were going to fail, he would, whatever his own
opinion of the novel, at once try another role in which to come
before the public.

So, six months after reporting favourably on *The Warden*,
Longman's reader was astonished by a work which he could
hardly believe had been written by the same author. *The New
Zealander* attempts nothing less than to appraise the nation's
condition and prescribe moral restoratives against a decline
which might be delayed though it couldn't be averted. The book
was rejected, but this didn't inhibit Trollope's enthusiasm as he

apparently revised it thoroughly with a view to trying it again. He was working on it at least until May 1856, when he again took up *Barchester Towers*, so that the version published in 1972, after over a century of neglect, probably differs quite a lot from the one sent to the publisher.[51] But even the revision is less likely to excite than embarrass. Few critics have commented on it at any length, most preferring a tactful reticence.

But the book has its significance. It demonstrates a role in which Trollope thought he could write to effect, a side of him difficult to guess from his other published work. Some of the views it reveals are interesting, but most of all it shows the gap between a consciously assumed authorial self and the unofficial self that emerges from his fiction at its best. In a few respects *The New Zealander* follows on from *The Warden*, most obviously in its discussion of the law and the press. But another and potentially a more telling connexion is that the book's whole organisation is based on an analysis of the country's main institutions. The work was to be framed by an introduction and conclusion which consist chiefly of moral exhortation. Its body was to be made up of four blocks mostly of three chapters each. These deal first with how the country is and ought to be run ('The Civil Service', 'The People and Their Rulers', 'The Press'), then with business and the professions ('Law and Physic', 'Trade', 'The Army and Navy', 'The Church'), then with the structure of government ('The House of Commons', 'The House of Lords', 'The Crown'), and lastly with culture ('Society', 'Literature', 'Art'). Two of the chapters, 'The Civil Service' and 'Trade', were apparently abstracted from the manuscript for use elsewhere.[52] But the positions marked for them in the original, and the thirteen chapters that survive, allow a number of provisional conclusions about Trollope's thinking in the mid-1850s.

It's surprising to find 'The Civil Service' intended as the first chapter after the introduction. Such a priority probably reflects not so much Trollope's own membership of the Service as his conviction in the worth of efficient administration. In February 1856, when he was still working on *The New Zealander*, he was to send to the *Athenaeum* an article on the third number of *Little Dorrit*. This was rejected and is now lost, but it is unlikely to have been sympathetic to Dickens' account of the Circumlocution Office.[53] The next chapter, 'The People and Their Rulers', states the general principles behind Trollope's theory of government. These were probably meant to underpin his case for the importance of the Civil Service, and for the role of gentlemen in public service generally – a subject on which he held well-known views (see, for instance, *An Autobiography*, 34). For he argues in favour of aristocracy in its etymological sense, government by the best. Not that this means an aristocracy of merit. How true aristocrats get selected Trollope leaves a mystery; how false ones are got rid of he admits is problematic (*New Zealander*, 13). Presumably he means simply gentlemen, with a few allowed exceptions. The confusions in this idea of course aren't limited to *The New Zealander*, but lie at the centre of Trollope's official thinking (and incidentally suggest that Dickens wasn't far wrong). Trollope needed to believe in promotion by merit, because that was how he had got on. But that couldn't mean merit as determined by competitive examinations, because of the need for practical experience and, especially, of an ideal of service which he believed almost exclusive to those he called gentlemen. What all this adds up to is a bourgeois takeover bid for the idea of aristocracy. Similarly with the idea of labour. Trollope believed labour should be honoured, but the specifics he recommended were all class-based: proper direction from above, basic education, individualism and self-respect. This blend,and sometimes confusion, of bourgeois and genteel values mirrors his own social position. For the duration of his career it was to remain a constant in his official thinking.

The same bias helps motivate Trollope's intense suspicion of the press (meaning the *Times* – for him the two were one and the same). What underlies this is a fear of democracy, stimulated almost certainly by de Tocqueville's influence.[54] He shifts revealingly from fear of the press to fear of what he sees as mob rule:

> A King too dominant, a minister too dominant, a party too dominant, have all been known, felt, dreaded, and finally overcome. Now we have a newspaper too dominant; that also is now known, and felt; will soon be dreaded, and must be overcome.
>
> For a man who has ever loved the idea of liberty how sad it is to see that the very landmarks of freedom which have been

longed for in one age, become, in the next, when acquired, the very strongest holds of tyranny! Look to the American States where every man is equal; from which all dominion of ascendant classes has been banished; where political power rests solely with the people, and there you will see such tyranny as is not compassed even at St. Petersburg. Who there can dare to advocate opinions contrary to those prevalent with the mob? (37)

Since it's difficult to suppose the *Times* ever guilty of encouraging mob rule, it's no surprise that Trollope later switched his attack to the new popular press, represented in the Palliser novels by *The People's Banner*.[55] The passage quoted is a fair sample of *The New Zealander's* rhetorical style, with its tub-thumping repetitiveness. It helps show why, though Trollope organised his critique around English institutions, he failed in this work to develop the perceptions he had reached by another route in *The Warden*. The nearest he came to those perceptions in *The New Zealander* is a passage on another of his habitual targets, the lawyer:

It is not that he fails to look on the truth as excellent; it is not that he is less averse to murder than another; it is not that he would have crime escape unpunished; but the habits of his education, of his trade, and his life will not allow him to see clearly. He has long since learned that no man in England is required to criminate himself, and he cannot bring himself to question the value of the lesson. How many lessons of the same kind have we not all learnt? (56).

This is an attack, as far as it goes, on institutional thinking. But Trollope was much better able to dramatise such a matter than to discuss it convincingly. That is why the unofficial view provided by the fiction goes deeper than his conscious and deliberate pronouncements. Trollope complains several times in *The New Zealander*, and often in his later career, that people are always mistaking habit-blindness for thinking.[56] The irony is that his own discursive thoughts are so frequently prejudiced or illogical. He cannot see, in the passage above, the need to protect innocence from oppression, although in *Phineas Redux* he will describe with force and sympathy a man's feelings in just such a case. And he cannot recognise the merits either of the system of advocacy or of trial by jury, the one because he thought it dishonest, the other because he preferred to trust a specialist's judgment to that arrived at by a group of ordinary people. Since these views are controversial, neither can be charged with habit-blindness. The trouble is that neither has been thought out properly. Trollope simplifies far too much. He fails to see what his fiction so often shows: that principle and dogma, however sincere, won't match human circumstance.

The chapter on the press is meant to illustrate the dangers which the two previous chapters were probably designed to meet. Good government at all levels, including the government of one's own opinions, would reverse the power of newspaper and mob. Then Trollope moves on to business and the professions, but it's unnecessary to follow him closely now that the main lines of his approach have been indicated. Considering *The New Zealander* as a profile of mid-Victorian England, its most obvious omission is industry. Trollope talks at various times of factory workers, miners, and of a railway contractor, but there is no separate chapter on the topic. Instead there is just the chapter on trade, missing from the manuscript, which from its title and from other material elsewhere seems almost certain to have dealt exclusively with commerce. The omission is hardly surprising, given Trollope's background and experience. It's possible that he would have written different novels if on his postal survey he had been sent to the industrial areas of the Midlands and North instead of to the rural South-west. At least he would have avoided defining England as 'feudal' or 'chival-rous', as he did at the start of the novel he wrote a few years later, *Doctor Thorne* (11; see also Chapter 6).

But a contemporary reader of *The Warden*, or later of the Barsetshire chronicles, might also have found some unexpected opinions declared by the same author in *The New Zealander*. This is another sign that Trollope was not only adopting a different form, but another writing identity. Where *The Warden* expresses a mild conservatism, ruefully accepting the hard necessities of change, *The New Zealander* shows some impatience. The nation's security is to be achieved 'by the mutability, not by the immutability, of our institutions' (149), and a protest is entered at 'paying worship to the dead at the expense of the living' (141).

Similarly Trollope rejects formalism and dogma in religion. He urges tolerance for Roman Catholics and Dissenters, and questions the obligation for non-conformists to pay Church Rates – not always enforced, but not abolished till 1868 (7). In a moment rare in all his writing, he mentions the 'two thousand labouring poor' for whom his figure of a typical clergyman ought to be responsible (99). Yet the book's sympathies for those working in fields, mines or factories remain conventional and distant. It has its decencies more by virtue of humane common sense. Writing during the Crimean War, Trollope advises that an enlisted man is likely to have the worst of his bargain with his country (178). And he insists on the benefits of education, especially on its superiority in the colonies. By this he doesn't always mean practical training, for he affirms that 'the happiness of any man to whom has been imparted the power of reading and enjoying a song of Burns' is to a certain extent ensured for his lifetime' (176). He discusses how the English middle class too often fails to amuse itself socially in its half-baked efforts to impress. Speaking up for country house architecture, the English school (especially Hogarth) in painting, and the need for a truly national gallery, he shows a firm if John Bullish taste. His attitude to art and literature certainly isn't philistine, but he avoids the exclusive idea of culture ('the best which has been thought and said in the world') which Matthew Arnold was to stress.

The New Zealander was compared by Longman's reader to Carlyle's *Latter-Day Pamphlets*.[57] Trollope's own remarks in several places on Carlyle suggest that he wouldn't have approved of the association,[58] but it's apt in a limited sense. *The New Zealander* was his attempt to set himself up, if not as Victorian prophet then as pundit. Its viewpoint is one of opinionated concern, its manner a written equivalent of Hyde Park oratory. The crucial fault is that it collapses again and again into moral sermonising. The plan Trollope chose, an account of his country according to its institutions, should have enabled a more searching critique. But Trollope persists in reducing every question to the Burns line he cites so often, 'It's gude to be honest and true'.[59] Equipped with this touchstone he can see and repudiate hypocrisy, as when he attacks the writer who 'asserts a doctrine not higher than that by which he lives, but higher than that by which he would wish to live' (49), rejects parliamentary purism, or insists on the worth of ambition and the naturalness of pleasure. But the maxim can't take him much further, especially as a restorative to hold off national degeneration. Why Trollope made it his slogan is worth considering.

Much of Trollope's writing shows a fear of runaway speculation. He had watched his parents go bankrupt after the failure of their financial adventure with the bazaar in Cincinnati; later, he had even saved some furniture from the bailiffs (*Autobiography*, 19–23). While a clerk in London he had invariably been in debt, persecuted by the collector (41–3). He had based his diagnosis of economic collapse in Ireland on previous extravagance and inflation of rents. And there were examples around him of speculative mania, including the rise and fall of George Hudson the railway king, and the suicide of John Sadleir the financier, whom he mentions in *The New Zealander* (211). His emphatic if simple solution represents his response to the economic development of Victorian England which took place through unprecedented and often risky investment, and which threw up scandals, suicides and the newly rich. This is the source and meaning of the nostalgic hope he expresses in *Doctor Thorne*, that England may never be a commercial country (12), and a central theme of the Barsetshire series. The essential myth of Barsetshire is of a haven where the old values, moral and material, are still current and capable of resisting commercialism in relationships as in cash. In *The Last Chronicle of Barset*, at the end of the series, Trollope includes a suicide speculator, Dobbs Broughton, and it's no coincidence that Josiah Crawley would never have been accused of theft if he hadn't been paid with someone else's cheque. *The Way We Live Now* is, of course, the novel in which Trollope made his most sustained attack on commercialism. But the tone of his attitude may be gauged from a by-the-way remark in *The Eustace Diamonds*, where he writes that for a major speech in parliament 'all the Directors of the Bank of England were in the gallery, and every chairman of a great banking company, and every Baring and every Rothschild, if there be Barings and Rothschilds who have not been returned by constituencies, and have not seats in the House by right' (485). This is an acid enough comment on the power of the moneymen, with its tinge of anti-Semitism. Trollope's own money dealings were always highly scrupulous, but in his attacks on commercialism, as in *The Struggles of Brown, Jones and Robinson* and (much later) *The Prime Minister*, it isn't always easy to separate the principle from the prejudice. The theme of honesty in Trollope is often not so much moral as ideological. As a prescription for delaying decadence it is at once too general and too limited. If *The New Zealander* could have had any life it was probably this that stifled it.

3 The Novelist Produces Himself (2)

Trollope's struggles to knock *The New Zealander* into publishable shape draw attention to a fact which could otherwise be easily overlooked – that after more than ten years of trying he had still not established a writing identity. It's tempting, but mistaken, to read back into the writer of those years the novelist he later became. In 1856 the possibilities were still open, and Trollope's persistence with his punditry suggests that he continued to think it his best chance of making a name. There is no record of why he changed his mind, but the most likely explanation is that *The Warden* turned out more successful than Longman's letter had led him to believe. So he returned to *Barchester Towers*, which as he had told Longman had always been planned as a sequel (*Letters*, p. 24, 17 February 1855).

Immediately he took a crucial step in beginning a working diary. Although he says in his *Autobiography* that he had 'always' kept one (102), the word shouldn't be taken literally. It must have seemed like always from the vantage point of the fifty or so books, not to mention articles and reviews, which he had completed when he made the statement. He is unlikely to have composed to such a plan works written as slowly, in comparison, as those of his first decade as an author. The immediate reason for keeping a diary is obscure. It may have been connected with another characteristic innovation, writing in railway carriages, which Trollope adopted at this time (*Autobiography*, 88). But it also seems possible that with *The New Zealander*'s rejection, and the partial success – it was now clear – of *The Warden*, Trollope decided that if he was to become a professional writer he must professionalise himself. That, to a civil servant who had long been concerned with an early form of time-and-motion study, could only mean arranging the most efficient schedule possible

54

for the production of words. It is possible to date exactly the new method's origin thanks to a marginal note in *The New Zealander* and to Trollope's papers in the Bodleian Library.[1] The last date in the margins of *The New Zealander* is May 1856; the working diary for *Barchester Towers* begins on 12 May of that year. That this was the new method's beginning is strongly suggested by the fact that Trollope had already written eighty-five manuscript pages of his novel before starting the diary. This also means that *Barchester Towers* in its published form can't have been one-third written by early 1855, as he had told Longman in his letter of 17 February (*Letters*, p. 24). It's possible, though it seems unlikely, that he slipped, having meant to say he had completed a third of the first volume. This would tally almost exactly with his numbering of the manuscript pages (eighty-five out of 240). Or, since he also said he hoped to finish the novel by 1 May if *The Warden* were selling, perhaps he planned a work of about the same length (completed, it's nearly three times as long). When he returned to *Barchester Towers* over a year later, he roughed out some notes on the back of his writing diary for the chapters he resumed with (8–12). These interestingly suggest that the introduction at that point of the Stanhopes, who add so much to the novel, may have been an afterthought; and also that Trollope had yet to work out his plot concerning Slope's love affairs and the deanery.

With *Barchester Towers* Trollope professionalised himself as an author in the sense that he adopted a regular plan of work and began to make money consistently from his writings. As Sutherland has shown, the prices he was able to command from his publishers and also his status in dealing with them began to rise from this time. Having obtained an advance of £100 on the half-profits of *Barchester Towers*, he received £250 for the copyright of *The Three Clerks*, £400 for *Doctor Thorne*, £400 again for *The Bertrams* but with a half share in the copyright to revert to him after three years, £250 for *The West Indies and the Spanish Main*, and £600 for *Castle Richmond*.[2] This means that from 1858 he was earning from his writing at least as much as three-quarters of what he earned from the Post Office, which in 1857 was £700 and from the end of 1859 £800 a year.[3] He could consider himself to have arrived as an author. In the *Times* of 23 May 1859 E. S. Dallas said Trollope was 'at the top of the tree'.[4]

But he added the qualification that his success was as an author 'of the circulating library sort'. The final advance was still to come.

The story of how Trollope was commissioned at a late stage in the planning of the new *Cornhill Magazine* to contribute its lead serial is known well enough not to need repetition here.[5] What I would like to emphasise is the impact of this unexpected opportunity on his career. Most obviously, the success of *Framley Parsonage* raised him immediately to the rank of a major novelist. He wasn't only a Mudie novelist – even if one of the most successful – any more. To take prices alone as a guide, he received £1000 for *Framley Parsonage*. For the next fifteen years he would receive not less than £2500 for any three-volume novel, and often substantially more, whether it was to be published first as a serial in a magazine or in parts. He gained a very wide readership thanks to the large circulation of the *Cornhill*. And he passed up few chances to undertake other literary work, though in 1861 he refused a lucrative offer to act as figurehead editor for the newly-founded rival *Temple Bar*.[6]

Secondly, and perhaps equally important, the *Cornhill* engagement helped define the general view of what kind of novelist Trollope was. When George Smith first called on Trollope for a novel, Trollope proposed *Castle Richmond*, which he had half finished for Chapman and Hall. But Smith, as Trollope describes it, 'suggested the Church, as though it were my peculiar subject. . . . He wanted an English tale, on English life, with a clerical flavour' (*Autobiography*, 122–3). And on that basis Trollope began his new novel in the train on the way home. What Smith had done was to identify Trollope as the chronicler of Barset. Trollope's own account doesn't suggest he considered the Church to be his special line. In this Smith displayed good judgement, since the three novels of the series published by 1859 are, with the exception of *The Macdermots of Ballycloran*, superior to Trollope's other completed work, and with his publisher's instinct he had recognised excellent chances of success for his magazine with an already established and developing product. The extraordinary thing is that Trollope either hadn't noticed the success and future potential of the Barsetshire novels as distinct from his other work, or, if he had noticed it, that he still preferred to try other kinds of writing. Though he was a poor judge of his own work, the latter alternative seems more likely.

Straightaway after *Barchester Towers* he had written a different type of novel with a quite different locale in *The Three Clerks*. Then he had experimented with *The Struggles of Brown, Jones and Robinson* (not finished till 1861) before returning to Barsetshire for *Doctor Thorne*. *The Bertrams*, the West Indies travel book, *Castle Richmond*, and a number of short stories all followed until Smith elicited *Framley Parsonage*. Trollope doesn't mention in his *Autobiography* that he had thought of writing a further Barsetshire chronicle before. It isn't at all clear whether he even considered these novels as a series until he wrote *Framley Parsonage* and drew his map of Barsetshire.

The sequence of events at this stage of Trollope's career is important because it helps determine whether he became a formula novelist, and if so how far. Sutherland finds that the phrase fits, though he praises Trollope for keeping up a much higher standard of work than it might imply.[7] But it was Smith who fixed, if he did not originate, Trollope's stereotyping as a clerical novelist. Although David Skilton dates Trollope's image as 'essentially the author of the *Chronicles of Barsetshire*' from late 1857,[8] I can find no evidence for this either from the *Critical Heritage* volume or from his own book. According to Skilton, the *Saturday Review* of 5 December 1857 finds *The Three Clerks* less satisfactory than the two previous novels, but in fact it says just the opposite. While finding plenty of faults in the new work, it declares: 'We think *The Three Clerks* a step in advance of Mr. Trollope's earlier works.'[9] *The Bertrams* was actually praised by the *Examiner* for providing another example of the novelist's versatility.[10] So, if *Framley Parsonage* established the Barsetshire image, Trollope didn't exactly choose to play up to it. He next went for another kind of subject in *Orley Farm* and a different form of publication, in monthly numbers. When he went back to the Barsetshire series with *The Small House at Allington* (also published in the *Cornhill*), he wrote a novel that had a minimum of clerical interest, though it reintroduced characters from earlier in the series, and he later jibbed at including it in *The Chronicles of Barsetshire*.[11] It was open to Trollope to continue turning out books like *Barchester Towers* or *Framley Parsonage*, but he chose to vary his topic in each of the novels and to end the series unreservedly after *The Small House at Allington* with *The Last Chronicle of Barset*. He seems to have feared that his readers might reject him not only for producing too much, but for producing too much of the same kind of material. So he began another series in the Palliser novels before the Barsetshires were finished. He took up difficult subjects, like the breakdown of a marriage in *He Knew He Was Right*, or prostitution in *The Vicar* of *Bullhampton*. Experiments such as *Nina Balatka* and *Linda Tressel*, both published anonymously, set abroad, and superficially unTrollopian in character, are further signs of his anxiety not to become stereotyped.

If Trollope produced himself as a formula novelist, it was less in his choice of subject than in his manner of work. The writing diary was part of this. He contracted with himself to write every day a certain number of words. This, with his habit of 'castle-building' now fully developed, allowed him to compose fiction of very even and on the whole surprisingly high quality, especially once he had perfected his routine. The pressure shows in carelessness early on. The *Saturday Review* commented in particular on slips and inconsistencies in *The Three Clerks*.[12] But the method's advantage is clear from *The Bertrams*, which probably couldn't have been produced without it – having been begun, the diary records, 'in Egypt, and written on the Mediterranean, in Malta, Gibraltar, England, Ireland, Scotland and finished in the West Indies'.[13] And this was a novel which Trollope had started only a day after finishing *Doctor Thorne* (*Autobiography*, 105; confirmed by the working diaries). No wonder *The Bertrams* is hardly free from faults, especially bad writing. In subsequent novels practice in the routine would help iron most of these out.

The third change that *Framley Parsonage* brought to Trollope's career was more fundamental to his writing than being defined as the chronicler of Barset – even than reaching the top rank among novelists. This was the new discipline of composing a serial. Starting with *Framley Parsonage*, Trollope wrote nearly all his novels in parts. As Mary Hamer has shown in detail, he did so whether or not he knew they were to be published serially, and in many cases (sixteen novels out of thirty-two) before he had placed them with a publisher.[14] This was probably no more than sound business sense, as almost all his work from his first serial onwards came out initially in parts. The only real exception is *Miss Mackenzie*, since *Harry Heathcote of Gangoil*, the only other novel not to be bought as a serial was a Christmas story for a special issue and so couldn't have been issued in parts. But Trollope also challenged himself with demands that exceed even those of composing for a serial. When he was beginning *The Last Chronicle of Barset*, he volunteered to write it so that it could be published in either twenty or thirty parts, observing to George Smith: 'There will be some trouble in this, but having a mechanical mind I think I can do it' (*Letters*, 6 February 1866, p. 178). He doesn't express any enthusiasm for the task in itself, adding that he could do the work for 'the sixpenny venture' (i.e. the thirty-number issue) 'more easily and more pleasantly'. In the event, Smith saved him the difficulty by deciding on thirty numbers, though the novel finally came out in thirty-two weekly parts. But in five later novels Trollope actually carried out the task he had proposed to Smith. Hamer, who calls attention to this double burden, suggests that Trollope must have valued the challenge, especially as he kept on with both schemes in the case of *He Knew He was Right* even though its publisher agreed to one of them only two days after Trollope had started writing it.[15] Perhaps there is another explanation. *He Knew He Was Right* came out in weekly numbers at sixpence each. The last novel for which this form of publication had been tried was *The Last Chronicle of Barset*. In his *Autobiography* Trollope says the experiment 'was not altogether successful' (236), so it seems possible that in composing *He Knew He Was Right* he deliberately left open the opportunity of publication in a different form (i.e. in twenty numbers of a magazine) in case it proved advisable. Three of the other five novels he wrote with alternative part schemes were completed before being placed with publishers, so in these cases the double arrangement was probably for the convenience of the market – especially as all three are very long works (*The Eustace Diamonds*, *Phineas Redux*, and *The Duke's Children*). In the last case, that of *The Prime Minister*, the novel was again to come out in separate numbers rather than as a magazine serial. As this form of publication was becoming less attractive at the period, Trollope may again have preferred the security of an alternative plan for publishing his novel.

Studied in detail, Trollope's working methods reveal a willingness to meet at least halfway the demands of the market. It can be argued, for instance, that he constructed his serials carefully, grouping or separating chapters to achieve effects of juxtaposition and contrast. This certainly happens, notably in Number Eleven of *The Last Chronicle of Barset*.[16] But then several questions arise. How would such effects work in a novel designed like *He Knew He Was Right*, to be published either in thirty-two or in twenty parts? If the novel had come out in the second form rather than the first, some of the effects Trollope might have planned in constructing his serial would inevitably have been sacrificed – as only a few of the part divisions could possibly coincide. Similarly, he made no bones when his novels were published with serial divisions differing from those for which he had provided. Dickens was well aware of the special problems in writing serial fiction for his weekly *All The Year Round*, which required very short parts.[17] But Trollope sold three of his later novels to the same periodical, though they were to come out in much smaller instalments than the ones he had written them for.[18] He commented on exactly this problem in a letter to William Blackwood: 'In writing a story in numbers a novelist divides his points of interest, so as to make each section a whole. It will often happen that his divisions should be recast to suit circumstances. But this cannot be done without a certain amount of detriment to the telling of the story' (*Letters*, 11 February 1880, p. 432). On that occasion Blackwood published the novel in question, *Dr. Wortle's School*, in the eight parts which Trollope had planned. The letter shows, however, that though Trollope knew how to exploit serial divisions effectively, he was prepared to bow to the expedients of the market. He would protest if a publisher tried to shortchange his readers, as he did in preventing both Strahan and Hurst and Blackett from publishing in two volumes works meant only for one.[19] Equally he was scrupulous in giving both full measure and full value. When he was told that Chapman and Hall had lost £120 on *The Duke's Children*, he offered to reimburse them (*Letters*, 13 August 1880, p. 444). But it isn't unfair to say that his integrity as a gentleman and as a man of business meant more to him than his integrity as a novelist. He would probably have preferred the same priority himself.

The benefit Trollope gained from composing in parts was, then, at least as much a business as an aesthetic stimulus. The working papers have nothing to show more revealing than the

relation, as he produced himself as a writer, between businessman and novelist. Composing in parts gave Trollope an extra
discipline by which to ensure production. The schemes of a
working diary and of writing within a framework of parts recall
the plans of another notable compulsive, Samuel Johnson, for
voluminous reading. Boswell records that Johnson numbered
the lines of a variety of classical works and drew up a table to set
the rate at which he would read them.[20] Trollope framed similar
and even more ambitious plans, but put them into effect as
producer more than consumer; though he did read, among
much else, nearly 300 early plays.[21] He had found a way of
turning his compulsions to profit. It was the official Trollope
who converted his desk into a portable production line, and,
administrator to his imagination, stood over it watch in hand.
Yet the result, given the unofficial Trollope's need to build
castles, to tell continual stories, was a kind of freedom. The
nature of that freedom may be illustrated from his first novel to
be subject to both constraints, the timetable of serial and of
diary.

It isn't a coincidence that *Framley Parsonage* is the novel to
introduce the multi-plot form which was later to characterise
Trollope's best work. In previous novels he had of course used
parallel plots, as in *The Kellys and the O'Kellys*, and sub-plots, as in
the love affair between John Bold and Eleanor Harding in *The
Warden*. The distinction of *Framley Parsonage* is that serial form
helped Trollope to develop and articulate coherently a variety
of separate but closely linked stories. It isn't necessary to take at
face value his remarks on the novel in his *Autobiography* (123).
Although, as Sutherland has put it, Trollope 'uses the language
of the cooking recipe' in describing how he made his plot,[22] it
doesn't follow that the novel is the 'hodge-podge' he made it out
to be. Certainly it contains a large number of stories. There are
the two major plot interests involving Mark Robarts and his
sister Lucy. Then, around these, are minor plots involving the
Grantly, Proudie, and Crawley familes, Miss Dunstable,
Nathaniel Sowerby, and Dr. Thorne – not to mention other
figures who play a still smaller role such as the Harold Smiths,
Frank Gresham, the Duke of Omnium, or the parliamentary
ciphers in the background. Yet the novel composes this mass of
disparate material into a surprisingly unified whole.

The key to the whole is power. This can be seen by reconstructing the necessary context the novel creates for itself, which is the political map of Barsetshire.[23] Excluding the de Courcys, whose influence is waning by the time of *Framley Parsonage*, six main forces are active in the county. The Proudies live in Barchester itself, the Grantlys to the south, Sowerby and the Duke of Omnium to the west, the Luftons to the north, and the Greshams to the east. When the novel opens, the balance of power is precarious. There is an alliance between the Grantlys and Luftons, countered by another between the Duke of Omnium and Sowerby. But the latter's estate is heavily mortgaged to the Duke, and if (as seems likely) it is absorbed by him, the Duke, who is already by far the richest landowner in the county, will become dangerously powerful. The other parties have not yet committed themselves firmly to either side, the Greshams because they have only just regained prominence, and the Proudies because they have objections to each opposing interest. They naturally resist the Grantlys and Luftons as Tory and High Church, but cannot altogether support the Duke on account of his immoral reputation, despite the lure of his rank.

The novel's action starts when Lady Lufton nominates Mark Robarts to the living of Framley. She does this in order to place a curb on her son, who is a friend of Robarts, and to consolidate her own influence in the parish, because she fears that the Duke's territorial ambitions threaten her son's estate as well as Sowerby's. Secondly, she agrees with Mrs. Grantly to encourage a match between her son and Mrs. Grantly's daughter, with a view to closing ranks and strengthening the connexions between the two families. Both plans misfire, but Lady Lufton's adversary does no better. The Duke's first scheme, to acquire Sowerby's property, is thwarted by Martha Dunstable who takes over the bankrupt's mortgages instead. Then, when the Duke tries to buy adjoining land in the Chase of Chaldicotes, Miss Dunstable forestalls him again. Heiress to a patent medicine manufacturer, she becomes the new champion of tradition. She grafts herself on to original Barsetshire stock by marrying Dr. Thorne, and, acting as a foil to the Duke, restores the county's balance of power. At the end, the new Thornes of Chaldicotes in western Barsetshire complement the old Thornes of Ullathorne in the east. More important, Dr. and Mrs. Thorne soften the internecine conflict of the previous arrangement by mediating between the two main power *blocs*: 'Here they live respected by their neighbours, and on terms of alliance both with the Duke of Omnium and with Lady Lufton' (*Framley Parsonage*, 522). Equilibrium is also restored in the county's representation in parliament, which remains divided west and east between Whigs and Tories. That the county's political balance reflects that of parliament demonstrates again the continuous theme in the novel of accommodations in power, ranging from the local (Mark Robarts' attempts to resist domination by Lady Lufton) to the national (the mock-heroic contest between gods and giants).

In the sphere of personal relationships power means not just politics but pride, the moral abstraction which provides the main official theme of *Framley Parsonage*. Mark Robarts, like all the other characters who fall to similar temptations, has to undergo the penalties of his worldliness. His sister Lucy, like the few who resist such temptations, will enjoy the benefits. But the moral theme carries nothing like the interest of the politics, even at the personal level. Here the core of the story is in Mark reaching a working relationship with his patroness, and in Lucy obtaining as a condition of accepting Lord Lufton the respect of the same formidable figure.

It would be possible to show how elements in the plot which I haven't examined, such as the role of the Proudies and Crawleys, fit into the political and moral economy of *Framley Parsonage*. But I hope enough has been said to indicate both the number of differing plot interests and their integration into a whole that makes sense on at least two major levels. Trollope had achieved nothing quite like this before. *The Bertrams*, also an ambitious novel, almost founders under the weight of fewer plot interests even though it's appreciably longer. But why should the serial form have helped him so much? One reason is put forward in his *Autobiography* when he says that the writer of a serial 'cannot afford to have many pages skipped out of the few which are to meet the reader's eye at the same time' (124). Realising this firmly, and with a long work to be released in many parts before him, he would keep up his readers' interest with a variety of stories while using the part-structure itself to articulate them. In this way serial form both favoured the proliferation of stories and provided a framework for controlling it. But the benefits went still deeper. I've mentioned that there are two layers to *Framley Parsonage*, the moral and the political. The first of these Trollope made his official theme, marking it carefully not only by parallels in his plots but by formal divisions and commentary.[24] Yet the novel's underlying structure is one of political manoeuvring resulting in consolidation of power in his imaginary county. This unofficial dimension to the novel isn't explicit. Trollope didn't point it up as he had his moral theme, and the likelihood is that it entered the novel less through deliberate planning than through an imaginative direction that developed spontaneously. If this is so, it was from the multi-plot structure that the political sub-text issued. To whatever degree he was aware of it, this is the element of the novel that has most to tell – partly about his own assumptions and wishes, but especially about how he saw the working, as a kind of self-stabilising mechanism, of the Victorian gentry. The discipline of the serial, and to a lesser extent of the diary, freed a part of his imagination by focusing his most conscious mind on the sheer mechanics of producing fiction. In the next chapter I shall discuss the underlying patterns revealed in the same way by the whole body of his writing. First, however, it remains to define the day-to-day habits by which he was to produce his writing for the rest of his career.

A fairly precise idea of Trollope's working methods may be pieced together from a variety of sources. He records in his *Autobiography* that his practice was to work for three hours every morning, of which half an hour was spent in reading what had been written the day before and the rest of the time in writing his usual quota of about ten pages of 250 words every quarter of an hour (234–5). He could achieve this rapidity of production, he says, only because he had prepared for it fully in advance. This he could do at the highest pressure when he had no distractions and could work fastest: 'At such times I have been able to imbue myself thoroughly with the characters I have had in hand. I have wandered alone among the rocks and woods, crying at their grief, laughing at their absurdities, and thoroughly enjoying their joy' (*Autobiography*, 151–2). Later in the same work he echoes this passage when he speaks of the novelist's need to live with his characters 'in the full reality of established intimacy' (200). And a few years after the *Autobiography* was written, but before it was published, he expanded on his account of how he composed in a short piece he contributed to *Good Words*.[25] The prior stage of composition, as has often been pointed out, is the 'castle-building' of his youth come to maturity. But it in turn couldn't occur without a stage still earlier, in which the developing writer 'in all his movements through the world . . . has, unconsciously for the most part, been drawing in matter from all that he has seen and heard' (*Autobiography*, 198).

If Trollope's account of how he composed his novels lays most emphasis on what preceded the writing, that doesn't mean he considered the writing unimportant. He often played down his labours as mechanical, but this shouldn't be taken too seriously. First, it's part of a defensive self-depreciation which had become habitual; the very first sentence of the *Autobiography* almost apologises for speaking of 'so insignificant a person as myself'. Second, he disparaged his writing because it seemed to him to come easily. But the reason it did so was not only that he had prepared for it thoroughly, but that he had long trained himself for rapid, fluent expression in his official work. It's worth comparing what he says in his *Autobiography* about report writing with what he says about novel writing. Extraordinarily, the reports were evidently written straight off without a draft. Trollope explains: 'It is by writing thus that a man can throw on to his paper the exact feeling with which his mind is impressed at the moment.' The saving in time he thought only a secondary advantage (116–17). He took trouble with this work, attempting to improve the style of official writing partly by his own example: 'I strove to do so gallantly, never being contented with the language of my own reports unless it seemed to have been so written as to be pleasant to read' (244). And he showed his standards were discriminating in criticising the style of the first books he reviewed – especially that of the Civil Service Commission's report.[26] This kind of conviction, and the exercise it demanded, helps explain the norm of straightforward clarity he consistently sustained in writing fiction.

But in one important respect Trollope's novel writing differed from his report writing. It has already been indicated that every day he wrote he read over what he had written the day before. He would then, according to the *Autobiography*, read over his work at least three more times before surrendering it to the publisher finally (153, 235). Since he says that one of these readings would be in print (though he adds that he had read a lot of his work in print twice), one of the other two readings presumably took place when the manuscript was complete and the other at some intermediate stage. He admits, correctly, that 'inaccuracies have crept through, – not in single spies, but in battalions' (153), but puts this down to insufficient supervision, not to hasty writing. In reports and novels alike, Trollope clearly valued what he considered as the freshness of first thoughts, unpolished but without sense of strain or labour; the difference is that he took greater pains with the novels, not only rereading his work but revising where he thought it necessary both in manuscript and in proof. The evidence for his revisions is in surviving letters to his publishers (especially George Smith) and others, and in the manuscripts of his novels (of which more later). These indicate that with some exceptions the work of rewriting was minor but not unimportant in that Trollope was able to sharpen phrasing and reduce awkwardness and inconsistency. He certainly cared about his writing, for after praising the skills of the printers in a letter to one of his editors he went on to declare: 'They should not alter my forms of expression, because they do not, and cannot, know my purpose' (*Letters*, p. 417, 3 April 1879). Though he doesn't often seem to have made a fair copy, sometimes someone else did so (usually this is likely to have been his wife), and occasionally he introduced corrections in proof.

Critics both contemporary and twentieth-century have often complained about Trollope's facility, his writing too fast and too much.[27] There are three factors to be considered here. First, Trollope was well aware that to succeed he had to write a lot. He observes: 'Short novels are not popular with readers generally. Critics often complain of the ordinary length of novels, – of the three volumes to which they are subjected; but few novels which have attained great success in England have been told in fewer pages' (*Autobiography*, 203–04). Second, far from making any bones about this demand of the market he seems positively to have welcomed it. He could conceive stories as fast as he could write them, and he had developed a regimen by which he could write them very fast indeed. But if he was to produce quantity, then quality would suffer. Of this again he was aware, laying claim only to 'whatever merit should be accorded to me for persevering diligence in my profession' (313–14). In other words, Trollope was able to tolerate less than perfect writing because he preferred to produce a lot of writing fast and because his habit of self-depreciation let him settle for competence instead of excellence. Third, the market in its appetite for fiction was itself prepared to accept writing that was less than perfect. Trollope's standards were high, but the question is whether if they had been higher still he would have been able to improve his work substantially by closer and more exacting revision.

The *Autobiography* provides evidence that Trollope had thought out his standards for novel writing. For all his mechanical skill in composition, he didn't consider any part of his product as arbitrary or expendable. He says, for instance: 'There should be no episodes in a novel. Every sentence, every word, through all those pages, should tend to the telling of the story' (204). In the same place he insists that subsidiary plots should 'all tend to the elucidation of the main story', and he cautions against extraneous dialogue. What is less clear is when Trollope formed such convictions and how consistently he lived up to them. He was willing to revise his early novels for second editions once he had become established, but this was probably more from commercial than from aesthetic motives. The new editions were in cheap one-volume form, and cuts had to be made to reduce printing costs. In a letter of 1861 Trollope explained in detail the economics of such an operation, and described his labour in reducing *The Three Clerks* by over sixty-four pages as very painful (*Letters*, pp. 89–90, 10 May 1861). The largest single cut, however, is a whole chapter – the one entitled 'The Civil Service', which amounts to a fold-in pamphlet expressing his views on competitive examinations. The chapter is certainly an indulgence, and one invited by the form of the three-volume novel. Yet Trollope was unwilling to introduce further cuts for a later cheap edition. He replied to Bentley: 'It gives more trouble to strike out pages, than to write new ones, as the whole sequence of a story, hangs page on page.' But he still admitted that the book contained an 'episode' which could be

left out, though 'even that wd require some care as it is alluded
to in different places' (*Letters*, p. 48, 8 August 1859). The episode
is probably Charley Tudor's story 'Crinoline and Macassar',
which can't be said to add much. It seems likely that Trollope
objected most to the labour needed for such a cut, which he
would somehow have to find time for in an already crowded
programme. It would be interesting to know what he thought
about revising *The Macdermots of Ballycloran*, which must have
taken more trouble than *The Three Clerks*. He cut it by three
whole chapters, streamlining it effectively for a more powerful
impact at its climax. He also made, on R. C. Terry's count, over
200 minor changes or deletions, most though not all of which are
improvements.[28] Yet even in his last novel, *The Landleaguers*, he
was capable of introducing a chapter as obviously out of place in
a novel as the one in *The Three Clerks* (chapter 41, 'The State of
Ireland').

Trollope didn't resort to the more blatant expedients for
eking out a novel to three volumes described by Charles and
Edward Lauterbach's informative survey of the nineteenth-
century three-decker.[29] Nevertheless, if *The Macdermots* and *The
Three Clerks* are better in one volume than three, perhaps the
standard production form of Victorian fiction was too permis-
sive for Trollope's best aesthetic interests. *Barchester Towers*
supplies an extra test case. When Trollope first submitted the
novel, Longman's reader advised that it needed drastic short-
ening. Trollope replied firmly: 'I do object to reducing the book
to two volumes – not because I am particularly wedded to three
but from a conviction that no book originally written in three
can be judiciously so reduced' (*Letters*, p. 25, 20 December
1856). The reader had actually called for a much sharper
reduction, from three volumes to one,[30] but Longman probably
felt this was too much to ask. The result was that Trollope
revised some passages to remove what the reader thought were
indelicacies, and either omitted or rewrote longer passages
which the reader considered ineffective (*Letters*, pp. 30–1, 1
February 1857). Ironically, it's possible that the reader's fears
were confirmed by a section in which the narrator humorously
complains that he needs twelve more pages to make up the 439
required (*Barchester Towers*, 489). The remark is part of Trollope's
game with his reader. That he meant it so is clear from the

comically precise number and from the fact that eight chapters before the narrator had asked just the opposite, that Mr. Longman would allow him another volume (420). Byplay of this kind can easily look redundant. In *Barchester Towers* it earns its keep not so much by its wit, which can be facetious, as by its role in creating and sustaining a relationship, central to the novel's effect, with the reader. In this work at least Trollope found a successful way of meeting both the needs of the market and the demands of his novel.

Again *Framley Parsonage* marks a turning point. The difference is that this novel was commissioned, so that Trollope had a contract agreed on in advance to supply a given quantity of fiction. This helps explain his answer to Smith's request that he cut a page from the serial. He complied, but added: 'It was as tho you asked for my hearts blood. And the fault must have been your own in giving me too long a page as a sample – I had even the words counted, so that I might give you exactly what I had undertaken to give & no more' (*Letters*, p. 54, 25 November 1859). Here again it's the businessman who speaks rather than the novelist. Trollope scrupulously fulfilled all his bargains with himself and with his publishers, and he expected identical care in return. He says in his letter about the difficulties of cutting a novel that he had subsequently taken pains so to reduce his work in the first writing that no further cuts would be required (*Letters*, p. 89, 10 May 1861). Probably he also felt that the measure he had given conscientiously should have been accepted as right. His reproach to Smith shows that he considered himself able to proportion his narrative to a stated length and still keep it both relevant and effective. Hamer has demonstrated how he did this with his first serial from the working papers and the section of manuscript to survive of *Framley Parsonage*.[31] The manuscript of *Orley Farm*, his first work to come out in monthly numbers, provides evidence that is equally important, if perhaps less flattering.

Orley Farm was begun on 4 July 1860, the day after Trollope had signed a contract with Chapman and Hall for a twenty-number novel.[32] It was completed on 15 June 1861, quite a long time by Trollope's standards, though comfortably on schedule for publication which had begun in March. No work after *Barchester Towers* was to take him longer to write, with the exception of his compendious, highly detailed *Australia and New Zealand*. Partly this was because of other commitments he set himself. His writing diary records that during this time he also wrote seven short stories and gave two lectures. In addition to his Post Office work he visited his brother in Florence, and Terry has established that it was at this period that he revised *The Macdermots of Ballycloran*.[33] But the manuscript of *Orley Farm* suggests another reason why it was so long in the making.[34] The novel was to be written in numbers one-third as long again as those of *Framley Parsonage* (sixty-four instead of forty-eight manuscript pages), and it was to be easily the longest Trollope had written to that date. It shouldn't be surprising if he found difficulty in tailoring his copy to the different length, and the manuscript suggests that this is just what happened.

The process of writing and rewriting *Orley Farm* is impossible to reconstruct fully, owing to the confusing state of surviving manuscript evidence and the absence of other records. but several points are clear. Trollope's writing diary reports that on 17 July 1860 he shortened the novel's opening number from seventy-six to sixty-four manuscript pages. That he may have had trouble with this opening number also seems indicated by his letter to Chapman, the publisher, which begins: 'I send back No 1 – which you may not consider quite complete as far as I am concerned' (*Letters*, p. 69, 23 August 1860). He can only be referring to *Orley Farm* because it was his first novel in numbers, and he wasn't to write another for Chapman and Hall until *Can You Forgive Her?*, three years later. A sixty-four page number should have been convenient for Trollope, as it would only mean adding a chapter to the forty-eight page, three-chapter numbers he had used for *Framley Parsonage*. But apparently he found it hard to get the proportions right at the outset. In addition to cutting the first number, he also reorganised it. Comparison of manuscript and printed text shows that he shifted material from Chapter 3, 'The Cleeve', and from Chapter 5, originally 'Sir Peregrine Orme Makes a Promise', into a new Chapter 4, 'The Perils of Youth'. These corrections, like quite a few others in *Orley Farm*, must presumably have been inserted in proof, for the manuscript shows no trace of the new chapter except for a note ending Chapter 3 where it was to finish in the published text. In turn the new chapter replaced the original Chapter 4, 'Mr., Mrs., and Miss Furnival', which with a few small alterations became Chapter 10. Trollope had significantly changed the order in which he introduced his subplots. Probably he had decided it would be a mistake to bring in the Furnivals as early as the opening number. His revision keeps the focus very distinctly on Lady Mason, the Ormes, and each family's heir – an emphasis which as I hope to show in Chapter 6 is important to the novel. Then the next number can move to the Masons of Groby Park and the commercial characters for purposes of contrast, before introducing the Furnivals in a block of three chapters which, without Trollope's revision, would have had to be messily separated.

The revised first number of *Orley Farm* shows Trollope shaping his material carefully for an apt, integral and properly balanced start to his serial. In the next two numbers he takes pains not only over introducing further characters and themes effectively, but over maintaining continuity between them. The second number begins with Sir Peregrine Orme before turning to the commercials and the Masons, and the third number with the commercials before turning to the Furnivals. Then the fourth number can start interweaving and complicating these various plots. But it evidently wasn't only at the beginning of his serial that Trollope had difficulty in proportioning his copy. On several occasions he added material which doesn't appear in the manuscript. Presumably this was done in proof – and most likely because extra copy was needed to fill out the number. That's what seems implied by the letter quoted above in which Trollope says Chapman might consider the opening number 'not quite complete'. He declared in a letter of the same period: 'I hate short measure as I do poison; but I hate inserting little bits to lengthen a chapter' (*Letters*, p. 93, 9 July 1861). Nevertheless, perhaps in his efforts at finding the right length for *Orley Farm*'s first number, he had cut too much. The text as printed in the World's Classics edition contains almost half a page of dialogue absent from the manuscript (1.35/1.25). This looks like filler because though it's relevant to the characterisation of Lucius Mason, it adds little to what has already been conveyed. Two similar insertions occur later, and I suggest for the same reason. Both are placed at the end of a number, where it would have been easiest to make up its length in proof, and neither is strictly essential. The first is the whole passage at the end of Chapter 32 beginning 'Mr. Mason and Mr. Dockwrath' – over a page and a half in the World's Classics edition (8.64 I.327–8). The second covers almost half a page at the end of Chapter 36, beginning with 'Young Peregrine Orme' (9.64/I.369).

Trollope's proof additions to *Orley Farm*, though only these three are of any length, suggest an ability to produce material to order much in the spirit of his own image of himself as a literary shoemaker.[35] This is emphasised by the fact that, despite the additions, most of the changes between manuscript and publication are cases of over-production. *Orley Farm* contains ten passages at least a paragraph in length which don't appear in the manuscript, and over a dozen shorter sections. These changes, like the three main insertions in proof, were probably made to adjust serial numbers to the required length. This seems the likeliest explanation in the case of two chapters, 22 and 65, that seem disproportionately long in the manuscript – over twenty pages. Trollope cut two passages in proof from each: an account, probably too circumstantial, of why Lady Mason spent Christmas at the Cleeve (6.17/I.215); a disquisition on breakfasts, not strictly relevant but in keeping with the narrator's special style of sociable wisdom (6.18/I.215); part of an inside view of Madeline Staveley (17.2/II.249); and part of an inside view of Felix Graham (17.10–11/II.254). Rather similarly, cuts in chapter 69, which is not in itself long, may have been needed to avoid reducing any one of the next three chapters. Trollope probably thought these too important to cut, as the first deals with Lady Mason's feelings after the opening day of the trial, the second with the cross-examination of the main witnesses, and the third with Furnival's defence speech. Instead of sacrificing material at any of these points, it was better to reduce a chapter in a lower key. The passages deleted – which, again, are all uncancelled in the manuscript – are from inside views of Felix Graham (18.1–2/II.290 and 18.5/II.292), and from conversation at the Staveley dinner table (18.8–9/II.294). None of them entails the loss of anything to be regretted.

Four other main cuts that Trollope apparently made in proof are more difficult to explain on grounds of need to save space. In the manuscript, the first comes near the start of the second number(2.3/I.39), but near the end of the first number in the text as published. It is a passage concerned with the unusual location of Lady Mason's drawing room – not exactly a topic of great moment, though it illustrates her house's picturesqueness, and helps characterise Lady Mason and Sir Peregrine through the comments it draws from them. Since the chapter in which it originally appeared was to have begun Trollope's second number, this, along with the trouble he had in getting his first two numbers right, may account for the apparent anomaly that he both inserted and cut in proof substantial sections from the same number. In this case, Trollope was right if in reading proof he found the passage redundant. Secondly, he deleted quite a long section from an inside view of Peregrine Orme in Chapter 37 (10.7–8/I.373). Though this cut may have been necessary to make room in the same number for one of the longest chapters in the book, Chapter 39, it seems more likely that Trollope simply found it repetitive. The other two unmarked cuts are also from inside views, and again they unnecessarily rehearse material already given. One concerns Mrs. Furnival (13.14/II.92), the other Augustus Staveley (17.32/II.268), neither a figure of much importance.

The shortest cuts in proof might seem most likely to have been made for aesthetic reasons rather than to save space, but such a view is discouraged by their location. Of the fifteen shorter deletions I've been able to trace, eleven occur in only three chapters, and each of those chapters is part of a number where Trollope was in danger of running over length. The three numbers are 17, 19, and 20, the last two of which – to judge from the space they occupy in the World's Classics edition – are longer than any others in the novel, while Number 17 runs them close. None of these involves material that is in any way decisive, though all avoid either over-emphasis or repetition. Again, then, Trollope was probably trying to save space. Nearly all of the shorter deletions in proof occur in the last quarter of the manuscript, as if he had worked himself into a routine in which he was liable to over-produce. The same conclusion is invited by the pattern of major additions and deletions between manuscript and text. All the additions come in the first half of the manuscript, and no less than six out of the eleven deletions I have discussed, all but one at least a paragraph in length, occur in the last quarter.

Trollope's corrections in proof, especially his cuts, generally improve his text by tightening it and reducing redundancy. Nevertheless, the evidence presented above suggests that what motivated the majority of corrections was the need to produce the number-length his publisher required. Corrections that appear both in manuscript and novel on the whole tell a different story. A few bear on characterisation, as when Felix Graham is made to seem less unfeeling towards Mary Snow in arranging for her to marry her suitor. The manuscript shows that Trollope originally had Graham go straight to Albert Fitzallen after talking with Mary, but that he then revised this so that Graham waited two days first, not having the heart to approach Fitzallen at once (15.1/II.166). A few other changes concern matters of emphasis. The best example is a sentence Trollope deleted from his description of Lady Mason's response to Furnival's speech in her defence. After the word 'pitiable', the manuscript originally went on: 'She at any rate knew that that codicil had not been so signed, and that she had sworn falsely' (18.54/II.326). Trollope must have thought this an unnecessary and tactless reminder. One other revision to his manuscript is more problematic. A passage of rhetoric against drunkenness is inserted in Chapter 57 (15.10 II.172-3, from 'Look at him' to 'protect us both!'). This may have been to make up the number-length, as the number in question would, without this addition, have been one of the shortest and Trollope is simply expanding on a topic he has already stressed. Such a probability is strengthened by the fact that the addition seems to be in a different hand from his own, so that he may have realised the number would be short and have sent material to make it up before it appeared in proof but when he no longer had access to that part of the manuscript. Probably the other hand was his wife's. From his own account she appears to have had more to do with his work than anyone else. He says in his *Autobiography* that no other friend ever read a word of his writing before it was printed, but that she had read 'almost everything, to my very great advantage in matters of taste' (63).[36] And from the few letters from Trollope to his wife that have survived – none at all in Booth's edition between 1859 and 1875 – there is one that shows her activity in writing for him a fair copy of *Doctor Thorne* (*Letters*, pp. 39-40, 2 February 1858). There is evidence of another hand elsewhere in the manuscript of *Orley Farm*, notably between pages 38–40 of Number 3. This looks like a fair copy as it contains few corrections; if so, it is probably Rose Trollope's work.

Most of the manuscript revisions to *Orley Farm* are, however, improvements to style. Some of Trollope's reviewers had complained, as I've pointed out, of his occasionally lax writing. This novel he deliberately revised for sharper and clearer emphasis. Perhaps he was helped by his revision of *The Macdermots*, which he almost certainly did at some time during the same period. His use in *Orley Farm* of precise and at times technical nomenclature possibly also reflects a wish to convey an appropriately legal atmosphere. On the first page of the manuscript, for instance, among a number of other tightened-up phrases, 'intimately connected with' replaces 'well known with reference to', 'landed estate' replaces 'large property', and 'left' becomes 'bequeathed'. Other revisions in the first chapter include 'devised' for 'bequeathed' (1.3/I.2, probably to avoid repeating the word, but also a more technical term), 'constructing' for 'building' (1.10/I.8), and 'bestowed upon his estate' for 'given to this place' (1.11/I.9). In revising his manuscript in this way Trollope was to some extent heightening a flavour of more formal language that he had already introduced. Generally he preferred plain, direct expression. This is illustrated by a comment he made as an editor: 'The word peruse we certainly never used in our life. We object to "perusing" as we do to "commencing," and "performing". We "read," and we "begin," and we "do".'[37] But the first chapter of *Orley Farm* is entitled 'The Commencement of the Great Orley Farm Case', and Trollope uses the word 'commence' along with other more formal expressions right from the opening pages. The effect is partly humorous, as if any tendency to over-dramatise were being gently mocked. As P. D. Edwards has pointed out, *Orley Farm* appeared at the start of the vogue for sensational fiction.[38] This Trollope obliquely exploits, in part through language that quizzically holds off heady involvement.

Stylistic revisions to the manuscript of *Orley Farm* are most frequent in the opening number, especially in the first chapter – as might be expected. But similar changes later in the manuscript indicate that Trollope stuck to his aim. He checks repetition in one place where he introduces two different phrases for 'thought of', which he was overworking (4.10/I.129). A few pages later he resists blandness, exchanging 'muddle-headed' for 'absurd' and 'his myrmidon' for 'the man' (4.13/I.131). Elsewhere, 'going down' becomes 'a journey', 'Think' becomes 'Reflect', 'days' becomes 'memories', and the phrase 'about Birmingham and elsewhere' is rejected for 'first at one provincial town and then at another' (5.11-13 I.17-71). Other efforts towards vigour include 'scapegrace' for 'young man' (1.44/I.32), and 'declared with energy' for 'gone on to say' (5.54/I.197). None of these revisions, it scarcely needs observing, adds any special strength or subtlety to the writing, but together they do improve the qualities of style that Trollope most valued – clarity and ease (*Autobiography*, 201-03). After a time the manuscript shows fewer such improvements, as if he had written himself into producing the style he wanted. Other changes continue to be made, but most are insertions and deletions of very minor interest.

The manuscript of *Orley Farm* invites several inferences about Trollope's practices of composition. These must remain provisional, especially as generalisations, for manuscripts in various conditions survive for as many as thirty-four of his novels,[39] and no one has yet examined and compared a sufficiently representative sample. However, given that *Orley Farm* shows more evidence of revision than most of the other novels whose manuscripts I have studied,[40] a number of points seem clear. Especially, Trollope appears to have taken more time and trouble both over revising his manuscript and correcting proof than he has usually received credit for. Here the stylistic revisions are particularly interesting. But more important to my mind is the evidence that many of the revisions, in proof especially, concern number-length. No doubt Trollope found in subsequent novels that adjusting his copy to the required length became easier, but *Orley Farm* helps indicate how he did it. The most convenient way to write a long novel is to include a variety of different stories. This he had done in *Orley Farm* as in *Framley Parsonage*. But in filling a serial local means of expansion are also useful. Study of deletions and additions in *Orley Farm* demonstrates three of these.

Dialogue is the least important, perhaps because Trollope already knew, as he was to say in his *Autobiography*, that it was too easily prone to irrelevance. Narrative commentary was a more natural area for expansion because of Trollope's unhurriedly talkative style at this stage of his career. Passages such as the disquisition on breakfasts, which he cut, and the tirade against drunkenness, to which he added, illustrate the flexibility of this dimension to his fiction. Finally and perhaps most important was the inside view. This was again a necessary element in his method, as I shall show in Chapter 5. At the same time, though, it offered opportunities for fairly unobtrusive extension. The serial reader had to be brought up-to-date with each main character's state of mind and with the typical rhythm of his thoughts as he reached a moment of crisis or decision. This was entirely legitimate, but the manuscript shows how easily Trollope was able to cut such passages if he wanted to reduce the length of a number.

The manuscript of *The Duke's Children* illustrates even more clearly the dangers of over-producing entailed by Trollope's methods. This is the only surviving manuscript of a novel by Trollope to reveal large-scale revision, chiefly in the form of cuts. According to his notes on the manuscript and working papers, the novel was reduced in April and May 1878 by nearly 50,000 words (just less than eighteen per cent of its original length).[41] Most of the alterations, especially the cuts, must have been made then, though it isn't always possible to distinguish corrections introduced at the time of writing in 1878. Passages that might be thought redundant were marked with red pencil, and these guides Trollope generally followed. Taken all together there can be little doubt that the novel gains from its reduction,[42] which so far as can be known represents alteration on a scale unique in his fiction. Most of the cuts are plainly designed to improve economy. Much slack or repetitive narrative and commentary is simply omitted – especially at the beginnings and endings of chapters, which seem to have been unusually prone to prolixity (e.g. 4.45–6/I.326, 5.1–3/II.11; 5.69/II.60, 7.93–4/II.260). Unnecessary circumstantiality is also much reduced (e.g. 1.7/I.5, 4.93/I.360, 6.58–9/II.141). Some of the cuts influence characterisation. Frank Tregear in his unrevised state appears almost an adventurer: over-clever, conceited, and unwilling to advance himself by his own efforts (1.31–4/I.24–6).

The Duke of Omnium would have turned out less sympathetic if
Trollope had not deleted several passages of indignation against
Mrs. Finn and his children's proposed marriages (e.g. 2.13-14/
I.111, 2.29-31/I.122). Silverbridge's feelings for Lady Mabel
Grex are toned down – probably necessary in view of his later
attachment to Isabel Boncassen (2.120/I.186, 3.92/I.261).
Trollope also left out some of the political background he had
first provided, perhaps recognising that as it developed the novel
had become more domestic than parliamentary (4.64/I.340,
where there is a brief reference to Irish Home Rule; 5.5-7/II.13,
on the subject of dishonesty and gamesmanship; and 7.61/II.239,
about Mr. Monk's wish for the Duke's political support). Some
heavy-handed attempts at low comedy or satire are cut too.
These mainly involve local politicians (Du Boung and Sprugeon
at Silverbridge, Mr. Williams the anti-Dissenter rector at
Polpenno), and sporting fanatics (Reginald Dobbes and hunts-
woman Mrs. Spooner). Finally, material concerning Major
Tifto is left out or revised, again with the effect of softening the
comedy (e.g. in Chapter 48), but also of playing down Tifto's
role as corrupter of the young (1.71-4/I.55-58).

Allowing for his much more drastic surgery on *The Duke's
Children*, the cuts Trollope made compare in kind and proportion
with those from the manuscript of *Orley Farm*. More straightforward narrative is omitted, but there are similar reductions in
general commentary. A discussion of convivial lunches, almost
entirely cut from Chapter 70 (7.125-6/II.283), recalls the chat
about breakfasts excised from *Orley Farm*; a cloying passage on a
woman's feelings about her home also disappears (8.17-18/
II.298). Trollope treated loose dialogue with equal ruthlessness,
cancelling at least fifteen passages of some length. A good
example of this kind of cut, though shorter than many, occurs at
the novel's end. The closing lines originally ran as follows:

'Well, sir,' said Silverbridge to the Duke when they were
out together in the park that afternoon, 'what do you think
about him?'

'I think he is a manly young man.'

'He certainly is that. And then he knows things and
understands them. It was never a surprise to me that Mary
should have been so fond of him.'

'I do not know that one ought to be surprised at anything. Perhaps what surprised me most was that he should have looked so high. There seemed to be so little to justify it. But now I will accept as courage what I before regarded as arrogance. Who knows. He may live yet to be a much greater man than his father-in-law. I am certainly very glad that he has a seat in Parliament.'

'It will be my turn next,' said Gerald, as he was smoking with his brother that evening. 'After what you and Mary have done, I think he must let me have my own way whatever it is.' (8.131/II.378–9)

Here Trollope deleted everything after 'arrogance', so that the novel finishes with an epigram that gracefully underlines the change undergone by the Duke. His original ending hit at least two wrong notes: false modesty in the Duke ('He may yet live to be a much greater man'), and facetious rebelliousness in Lord Gerald. The revision is both more concise and more apt in drawing attention so tactfully to an accord reached against the grain.

Trollope shows equal discretion in deleting over twenty fairly extensive passages of interior view. Most involve the Duke himself especially early on, and, especially later on, Lord Silverbridge. The effect in the first case, I've already suggested, is to render the Duke less irritably tormented; since in the cancelled sections his indignation tends to exceed its object, their removal makes him more sympathetic. In the case of inside views of Lord Silverbridge the largest number of deletions concern his relationship with his father. But these don't add very much, and so Trollope probably thought in cutting them. Generally, his reductions in passages of this type reinforce the conclusion suggested by *Orley Farm*: that interior views, though integral to his method as a novelist, too easily invited redundancy.

One main effect of Trollope's revisions to *The Duke's Children* is indicated by C. P. Snow's comment that it is 'one of the most elegant verbally of all Trollope's novels'.[43] This judgement carries more weight because it was delivered in apparent unawareness that the novel was revised in manuscript, and that the manuscript is in Trollope's own hand. (Snow thought it might, like other late works, have been dictated.)[44] Perhaps the

word 'elegant' isn't quite right, as it suggests a stylised
sophistication foreign to Trollope. But his writing in *The Duke's
Children* has a plain but graceful authority thanks to more
concise, more exact phrasing and to elimination of ill-judged or
unnecessary passages. In the single case, then, where Trollope
substantially reduced a manuscript, he improved it appreciably.
The question is why he made the cuts. I do not know of any
evidence that points to an answer, but think it most likely that
the publisher asked for shorter measure. Bearing in mind
Trollope's reluctance to reduce his work, as with *Barchester
Towers* and *The Three Clerks*, it seems improbable that he would
of his own accord have undertaken the task. But if his revisions to
The Duke's Children are owing to an external constraint, a further
question arises. Would all of his novels have benefited from
similar reduction? To this the best answer seems to be a perhaps.
For in writing *The Duke's Children* Trollope faced special
temptations to expand beyond need. The novel is the last in a
series, dealing with characters and events he had written about
previously. Prolixity must have been difficult to avoid in
reminding his readers of these. Similarly, it must have been hard
to judge how much political circumstance to include, if we
remember the importance of this element in the earlier novels of
the series. Then again Trollope was nearing the end of his
career, and slack writing may have crept in insensibly –
especially as he wrote about familiar characters and themes.
And he had failed to appreciate what a reviewer of this very
novel was to suggest in pointing out that *The Duke's Children* was
'of more than average length',[45] even after what we now know to
have been extensive reduction. The market was moving away
from the old three-decker, and though Trollope continued to
supply it with his short, more experimental novels (such as, at
this period, *Cousin Henry* and *The Fixed Period*), he kept on with
the standard form till the end.

The questions provoked by Trollope's working methods
cannot finally be approached without recognising how tightly
those methods are bound up with his whole practice as a novelist.
He liked to write a lot, he liked to write fast, and he liked
to write – as far as he could – spontaneously. Outlines for several
of his novels in the working papers actually confirm, as far as
they go, his extraordinary statement in his *Autobiography*: 'With

nothing settled in my brain as to the final development of events, with no capability of settling anything, but with a most distinct conception of some character or characters, I have rushed at the work as a rider rushes at a fence which he does not see' (151). For the outlines chiefly limit themselves to character sketches – 'a collection of characters in search of a plot', as Bradford Booth put it[46] – and even then Trollope sometimes changed his plan in the telling, as he did in developing Melmotte in *The Way We Live Now*.[47] The reason that Trollope revised, on the whole, so little was not only that he had schooled himself into becoming a highly efficient writer, it was also that he considered his own first thoughts, sometimes wrongly, as freshest and best in principle. The result is a fatty layer in some of his novels of loose and redundant writing. But if he had taken more trouble with revising his work it isn't wholly clear that quality would have advanced as quantity receded. For fast writing allowed an imaginative release which more deliberate composition and refinement might well have checked. *The Warden* is the work over which Trollope took most care, not all to its advantage.

Trollope's writing diaries and his habit of composing in parts were the means by which he advanced, consolidated, and never had to abandon the position he established for himself as a writer. His success, in common with that of other Victorian novelists, was in part determined by his willingness to fill, regularly, the three volumes demanded by the market, and by his ability to provide fiction that read well in serial. Both his preferences and his methods were then perfectly adapted to the conditions obtaining for publication of novels during most of his career. But he wasn't a formula novelist. He persistently refused to become typecast, showing a continued readiness to experiment within the limits he accepted. His motive for writing wasn't to reproduce what had sold well before. It was to produce, profitably, what he couldn't help imagining. One reason why he reveals so little of his inner life in the *Autobiography* is that so much of it was composed by his fiction: 'I was continually asking myself how this woman would act when this or that event had passed over her head, or how that man would carry himself when his youth had become manhood, or his manhood declined to old age' (274). His testimony is strikingly confirmed by Josiah Crawley's emergence from a few sentences in *Barchester Towers* to a supporting part in *Framley Parsonage*, and then to the central role of *The Last Chronicle*.[48] Trollope's mechanical habits of writing paradoxically encouraged not fiction to order, but expression of what lay deepest. His fertility in generating character and circumstance suggests a variant of Parkinson's Law, in which fiction expands to fill the available space. To what filled that space, in the underlying preoccupations revealed by the stories, I now turn.

4   Self and Society

Reading Trollope, as with other Victorian novelists, one is likely to be struck by the extraordinary combination of panoramic sweep and precisely focused detail. Henry James called *Middlemarch* 'a treasure-house of details, but . . . an indifferent whole': Orwell declared that Dickens' novels had 'rotten architecture, but wonderful gargoyles'.[1] With Trollope, the image that comes to mind is a picture rather than a building. A work by Frith such as *Ramsgate Sands* (exhibited 1854) or *Derby Day* (1858) might fittingly represent the broad canvas of closely studied portraits suggested by Trollope's habitual use of pictorial metaphors in talking of his craft. This seems apt, for while his best and most characteristic works are on the largest scale, some of his best and most characteristic powers subtly inform the small but charged incidents, the minor expressive occasions of life. Mr. Harding and his plangently abandoned 'cello, Lily Dale writing two words in her book, Adolphus Crosbie asking pointblank for a loan of £500 – such scenes as these, all from *The Last Chronicle of Barset* and all at varying distances from its central story, illustrate the small scale at which Trollope worked on one, vitally important, level of his fiction.

Frith's paintings, portraying the variety as well as the crowdedness of contemporary life, are very carefully composed. Robert Tracy points out an appropriate example in *The Private View at the Royal Academy in 1881* (1883). Here a gallery (it's impossible to avoid the word) of Victorian celebrities includes not just Lord Leighton at the centre and Gladstone nearby – President of the Royal Academy and Prime Minister respectively. On their left stands Oscar Wilde with a group of aesthetic admirers; on their right, in 'striking contrast', none other than

Anthony Trollope.[2] This kind of juxtaposition is also the way
Trollope works in organising his stories, as Tracy says and as
Jerome Thale argued in a pioneering article at a time when
critics were still complaining about irrelevant sub-plots and
desultory narrative.[3] For the revolution that took place in
criticism of Dickens and George Eliot has spread to Trollope
studies too. No one now thinks of *Bleak House* or *Middlemarch* as
'loose' and 'baggy', as Henry James, in a famous phrase, once
described the typical nineteenth-century novel.[4] In the same
way, ingenuity in demonstrating the coherence of Trollope's
novels has become almost as commonplace as protests once were
about their shapelessness.[5]

Perhaps in some ways the reaction has gone too far. While it's
necessary and valuable to know about the relations between
plots and sub-plots in Trollope's novels, and about the steps he
took for marking them in constructing his narratives, that isn't
the whole story. For one thing, the analogy between novel and
picture soon breaks down. Narratives aren't composed like
paintings. Most obviously, this is because they take much longer
to read and because they can contain, perhaps dispose, far more
material. But there's also a limit to what relations between plots
and sub-plots can tell. No reading of a Victorian novel, however
inventive, could possibly reconcile its every detail even to a
complex pattern of story or theme. Then again, as I've tried to
show with Trollope's *Framley Parsonage*, a different kind of
organisation may be working beneath the surface. This is where
Thale's article provides a further lead. In proposing a solution to
the problem of structure in Trollope, the illustrations Thale uses
all exemplify what Trollope's best contemporary critic, R. H.
Hutton, brilliantly identified as the distinctive quality of his
work: a searching insight, based on close observation, into how
people present themselves to each other in social life.[6] The
trouble is that this, like a society painting, leaves something out.
Hutton's essential criticism of Trollope is that 'he gives us no
strictly individual life, – no life beneath the social surface, – at
all; that he never completes the outline of any character as it
might be observed in society, by sketching it as it would be seen
and appreciated or misconceived and falsely coloured by the
inner self'.[7] It is a penetrating charge. Yet, as David Skilton has
suggested, in making it Hutton must have been blind to the long

passages of interior view which run through Trollope's novels.[8] These I shall discuss in my next chapter, but what they point to is that Trollope isn't just a society novelist – or 'social naturalist', as Hutton called him,[9] he is also a moral psychologist, a novelist not only of society but of the self. As J. Hillis Miller has put it, his fiction 'concentrates with admirable consistency on the question of what constitutes authentic selfhood'.[10] Yet it does so – and to this extent Hutton was right – in what always remains a social context, in which relations to others matter at least as much as relations to self. Trollope returns again and again in his fiction to the problem of how such relations are negotiated, so much so that it is in his repeated attempts to resolve it that the inner unity of his fiction is to be found. This is composition not of a painterly kind, but like the pattern created among filings on a piece of paper by a magnet beneath. If such a metaphor suggests an imagination powerful but inert, impelling rather than actively shaping and transforming its material, it's necessary to consider first the meaning and value of what it turned out.

To begin with, one of the poles in Trollope's fiction is his commitment to the autonomy of the individual person. The identity of his characters expresses itself on every plane of their lives, often in events which bear less than momentous importance for anyone else. One typical example is the writing of letters, a frequent device in Trollope's novels and one at which he excels. In *The Last Chronicle*, for instance, Grace Crawley has to write to the suitor whom she feels obliged to refuse despite herself. It seems a very small incident as regards the novel, though not for the character personally, but Trollope observes that she will not even discuss what she has to say with her friend, let alone ask for aid in how to say it, for 'she feared that she could not secure that aid without compromising her own power of action, – her own individuality' (I,378). Trollope values highly such jealous independence, and is especially sensitive to those whose autonomy is threatened in some way. This is one reason why his portrayal of women has so much interest, but its importance goes deeper, for it's in their independence – obstinate even to bloodymindedness – that the ambiguous attraction of many of his characters most strongly makes itself felt. In *The Last Chronicle* Josiah Crawley refuses to resign his curacy when the Bishop tries

to inhibit him, then does resign it when he has won his point and
nearly everyone wants him to stay. 'It's dogged as does it' is his
slogan – almost in the original sense of 'battle cry'. Adopted
from a hard-bitten navvy, it would suit any of Trollope's more
intransigent individualists. Will Belton in *The Belton Estate*,
Frank Fenwick in *The Vicar of Bullhampton*, Dr. Wortle in *Dr.
Wortle's School* – such characters seem to live by self-assertion. In
other novels Dr. Thorne brandishes a pair of human thigh bones
at Lady Arabella Gresham, and Mr. Scarborough successfully
defies the whole law of entail; but even figures who play a less
central role are capable of commanding the same slightly
shocked respect. In *Is He Popenjoy?* the Dean of Brotherton all too
literally personifies the church-militant when he assaults a
marquis, and in *The Last Chronicle* Archdeacon and Henry
Grantly are as cross-grained as any possible father and son, each
in assertion of his own independence.

Trollope's view of identity begins, though it doesn't end, with
the axiom: 'Every man to himself is the centre of the whole
world' (*Can You Forgive Her?*, I,376). The force and value of
individuality is as important to him as to Mill in social science,
or Samuel Smiles in popular ethics. He stands with them rather
than with the Evangelical belief that the self should be subdued,
not accepted, and in this he differs from most Victorian
novelists. It's illuminating to compare Trollope's idea of the
centrality of the self with George Eliot's, expressed in the
parable of pier-glass and candle in *Middlemarch*.[11] To George
Eliot's generalising mind, the radiation of scratches from the
centre of the reflected light is just an optical illusion: move the
candle to represent the influence of another person's egoism,
and the same phenomenon is repeated elsewhere. So Olympian
a view wouldn't have recommended itself to Trollope, who
respects each person's independence and accepts the inescapable
limitations of having a personality to affirm. George Eliot,
grafting positivist ethics on to Evangelical morality, believes
that the general Good advances by individual acts of self-denial.
There is truth in this, but Trollope would recognise with Mill
the co-operation, in creating that general Good, of 'pagan self-
assertion' with 'Christian self-denial' (Sterling's phrases, quoted
in the essay *On Liberty*[12]), and would hold further that it's only
the strong self which can realise needs beyond its immediate

interests and deny itself in their favour. To him, the priority of
the self is a necessary condition of its existence.

Dickens presents an even plainer contrast: though he expresses in his novels a much more vividly sensitive image of
Victorian life, his characters often reflect an imaginative world
which Graham Greene has called 'Manichaean'.[13] There's
nothing in Trollope like the intelligence, at once compassionate
and tough-minded, of Dickens' presentation of Pip in *Great
Expectations*. But then there is nothing either like the strange and
wonderful extremes to which the imagination of his more
popular rival ran. Dickens' sheep neither fall nor rise to
selfishness; his goats are selfish and nothing else. At one end
there is the anarchic unrestraint of Quilp, the solipsism of Mrs.
Gamp, or the magnificent self-reference of Pecksniff; at the
other, the passivity of Oliver Twist and Little Nell, or the self-
effacing sentiment of Esther Summerson and Arthur Clennam.
What Dickens does with these characters goes beyond what they
are, but only rarely – as with Pip in *Great Expectations* – did he
convincingly present a mixed type, egoist before self-denier.
Trollope, on the contrary, saw many more shades of grey than
clear examples of black and white. Even the reform of Pip
might have appeared to him as too good to be true, for in his
view egoism and self-denial were less stages in the growth of
personality than mutually dependent elements. Crawley, who
sacrifices comfort, position and even the well-being of his family
to the Church, is independent to the point of arrogance and
beyond. Plantagenet Palliser, whose two most important acts
are resignation of power – political in *The Prime Minister*,
patriarchal in *The Duke's Children* – tends to be touchily
dominant, wrapped up in self. While Dickens bifurcates egoism
and unselfishness, Trollope shows how personality can be
affirmed through self-sacrifice. In another political novel,
Phineas Finn regains his integrity at the cost of his career; and
the hero of Trollope's last completed work, *An Old Man's Love*,
fulfils himself more satisfactorily by denying himself for the sake
of the girl he loves than he could have by marrying her. These
moral victories carry all the more conviction for being founded
on a celebration of the energy of the self.

Nevertheless, although Trollope values more highly than
most Victorian novelists the full expression of the individual self,

he is as alive as any of them to the dangers of egoism unbridled. Powerful and necessary as may be each person's need to assert himself, to establish his independence and justify it, it is beyond any other instinct susceptible to perversion. Several of Trollope's best novels crucially concern themselves with a study of obstinacy from both psychological and social viewpoints. The seriousness of this concern is reflected not only in the length and density of these works, and in an imaginative coherence which has still to be fully recognised, but by the fact that in each case he returned to a theme he had handled earlier to explore each of its elements in the round. It has been noticed that *Rachel Ray* develops the plot of a story published previously, 'The Court-ship of Susan Bell'.[14] Similarly, both *The Small House at Allington* and *The Belton Estate* probably spring in part from 'The Parson's Daughter of Oxney Colne'; and in reworking his abortive play *The Noble Jilt* as the novel *Can You Forgive Her?*, Trollope may also have made use of another story, 'The Mistletoe Bough'.[15] These are early and not especially important examples of Trollope transforming a previous idea. Of much more interest are the relations between *Linda Tressel* and *John Caldigate*, and between *Lady Anna* and *The Duke's Children*. *Linda Tressel* is about a girl's persecution by her Calvinist aunt and guardian. Denied the company of young men, and pressed fiercely to marry a man much older than herself, Linda dies because her own will is made of no account. The same conflict reappears in a different form in *John Caldigate*. Like Linda's aunt, Mrs. Bolton is a Calvinist and a tyrant (the two often went together to Trollope's anti-Evangelical mind). Unable to prevent her daughter marry-ing the man she loves, Mrs. Bolton tries to repossess her by force when a charge of bigamy is brought against her hated son-in-law. She justifies herself on religious grounds, much as Madame Staubach does in *Linda Tressel*, making full use of the accusation against John Caldigate. But, as Trollope chillingly shows, both women's religious fervour is a direct though unconscious rationalisation of a desperate will to power.

Linda Tressel is a short novel, concentrating on its single topic with an almost claustrophobic intensity. *John Caldigate* surpasses its prototype not in developing that subject further, but in proliferating, through its complex plot, other and different examples of obstinacy. Not only Mrs. Bolton is intransigent, so, necessarily, is her daughter; and, with less justification, her son Robert, the lawyer retained by Caldigate, and even the judge. Blinded by self-conceit, these three can allow, no more than Mrs. Bolton, the possibility of Caldigate's innocence. Once committed to a judgment, they hold it so resolutely that their whole personalities seem at stake. All Caldigate can do is to resist with equal determination. His wife and father support him to the utmost – though Trollope doesn't dodge the implication that their belief in him also has its arbitrary part. Truth begins to appear relative, dependent on prejudice, until Caldigate's story is confirmed. Trollope's fiction often springs from such a tension between prejudice and a truth which he is convinced will finally come to light. That conviction is at once threatened and enabled by his confidence in individual power, for, if a strong will may impose its prejudice on others, it may be checked by another strong will. As he says in *The New Zealander*, 'In all cases of despotic rule, of power grown too powerful, the fault is with the subject, not with the ruler; with the men, not with the master' (39). Tyrants depend on slaves – it is because Linda Tressel 'had not learned to recognise the fact of her own individuality' (*Linda Tressel*, 297) that she can be stifled out of existence by her aunt. But limit the will even of a tyrant, and the world's sum of energy goes down. Better trust truth to emerge from conflict, suggests Trollope, than shackle the independence of the self.

The link between *Lady Anna* and *The Duke's Children* is of a similar kind, though the later novel extends its predecessor differently. Each pivots on a conflict between parent and child in which the parent wishes the child to act out in the same way the crisis of his own early life. In *Lady Anna* the issue is loveless marriage. Countess Lovel, her name echoing the theme, had married greatly above herself – only to be disowned when her husband claimed he was married before. Having spent her whole life fighting to vindicate her right to the rank and wealth which had tempted her, victory is in sight when her opponents suggest an amicable settlement through her daughter's marriage to the young man on whom the title is entailed. Even though it isn't strictly necessary to her purpose, the Countess prosecutes this scheme with all her might because of an unconscious need to demonstrate vicariously that her own marriage was justified. The principles are at stake on which she has based her life, and when Lady Anna refuses to copy her error she breaks down and retires from the world. In *The Duke's Children* a more complex version of this drama appears.[16] Years before, Lady Glencora Palliser had married her husband without loving him, wrenched from her infatuation with Burgo Fitzgerald. Discovering after her death that she had secretly encouraged her daughter to marry a man he considers unsuitable, the Duke suspects that she has been trying to successfully re-enact her own early life. He counters in kind, attempting to replace the girl's suitor with a surrogate for himself, but the analogies with his own marriage are false, and the plan fails. By the end of the novel he has been brought to accept a second union at odds with his own when his elder son marries an American girl.

It isn't too much to say that in each of these novels the parent's integrity is at issue as much as the child's. The Duke of Omnium and Lady Lovel each feel that their lives would in some way be falsified if their children's actions were to contradict their own personal histories, and yet, for the children, the fight to marry whom they love is their crucial test of self-realisation. The Duke is able to accept his daughter's marriage when he comes to understand that it doesn't really correspond with the marriage his wife had wished for herself; but Lady Lovel can in no way compromise, for the fundamental choice of her life has been put in question. The obstinacy shown by each parent suggests that for Trollope the struggle to maintain an identity cannot be decided in one action or on one front. It is a struggle which continues through life, although some events exercise a more determining influence than others. Chief among these is marriage, and it is to conflicts over marriage that Trollope again and again returns – not because of sentimentality in himself, or a wish to gratify it in his audience, but above all because he recognised marriage as a bond which made possible both integration of self and integration between self and society.

The novel which most fully demonstrates this idea is *He Knew He Was Right*, but once more an earlier and a shorter work helped prepare the ground. *The Golden Lion of Granpère* was written immediately before *He Knew He Was Right* in 1867, though it wasn't published till 1872. It dramatises a contest between father and son over the son's wish to marry his adopted sister, but although there are hints of sexual rivalry the battle is

provoked, as always in Trollope, by the unyielding independence of each person. Michel Voss, Trollope observes, would
probably not have objected to the match had it been put to him
'with a proper amount of attention to his judgement and
controlling power' (15); nor, if his father had been less
overbearing, would George Voss have been so ready to rebel.
The novel is humorous in tone, drawing ironic comedy from
each man's self-deception and the rubs arising. But there is also a
psychological interest in their perversity, the twisted outgrowth
of a fierce need to assert themselves. As Trollope remarks of the
father, so of the son: 'It was singular to observe how cruel he had
become against the girl whom he so dearly loved' (225). In *He
Knew He Was Right*, this deceptively casual comment has developed into perception of a different tone and order: 'They who
do not understand that a man may be brought to hope that which
of all things is the most grievous to him, have not observed with
sufficient closeness the perversity of the human mind' (364).

The relation between *He Knew He Was Right* and *The Golden
Lion of Granpère* isn't as close as in the two other pairs of novels,
depending more on community of psychological insight than on
similarity in story. Yet in one respect the development from
earlier work to later corresponds: in *He Knew He Was Right*, as in
John Caldigate and *The Duke's Children*, Trollope pursued his
subject through a number of varying conflicts, all with the effect
of casting light on it from different points. The central problem,
reflected ironically in the title, is how, if a strong identity is all-
important, it may be sustained in any relationship by each
person. Obstinacy is the law of life for all Trollope's leading
characters, as well as for many minor figures in his work. Even
Septimus Harding, mild as he appears, has the strength of will to
resign against the opposition of all around him in *The Warden*.
But if, to assure stable identity, one's purpose must be secured,
an impasse may be created by the equal and opposite will of
another person. This is what happens in all the stories which
make up the complex pattern of *He Knew He Was Right*. The
peculiarity of the novel is that the same quality which supports
the identity of some of the characters, such as Nora Rowley or
Dorothy Stanbury, in others threatens health, sanity, and even
life. Miss Stanbury, Camilla French, and, in the main plot,
Louis Trevelyan, are all in some measure victims to the spirit of

obstinacy that is vital elsewhere. Plot and sub-plots vary the same essential theme, so that the novel's meaning grows from the different developments on each side.

Common to each plot is a struggle over marriage, present or in prospect. The partners either clash with each other, as do the Trevelyans, or with someone who holds inhibiting power. Dorothy Stanbury and Brooke Burgess rebel against Dorothy's aunt, who will not countenance their marriage because of a feud many years earlier. Miss Stanbury, genteel but poor, had been prevented by family quarrels from marrying a Burgess (the name suggests why), but had then inherited most of his wealth. Possessed by a need to justify herself, she will allow no member of her family to enjoy the legacy which she is determined to return at her death; unconsciously, perhaps, she won't have her niece succeeding where she had failed. Here again Trollope shows how the integrity of a self may depend on the conviction of a lifetime. Yet, however painfully, Miss Stanbury comes at last to contradict herself. She does so by virtue of a growing love for her niece which she cannot suppress and which calls out her goodwill. Love in Trollope, for those characters who can experience it, is a commitment of the whole being which can be denied only with crippling results. So marriage is crucial for Trollope's lovers, since the maintenance of identity may depend on a fulfilment of love which is possible only within the given social order. It is in this way that Dorothy Stanbury's opposition to her aunt is justified, as also Nora Rowley's opposition to her father in the parallel sub-plot, for if marriage is disallowed, lovers in Trollope can have no recourse but dogged persistence to defend the fundamental choice that defines them. In two further sub-plots, however, resistance to marriage comes from within the couple itself. Caroline Spalding, an American girl, tries to call off her engagement to an English peer because she fears that her social origins will be held against her, but she is in love with him, and so he is justified in bringing her back to their purpose. In contrast, the hapless Gibson is subdued to matrimony by the joint efforts of two husband-hunting females. Then, when he changes his preference, a second battle is fought between the sisters themselves. Murder and madness threaten, in farcical parody of the main plot, until the unlucky sister eventually yields.

A struggle for identity centring on marriage: the point at which all the sub-plots intersect is also the crux of the main plot and the novel's thematic core. Louis and Emily Trevelyan quarrel not because he really suspects her of infidelity, or because she has any wish to be unfaithful, but through each partner's need for self-assertion. Husband claims too much authority over wife: wife demands too much autonomy in return. With such embattled and embittering attitudes on each side, a trivial dispute becomes self-compounding. Both refuse to draw back because they fear to compromise themselves. Instead, they justify their positions with arguments that make it progressively more difficult for them to yield. Trevelyan, brooding in solitude, reaches psychological impasse: a vicious circle of rationalisation inscribing ever more sharply a fixed idea. He cannot submit because, as Trollope puts it in a phrase worthy of R. D. Laing,[17] 'He could not thus swallow down all the convictions by which he had fortified himself to bear the misfortunes which he had endured' (634). That way madness lies, but Emily Trevelyan never declines so far. With a baby to care for, and relatives around her, she avoids her husband's fatal isolation and at last, after a long separation, gives in, shocked at his ruin in body and mind. Trevelyan is too dilapidated to survive for long, yet on his deathbed her will reasserts itself. She asks whether he really thinks she has been unfaithful, and, admitting by the faintest sign that he has been wrong, Trevelyan dies. Such persistence looks remorseless, but she could no longer sustain her integrity without some acknowledgment that her part in the quarrel wasn't unjustified, so powerful, in Trollope, is the need for self-determination, to know one is right.

The phrase which gives the novel its title echoes and re-echoes through plot and sub-plot alike. Trollope presents a chaos of self-assertion, in which the whole principle of society seems threatened. Yet it is only a threat, since what the successful characters fight for is association: associations which as well as realising their own deepest selves call a renewed society into being. The principal sub-plots all end in marriages that help change society. Brooke Burgess and Dorothy Stanbury not only reconcile the feud between their respective families but bring about, in the terms suggested above, an alliance between trade and gentility. Nora Rowley's marriage to Hugh Stanbury also

registers change, showing journalism in process of being accepted
as a profession – especially as the wedding takes place under
aristocratic patronage. Finally, the marriage of the patrons itself
points to social renewal, with an American bride promising to
leaven the English aristocracy. Whether or not Trollope was
right to place upon marriage the twin burden of effecting and
representing social change is a question to be faced in Chapter 6.
But in each of the new marriages in *He Knew He Was Right* self
and society are finally united in marriage, the deepest energy of
the self embodied in social as well as personal reintegration. It is
the character who most insists on his autonomy who is
destroyed, as if death and madness inevitably followed from lack
of social relation.

The world of *He Knew He Was Right* may be seen as a model
designed to resolve one of Trollope's most urgent preoccupations: how is society possible, if all must be individuals? Novels
such as *Framley Parsonage* and *Is He Popenjoy?* play variations on
the same theme, but in other works Trollope sometimes reversed
the question. His double commitment to individuality and
community is the conundrum that generates his fiction, as he
seeks with the impartiality of obsession to answer it every
possible way. Its source, as I have suggested, lies in the bitterness
of his childhood, when he was isolated and an object of
contempt. Denied full association with his schoolfellows, Trollope
formed an identity the hard way and remained painfully aware
of the difficulties in maintaining it. That is why, among the
Victorian novelists, he most emphasises the importance of
individuality; yet also why he is the most sensitive to what
threatens it. The problem for the two principal characters of *The
Last Chronicle* and *Phineas Redux* is how identity may be sustained
under circumstances of maximum pressure.

The typical position of Trollope's characters is at the centre of
social attention. Sometimes this takes the form of a press
campaign, suffered by Harding in *The Warden* and in the Palliser
novels by Phineas Finn and the Duke of Omnium. At other
times, it is a trial that focuses the social gaze: on Lady Mason in
Orley Farm, and Josiah Crawley in *The Last Chronicle*, or on the
figures whose names supply the titles of *Phineas Redux* and *John
Caldigate*. Trollope's first novel, *The Macdermots of Ballycloran*,

vividly, if crudely, describes the feelings of a man exposed to the same predicament, but the mere fact of public attention is in itself both painful and disorientating. For Trollope, the world's knowledge of one's misfortune is always far worse than the misfortune itself could be, and this remains as true for the hero of his last novel, *An Old Man's Love*, as for any other figure, such as Lily Dale in the Barsetshire series or the illegitimate Ralph Newton in *Ralph the Heir*. Not only is this theme remarkably persistent in Trollope, but comparison with other novelists of his time suggests it is quite distinctive. In *Vanity Fair*, Becky Sharp may be hurt by social censure, but she isn't crushed or unfixed in any way. She feels the slights, but not as a personal impeachment. In Trollope, on the other hand, even so amoral a character as Ferdinand Lopez feels as a burden 'hard to bear without wincing' the secrecy he has to maintain about his social origins (*The Prime Minister*, I,3). Arthur Clennam, hero of *Little Dorrit*, is shown to suffer when Dickens makes him an unconvincing scapegoat after Merdle's ruin, but he undergoes no permanent damage. Wishing to exonerate his partner, he even courts the role. Trollope is in most respects closer to George Eliot than to Dickens, but in *Middlemarch* it isn't so much public opinion that troubles people as 'the hampering threadlike pressure of small social conditions' (in this context on Lydgate).[18] Although social disgrace is felt very strongly by Bulstrode, the banker whose guilt is exposed in the same novel, it is a sense that invades even Trollope's most exemplary figures, and injures them no less for their innocence. We must go to Meredith's *One of Our Conquerors*, much later in the century, to find a consciousness of social pressure that approaches Trollope's. There we see in Victor Radnor the fatal inconsistencies of an attempt to vindicate unsocial behaviour (in the shape of a good but adulterous union) by winning social success; and in his wife Nataly the crushing effects of social persecution, rendered all the more inescapable because Radnor, in pursuit of his goal, reduces her to propitiate the society whose standards they transgress.

The Last Chronicle of Barset and *Phineas Redux* are the novels which dramatise most strenuously Trollope's sense of social pressure. Here again a link with his childhood experience appears, for the central character of each work undergoes an ordeal parallel to one of the first incidents described in the *Autobiography*, when the young Trollope was punished for a crime he didn't commit. Both Crawley and Phineas Finn suffer crises of identity which project that ordeal. Wrongly accused on strong circumstantial evidence, each is eventually found innocent – almost as if their stories could be Trollope's unconscious vindication. Writing fifty years after the event, he could say 'it burns me now as though it were yesterday', and be tempted to publish the names of the culprits (*Autobiography*, 5). Neither novel, however, shows much sign of wish-fulfilment. Each is distinguished by an insight verging on the relentless into the stresses on identity resulting from social pressure.

For all Trollope's celebration of individuality, the characters of his works often depend to a marked degree on the good opinion of others. As with John Caldigate, so with them: 'Not to be approved of, not to be courted, not to stand well in the eyes of those around him, was to him positive and immediate suffering' (*John Caldigate*, 350). In Trollope, identity is not simply the expression of an inner being that precedes existence, but is assimilated in part to the relations that envelop it. If the quality of those relations changes, the person's identity either alters with it or a dangerous discrepancy develops. *The Last Chronicle* explores the first of these alternatives, *Phineas Redux* the second. Josiah Crawley, a clergyman driven almost to madness by the poverty in which he and his family live, is unable to account for a cheque he has cashed and is accused of theft. When the Bishop tries to suspend him, Crawley defends himself fiercely, asserting his right to keep his benefice pending the legal decision. A man of pronounced individuality, his natural stance is in opposition – whether crushing the Bishop on his own territory, or resisting the help of well-meaning friends. Yet, despite such militant independence, Crawley comes to disbelieve his own memory and accept that he may be guilty, though unintentionally, of theft. Aware of some confusion in his mind over the cheque, and of the general feeling that he misappropriated it, he is influenced by that feeling so far as to reverse his earlier action and resign of his own free will. By doing so he can both act in accordance with the general view and sustain his autonomy, for he is deferring neither to the Bishop, whom he has already defeated, nor to the advice of his friends, who all argue against resignation. The intense psychological stress he suffers during the early part of the novel relaxes when there is no longer a discrepancy between the account he gives of the cheque and the view generally accepted, and when he can act on that basis – firmly, controversially, and (as if it proved his integrity) against his own interests.

The Last Chronicle, like *John Caldigate* and *He Knew He Was Right*, corresponds to other major novels by Trollope in the coherence of its inner structure. The story of Josiah Crawley is set in a context which places his achievement in relief, for other characters either assert themselves excessively, or defer excessively to social claims. In Barsetshire, all is contention. Archdeacon Grantly strives to maintain his authority as a father, Henry Grantly his independence as a son; Mrs. Proudie attempts to rule the diocese, the diocese refuses to be ruled; Lily Dale is advised on all sides to marry John Eames, she resolves on spinsterhood. In London, on the other hand, convention is the general rule. All subsists on credit, by an effort of outward show – whether in finance, as with Dobbs Broughton, or in personal relations, as with Conway Dalrymple and Mrs. Broughton, or John Eames and Madalina Demolines. Everyone tries so hard to be other than he is that social life becomes emptied of meaning. In the two worlds of his novel Trollope has embodied a basic contrast: the Barsetshire characters, who fear public opinion, protect themselves by self-assertion, while the London characters govern their lives by it and so forfeit any true identity. Crawley's distinction consists in his ability to remain an individual while deferring to social claims – in coming to accept the general view about the cheque, but in contradicting the advice just as generally given.

Crawley's story suggests, though it doesn't fully develop, an interesting idea about madness. If madness may be defined in terms of a discrepancy between one person's view of himself and that of those around him, then it may be induced by such a discrepancy, even if its source is arbitrary or accidental. Crawley approaches insanity in the depth of his depression, but he recovers by coming to accept the collective opinion, and then differing fiercely in the action to be taken. In *Phineas Redux* Trollope extends the theme by placing his hero in a more uncompromising position. Accused on strong circumstantial evidence of a murder he didn't commit, all Phineas Finn can do is to deny his guilt and depend on the support of his friends. He undergoes the trial with honour, and is triumphantly vindicated by the arrival of fresh evidence, but when the ordeal is over he breaks down and the damage to his personality becomes manifest. What affects him so critically is the knowledge that almost everyone has believed him guilty, including even colleagues and friends; and this is compounded by his isolation in prison and the dock. In a deep sense, the issue of the trial is mistaken identity. Crawley knew it wasn't in his nature to be a thief, but was brought to admit the possibility of unintentional error by the pressure of evidence and belief against him. Similarly, Phineas knows he cannot be a murderer, but for him there's no means of meeting the opposite case. Instead, the strength of belief in his guilt seeps into and distorts his awareness. Trollope suggests the strains on Phineas by concentrating on the reactions of the outside world to his arrest, keeping the prisoner isolated and offstage. The effect is vividly realised when, alone for the first time after his release, Phineas 'stood up in the middle of the room, stretching forth his hands, and putting one first to his breast and then to his brow, feeling himself as though doubting his own identity' (*Phineas Redux*, II,292). Even knowing it to be false, Phineas has suffered so much from public accusation as to need physical reassurance that he is intact – still, at least outwardly, the same person.

The basic congruity of theme between *Phineas Redux* and *The Last Chronicle* is emphasised by the repetition in each novel of the same Latin proverb: 'no one at an instant, – of a sudden, – becomes most base' (*The Last Chronicle*, I,438; *Phineas Redux*, II,164). Perhaps it's significant that the phrase is a rule of grammar, as if its truth were equally an axiom, for it guarantees the consistency of identity in a world which, like that of Trollope's youth, continually threatens it. Such a threat is unusually dangerous for those as insecure as Crawley and Phineas, one struggling against poverty to keep up gentlemanly status, the other aiming without money or position for a career in politics. Crawley comes under suspicion of theft through his need to accept charity, Phineas under suspicion of murder through a quarrel with his rival for an appointment he needs to stay in parliament. Earlier in his career Phineas had suffered a crisis which caused him to feel that 'he would never set himself aright, even unto himself, till he had gone through some terrible act of humiliation' (*Phineas Finn*, I,311), recognising at some level that he must eventually pay, psychologically, for his ambition. Since it is his exaggerated awareness of insecurity that brings him to quarrel with Bonteen, which in turn leads to his being accused of murder, his ordeal may be seen as a paradigm of the stresses suffered by the man who tries to rise in society, just as Crawley's is a paradigm of those suffered by the man who is literally degraded.

Trollope's insight into the stress of social pressure helps explain why, though among Victorian novelists he is the strongest champion of individuality, he also possesses most confidence that the individual may be fulfilled in society. More than Dickens, George Eliot or Meredith, he believes that self and social role may correspond. People in Meredith tend to be radically self-deluded by virtue of a position they aspire to or already hold, like Willoughby in *The Egoist*, Victor Radnor in *One of Our Conquerors*, or Richard Feverel, whose ordeal is the outcome of his father's attempt to form a fit successor. In George Eliot there is another kind of dissonance in which individual idealism is constrained by social conditions. Dorothea's tragedy in *Middlemarch* is that the fullness of her nature cannot be realised within the 'imperfect social state' in which she finds herself. Her influence on others may be 'incalculably diffusive',[19] but her gifts are not channelled to account. The contrast is clearer still with Dickens whose heroes and heroines rarely if ever end their careers in significant relation to society; instead they tend to withdraw into families which appear self-subsisting, cut off from the world, and which, apart from their incomes, are so. Pip, at the end of *Great Expectations*, is an exception to this in that he has to make his own way in life; but his career is abroad and it has no meaning in itself other than as a means of honourable support. For Trollope, on the contrary, there is always a link between identity and social role, whether that role entails a job or profession or neither, whether the person is a clergyman like Crawley, an aspiring politician like Phineas Finn, or a leisured gentleman like Trevelyan; or whether a confirmed spinster, wife, or marriageable girl.

Trollope remarks in his *Autobiography* on the craving for

approval which grew out of his loneliness and rejection in early life (14, 52–3). It is now possible to see in the bitter experience of his youth the roots not only of his career as a novelist – in those long stories with which, in solitary reverie, he indulged himself – but also of the characteristic fictions through which the strains he underwent were worked out. If his novels typically move through struggle and discord towards an adjustment of relations between individuals and society, then it's largely because that is a kind of resolution he wished to believe in himself. What gives them their distinction is the thoroughness with which he imagined the struggle, if not always the resolution. Acutely sensitive to stresses on identity, he compensates with a dynamic conception of the self; and in his model of society it is the power of the individual will that enables social advancement. Nevertheless, there is still the question whether Trollope doesn't pay too high a price for the accommodation between self and society which his novels effect more often and more typically than those of his major contemporaries. This has been a recurrent doubt in criticism of his work. Though it hasn't often been pursued very far, a review of 1861 put it pungently if onesidedly:

> There are no men and women in 'Framley Parsonage': they are never viewed as men and women; but only with regard to their relations to Society. The only conscience in the book is, 'What will the world say?' the only morality, 'Such conduct does not become such a position'. Unfrock Mark Robarts and he does not exist. Deprive Lord Lufton of his title, Miss Dunstable of her wealth, and they cease to be.[20]

More recently a similar charge has been pressed by George Levine, who argues that Trollope's realism tends to deny the idealism of the individual self and to enforce a worldly wisdom of acquiescence in social convention.[21]

The novels suggest that the truth is more complicated. While they generally move towards accommodation between individual and society, adjustments have to be made on both sides. Whatever the strains upon them, neither Crawley nor Phineas Finn surrenders his identity, and each is finally vindicated. In *He Knew He Was Right*, the need for an ability to accept change is demonstrated in both individuals and society. Trevelyan's attitude to social change is suggested by his contempt for his friend's profession as a journalist, his attitude to personal change by his refusal to compromise with his wife. This inability to accommodate destroys him. On the other hand, Miss Stanbury begins by opposing change of all kinds, yet by the end she has come to accept a renewal of her own closest ties parallel to those in the novel's society. The same is true even of the novel chosen by Professor Levine to exemplify his argument. *Can You Forgive Her?* ends not only with Alice Vavasor consenting to marry John Grey, but also with Grey himself agreeing, against all his previous resolutions, to enter politics. He must learn the same lesson as Plantagenet Palliser, in the parallel story, to treat his wife as a person in her own right. The nature of the compromise is evident not in the comic third plot, but in the tolerant humanity which all four partners in the main plots must develop if they are to come to terms with each other – and with themselves. For it isn't as a sacrificial offering that Alice Vavasor returns to John Grey, though she harbours some residual doubt. Trollope has imagined her position more subtly and more thoroughly. She had broken her engagement to Grey, not because she did not love him, but because of an insecurity which called on her to assert herself. Motherless, and with her place in the world ill-defined (a fact Trollope underlines with his novel's opening sentence), she has to maintain her independence against a man who is all too self-assured. It's in this way that the jilting is to be understood – a jilting which will make for a stronger relationship between them, just as the Palliser marriage truly begins only after Glencora has come near to desertion.

I have argued that Trollope believed firmly in each person's right to independence. If he did, then it isn't possible to agree with Professor Levine that his 'ultimate value' is the survival of society – even if, as I have also tried to show, 'the well-being, even the identity, of all people is dependent on it'.[22] The truth is that the relation between individual and society must be reciprocal, each modifying the other. Just as the self depends for existence on association with others, so only through conflict with individuals can society change and renew itself. Trollope's double perspective presents what for him was not only the arbitrariness of conventions but their necessity, not only the dangers of the individual will but its motive power. Professor Levine's argument refines the tradition in Trollope criticism identified at the beginning of this chapter, a tradition which represents him as a society novelist, with little insight or concern for the individual in his or her inner self. What is valid in this view consists chiefly in Trollope's sense of social relationships as a kind of envelope within which alone people can live and find fulfilment. That sense sprang not from complacency with the conventional world, but from concern for personal identity which experience had taught him to be fragile. Trollope didn't believe that people could develop and pursue aspirations in isolation from society. But that doesn't mean he was content to accept uncritically the conventions of his period. His dream is of reconciliation, his nightmare of estrangement, between self and society, and his fictions act out each alternative. If the emphasis falls finally on reconciliation, it hasn't simply been dreamed but worked for and dramatised.

Professor Levine's real antagonist is the official Trollope. This is the figure who prescribes matrimony for all Alice Vavasor's difficulties, and pretends to solve Crawley's with a comfortable living. Similar doubts spring up when Trollope's stories are compared with the history of his time. In what sense is the plight of an underpaid curate representative? – or that of a member of parliament unjustly accused of murder? And how could marriage have been so important a means of social change as the novels portray it? – unless by the notion is intended only the small change of genteel and upper-class life? Looked at from this point of view, the novels appear disconnected from their real foundations, and Trollope's achievement dwindles into the superficial and ephemeral.

If such an assessment of his work is mistaken, the reason is what the novels have to show unofficially. That has been the subject of this chapter in the form of those struggles for identity which they continually re-enact. The question now is what significance those struggles have to Trollope's representation of Victorian life. Surprisingly enough, an answer is suggested by R. H. Hutton, the same contemporary critic who stated the classic case against Trollope as merely a novelist of society. Reviewing a new edition of Jane Austen just after Trollope's death, Hutton was challenged to fresh insight by comparing the two novelists' work. What he grasped was the different picture each writer reflected of personal identity in social life:

Everybody in Miss Austen, from the squires and the doctors down to the lovers, is leisurely, giving one a great sense of perfect seclusion, ample opportunity, plenty of space, and plenty of time. Everybody in Mr. Trollope is more or less under pressure, swayed hither and thither by opposite attractions, assailed on this side and on that by the strategy of rivals; everywhere someone's room is more wanted than his company; everywhere time is short. . . . Miss Austen's people are themselves alone. Mr. Trollope's people are themselves so far as the circumstances of the day will allow them to be themselves, but very often are much distorted from their most natural selves.[23]

It is a brilliant contrast, and one that helps explain the bias in Trollope's fiction that Hutton had earlier recognised. The reason why Trollope allowed so much influence to relations with others, to public opinion, is that in the world he inhabited individuality could no longer be taken for granted. Hutton touches briefly on the social changes that effected this development. This isn't the place to go further, but I would suggest that one of Trollope's main achievements is to display the pressures on identity of a new kind of social life. At a time when individualism was the orthodox cry, Trollope revealed despite himself some of its limits and contradictions.

Professor Levine has an excellent phrase to describe the essential note at the end of a Trollope novel. It is a note, he says, of 'unembittered disenchantment'.[24] The phrase catches finely the tension beneath Trollope's acceptance. His imagination is exercised again and again by the kind of dilemma I have discussed. Two final examples will show how equally it was balanced for him. In his *Autobiography* Trollope describes the difficulties for a statesman who is also an idealist. He defines the average politician as 'a good, round, smooth, hard, useful pebble' (309). Such men, he has stated, have submitted themselves 'to be shaped and fashioned, and to be formed into tools' (308). And this, he acknowledges, is necessary if people are to work in unison for common aims. But his interest is in a person 'who could not become a pebble, having too strong an identity of his own', and it is the troubles of such an individual that he describes in the story of Plantagenet Palliser. One limitation of this story is that he can only indicate vaguely what political ideals might amount to. That doesn't, however, affect my point, which has to do not with what he could put into words but with what he could convey through his fiction. In this light, Palliser's career is another re-enactment of the drama his novels kept staging. Trollope's view of Palliser is interested, marked by special pleading for the Establishment figure,[25] but it demonstrates again his unofficial theme of the trials of identity.

The second example puts the opposite viewpoint – one of confidence in the value and necessity of adaptation. Trollope suggests in a simile from *Rachel Ray* how society can keep its continuity despite both constant change and inflexibility among some of its members:

> A man cannot change as men change. Individual men are like the separate links of a rotatory chain. The chain goes on with continuous easy motion as though every part of it were capable of adapting itself to a curve, but not the less is each link as stiff and sturdy as any other piece of wrought iron. (234)

Trollope emphasises both the continuity of the chain and the individual obduracy that gives it its strength. That he should have chosen a mechanical metaphor is wholly apt, in the context of a society which had transformed itself through rapid industrial development. That he didn't recognise all his metaphor implied helps define the limits of his perception.

5 *The Interior View*

No one needs to be told that one of the achievements of modern fiction has been the development of techniques for conveying inner processes of feeling and reflection. It isn't always remembered, however, that this was a development which couldn't have taken place without earlier writers preparing the way. Perhaps worse, in their pursuit of new territories critics have tended to neglect those which seemed to have been assimilated long ago. In this chapter I shall argue that Trollope, like other Victorian novelists, had ways of representing inner experience which haven't been sufficiently studied. The interior view plays a central part in his fiction though its importance has rarely been noticed. To recognise its importance is again to question the notion that his novels concern themselves with society over the self. It is to demonstrate a kind of resource with which he hasn't been credited, and to raise the question of how effectively he employed it. Finally, it is to identify another channel through which the unofficial Trollope expressed himself.

First, however, Trollope's method of interior view has to be placed in context. To compare Victorian and modern representations of mental process is already to assume one basic similarity. For a new inwardness, however differently embodied, is itself an important departure – always excepting Sterne – from the novel of the previous century. There the quality of mental life is rendered in three distinct ways, none of them very much like the methods introduced later. Defoe adopts the form of the memoir, with its retrospective distance and unconscious revisions (compare, for instance, the three accounts he has Crusoe give of arriving on his island, each as if written at a further remove from the experience).[1] Fielding intimates little of his characters' inward lives, as if it would be indelicate to pry; but when he

105

does, he employs brief soliloquy or outward detail. He objected
to the most immediate form of representation at his period,
epistolary fiction. In this characters express – sometimes reveal –
their own thoughts and feelings, usually to a sympathetic
reader. As Ian Watt has pointed out, such closeness to inward
experience influenced through Jane Austen a growing interest
in conveying mental process in the fiction of the next century.[2]
Novelists began to explore character from within: Jane Austen
through the filters of irony, the Brontës by first person narration,
or by forms that could take its pressure. But in Dickens and
Thackeray the inner world is rarely evoked so directly, however
much their characterisation may imply of unacknowledged
wishes and submerged motives. Even their first person novels
are less introspective. In the third person their method is mainly
external, whether branching into ironic implication as with
Thackeray, or soliloquy as with Dickens. Each has its own
rewards, such as the hints at Amelia's selfishness in *Vanity Fair*,
or Dickens' virtuoso performances in *Little Dorrit* of Miss Wade
and Flora Finching. But for all that the reader remains on the
outside: confidant of a sly commentator, or audience to
theatrical impersonation.

Nevertheless, and through the medium of Jane Austen and
the Brontë sisters, the interior view has become an established
technique in English fiction by the 1860s. Two of the major
novelists to use it are also women: Mrs. Gaskell and George
Eliot. To them should be added Trollope and Meredith. It
would be misleading to suggest that this was a tidy development,
or perhaps even to trace more than the obvious lines of
influence. Though Trollope admired Jane Austen, though Mrs.
Gaskell wrote a life of Charlotte Brontë, though George Eliot
drew on both these sources and others, the significant fact is that
all these writers were extending the boundaries of fiction
inwards. And, building in various ways on the groundwork laid
by their predecessors, they did so in some independence of each
other. Perhaps this is one reason why their techniques are so
different. Mrs. Gaskell's interior views screen emotional evoca-
tion with commentary, while Meredith's can be consciously
experimental, even operatic, in representing the sensibility of his
characters, physical as well as psychological, to events, atmos-
pheres and especially to the presence of others. George Eliot is

concerned above all by the conflicts and temptations of the moral consciousness. Like Meredith, she combines metaphor with free indirect speech to recapture mental process. Experiments with metaphor were to take on increasing importance in the next generation, but that direction is never followed by Trollope, whose speciality is to recreate mental rhythms through repetition and rhetorical patterns of speech.

Not much in this brief account will have been new, but the problem still remains why Victorian resources for rendering inward experience have gone neglected in comparison with the celebrated achievements of the moderns. One reason lies in misleading terminology. It has become conventional to distinguish between Victorian and modern interior views with the respective labels of 'analysis' and 'representation'.[3] There is more truth in this than in some oversimplifications, but it leaves no room for the important element of representation in Victorian interior views, and forgets too easily that even modern writers cannot represent consciousness directly, but only through conventions. There is also a further reason: while Anglo-American critics were busy unscrambling the codes of James Joyce, Virginia Woolf or William Faulkner, philologists on the Continent were discovering, in earlier fiction, the subtle notation of free indirect speech. As Dorrit Cohn has indicated, English and American critics have paid this material scant attention until recently, even when it involves English literature, and although it has long been available.[4]

Trollope provides an especially clear illustration of this neglect, for he is a novelist whose style and technique in general have until lately occasioned less interest than disparagement. Few people have so much as appreciated that the interior view is an essential part of his method, let alone discussed its qualities. The first seems to have been Lisa Glauser, a Swiss, who included Trollope in a survey of *erlebte Rede* (roughly, the German term for free indirect speech) in English nineteenth-century fiction.[5] Glauser places Trollope in the tradition of the previous century. She argues that he depends chiefly on social comedy in a novel such as *Barchester Towers*, but that he was also capable, as in *Rachel Ray*, of developing free indirect speech as a means of characterisation and emotional heightening. She doesn't find his handling of the method especially distinguished, and claims

that he devalued it in *The Way We Live Now* (her third and last
example) by using it superficially and indiscriminately. Glauser's
account has its limitations, perhaps inevitably in a pioneering
study. A sample of three novels out of forty-seven is almost
bound to give a false impression, which is further compounded
by a too obedient application of received ideas of literary
history, the sole authority being Joseph Baker. (*The Way We Live
Now*, for instance, is viewed as nothing but Trollope venting his
spleen.) Nevertheless, Glauser's monograph broke new ground,
and her discussion is useful where it depends on close observation rather than received opinions. It might have been still more
valuable, in Trollope's case, if she had dealt with novels of
greater psychological interest, such as *The Last Chronicle of Barset*
or *He Knew He Was Right*.

The only Trollopian to take up Glauser's study is one of the
few English critics to have commented even briefly on Trollope's
interior view technique. David Skilton calls attention to the
curious critical neglect of the world of private feeling in
Trollope, and proposes an explanation.[6] Trollope, he thinks,
didn't quite solve the problem of how to present his characters'
internal meditations. Since these always involve actions which
have already happened, they can be mistaken too easily for
repetitious summary – a danger which a modern novelist would
probably avoid by using 'stream of consciousness' style instead.
This is an interesting guess, and one partly borne out by Roy
Pascal's remarks on Trollope in his informative survey of how
free indirect speech developed and reached critical definition.
Pascal confirms the importance of interior views in Trollope by
indicating that free indirect speech is abundant in his novels
'from the earliest to the last', and by focusing his analysis on
presentation of characters' thoughts rather than their speech.[7]
The two novels he refers to are *Barchester Towers* and *Is He
Popenjoy?*, though he could have taken his own phrase literally –
both *The Macdermots of Ballycloran*, Trollope's first novel, and *An
Old Man's Love*, his last, contain examples of the technique. The
reason behind Pascal's selection of texts is to illustrate not only
how Trollope used free indirect speech at both ends of his
career, but how it was open to abuse by a novelist who, he
claims, sometimes employed it too easily. Pascal suggests that in
his best work Trollope showed more discrimination. But it isn't

within the scope of his discussion to consider Trollope's successes, and for this reason it has some of the same limitations as Glauser's.

To recognise the special value of Trollope's interior views it has taken the perception of a contemporary novelist who has sometimes been compared with him. Trollope wasn't interested in representing consciousness directly, as Skilton seems to assume (for example in calling his interior views 'internal monologues', which they are not). As Snow has suggested, what Trollope shows instead is a character's continuous inner reflection as it shapes or influences his moral choices.[8] To explain this more clearly, and to define as fully as I can Trollope's handling of the interior view at his best, I shall discuss in detail an example of this kind of writing from *The Last Chronicle of Barset*. It occurs as a single paragraph in Chapter 12, when Josiah Crawley has roused himself from his morbid broodings to go among the brickmakers. His wife has just tried to prevent him from going out, fearing that he may be tempted to commit suicide, but he has read her unspoken forebodings, and she has given way to his assurance that she need fear nothing.

She did let him pass without another word, and he went out of the house, shutting the door after him noiselessly, and closing the wicket-gate of the garden. For a while she sat herself down on the nearest chair, and tried to make up her mind how she
5   might best treat him in his present state of mind. As regarded the present morning her heart was at ease. She knew that he would do now nothing of that which she had apprehended. She could trust him not to be false in his word to her, though she could not before have trusted him not to commit so much
10   heavier a sin. If he would really employ himself from morning till night among the poor, he would be better so, – his trouble would be easier of endurance, – than with any other employment which he could adopt. What she most dreaded was that he should sit idle over the fire and do nothing. When
15   he was so seated she could read his mind, as though it was open to her as a book. She had been quite right when she had accused him of over-indulgence in his grief. He did give way to it till it became a luxury to him, – a luxury which she would

not have had the heart to deny him, had she not felt it to be of
20   all luxuries the most pernicious. During these long hours, in
which he would sit speechless, doing nothing, he was telling
himself from minute to minute that of all God's creatures he
was the most heavily afflicted, and was revelling in the sense
of the injustice done to him. He was recalling all the facts of
25   his life, his education, which had been costly, and, as
regarded knowledge, successful; his vocation to the church,
when in his youth he had determined to devote himself to the
service of his Saviour, disregarding promotion or the favour
of men; the short, sweet days of his early love, in which he had
30   devoted himself again, – thinking nothing of self, but everything of her; his diligent working, in which he had ever done
his very utmost for the parish in which he was placed, and
always his best for the poorest; the success of other men who
had been his compeers, and, as he too often told himself,
35   intellectually his inferiors; then of his children, who had been
carried off from his love to the churchyard, – over whose
graves he himself had stood, reading out the pathetic words of
the funeral service with unswerving voice and a bleeding
heart; and then of his children still living, who loved their
40   mother so much better than they loved him. And he would
recall all the circumstances of his poverty, – how he had been
driven to accept alms, to fly from creditors, to hide himself, to
see his chairs and tables seized before the eyes of those over
whom he had been set as their spiritual pastor. And in it all, I
45   think, there was nothing so bitter to the man as the
derogation from the spiritual grandeur of his position as priest
among men, which came as one necessary result from his
poverty. St. Paul could go forth without money in his purse or
shoes to his feet or two suits to his back, and his poverty never
50   stood in the way of his preaching, or hindered the veneration
of the faithful. St. Paul, indeed, was called upon to bear
stripes, was flung into prison, encountered terrible dangers.
But Mr. Crawley, – so he told himself, – could have
encountered all that without flinching. The stripes and scorn
55   of the unfaithful would have been nothing to him, if only the
faithful would have believed in him, poor as he was, as they
would have believed in him had he been rich! Even they
whom he had most loved treated him almost with derision,

because he was now different from them. Dean Arabin had
60 laughed at him because he had persisted in walking ten miles
through the mud instead of being conveyed in the dean's
carriage; and yet, after that, he had been driven to accept the
dean's charity! No one respected him. No one! His very wife
thought that he was a lunatic. And how he had been publicly
65 branded as a thief; and in all likelihood would end his days in
a gaol! Such were always his thoughts as he sat idle, silent,
moody, over the fire; and his wife well knew their currents. It
would certainly be better that he should drive himself to some
employment, if any employment could be found possible to
70 him.[9]

The passage falls naturally into three sections, marked by
changes of mood, tempo and tense. The first of these, ending in
line 20 at 'pernicious', describes Mrs. Crawley's thoughts about
her husband; the second, ending in line 44 at 'pastor', Crawley's
own reflections on his sad personal history; and the third, until
almost the end of the passage, his indignation at the injustice of
his present position. But these divisions must not be drawn too
rigidly, for perhaps the most remarkable feature of the passage is
its continuity. There are two interior views here, not just one,
and the time of the paragraph isn't even predominantly in the
novel's 'present'. The narrative glides with deceptive ease
between the minds of Mrs. Crawley, her husband and the
narrator, who is their intermediary; and between the different
temporal levels of Crawley's reflections.

Before going further, it's necessary to establish a way of
discriminating accurately between the changing modes of the
narrative. Graham Hough has provided a helpful basis by
indicating five different voices in Jane Austen's *Emma*: the
authorial voice, objective narrative, coloured narrative, free
indirect speech, and direct speech.[10] These distinctions are
essentially sound, but for wider uses I propose two modifications.
First, the category of 'authorial voice' doesn't allow for a
projected narrator; it would be clearer to use the term
'subjective narrative' instead, and to state whether this is the
author speaking in his own person, as is the case with this
passage, or in a created role. Second, it is important to
distinguish between free indirect speech as representing spoken

or unspoken monologue. This is an essential pointer to whether the presentation is from without or within. Hough finds neither kind of much importance in *Emma*, perhaps because he makes little of unspoken monologue. But this has a value all its own, for instance the vivid impression of Emma's self-reproach when she reflects on how she has herself helped create the possibility of Knightley's marrying Harriet (Chapters 47 and 48). It is sensible to use a different name for each register. I follow Cohn in preferring 'narrated monologue' for thought, and for the spoken voice suggest 'narrated speech'. These terms clarify a distinction blurred by 'free indirect speech', and their phrasing makes them unambiguous. To sum up, there are now six categories in all. Subjective narrative represents the narrator's point of view, whether the author or a created narrator is in question. Objective narrative comes from the same source; it is confined principally to describing objects and events without obvious influence from the narrator's opinions or values. Coloured narrative represents the influence of a character's viewpoint, absorbed into the narrative for sympathetic or ironic effect; narrated monologue repeats the character's own words in reflection, but in the third person and the tense of narration; narrated speech is the equivalent for spoken words; and direct speech is self-explanatory. It only remains to add internal monologue and stream of consciousness style to render this list of fictional voices complete. These represent thought at the more and less formulated stages respectively. The first occurs rarely in Trollope, while of course the second is a later development.

It is now possible to define more clearly what kinds of narrative occur in the extract. The first sentence is plainly objective, without colouring either from the narrator or characters. As the second sentence unfolds, however, a point of view is felt, and even a slight mental intonation. From here until about line 20 the focus is primarily on Mrs. Crawley, and Trollope slowly introduces colouring to suggest the character of her thinking. There is an impression of her need for immediate relief – she sits down 'on the nearest chair' – and also, in the rather awkward repetition of 'mind', of the perplexing nature of her concern. These two suggestions, unobtrusive enough at first, are gradually heightened in the lines that follow. The next two

sentences are short, for Mrs. Crawley is resting momentarily on
the assurance she has gained; a fact emphasised by the repetition
of 'present', and by the position of 'now' in the fourth sentence
between verb and object. Perhaps without the reader noticing,
Trollope is already beginning to represent Mrs. Crawley's
thoughts in their own idiom. There are two cumbersome
euphemisms for the possibility of her husband's suicide – 'that
which she had apprehended' and 'so much heavier a sin' – and a
succession of tortuous negatives. These are signs of entry into
narrated monologue. Trollope is dramatising Mrs. Crawley's
anxiety by imitating the manner in which she would express her
fears to herself.

However, no sooner has this partial heightening of tone been
reached than it begins to flatten out as Mrs. Crawley applies her
mind to the problems now confronting her. The syntax becomes
more direct, even loose – as with the interpolated clause 'his
trouble would be easier of endurance', which crops up as if
grasped suddenly, as a clarification, during the actual process
of thinking. The next three sentences are succinct and straightforward. Now that her fear of suicide has receded, Mrs. Crawley
can define the immediate danger and a way to meet it, fully
confident that she understands her husband's condition. But
here an ambiguity occurs, one inherent in the form of free
indirect speech. There is no way of telling whether the two
sentences in lines 16–20 represent the character's view or the
narrator's, whether Mrs. Crawley is assuring herself that she has
read her husband's mind correctly, or whether Trollope is
confirming her opinion. The reader is more likely to follow the
first alternative than the second if he has been sufficiently alive
to Mrs. Crawley's voice for its influence to continue; but because
the observation is reported without much heightening it
remains, in the proper sense of the word, equivocal. This
indeterminacy serves two ends. First, Trollope both conveys a
moral judgement on Crawley, and dramatises it by presenting it
from Mrs. Crawley's viewpoint. Whether or not she actually
expresses it to herself he is, in effect, underwriting it. Second, by
temporarily suspending the distinction between his own voice
and Mrs. Crawley's, he prepares the way for the shift into her
husband's voice which is shortly to come. Some colouring
lingers on, nevertheless – especially in the double repetition of

'luxury', which emphasises, by its own excess, the extravagance of Crawley's grief.

It isn't clear exactly at what point the narrative leaves Mrs. Crawley's mind and enters her husband's, but after a few lines it becomes evident that her viewpoint has dissolved completely. The tense moves from past to conditional and then past continuous; the tempo slackens as if to register a more deliberate manner. At the same time there is some intensification: hyperbole in Crawley's view of his condition, and a certain moral charge in the word 'revelling'. At this stage it still isn't entirely plain whether the charge reflects Mrs. Crawley's perspective or Trollope's, but as the passage continues the narrative voice comes more into the open. It emerges by degrees, so that for a time the area of indeterminacy ranges between Trollope and Crawley, rather than between Trollope and Mrs. Crawley. For instance, the phrase 'as regarded knowledge' in lines 25–6 is ambiguous. If attributed to Crawley, it is an ironic reflection that his expensive education brought him knowledge and nothing else; if to Trollope, it implies that, in other respects, perhaps involving self-discipline and emotional maturity, Crawley could have learned more. Again Trollope may seem to have his cake and eat it, but the principal aim is probably to ease the reader from Mrs. Crawley's mind to her husband's as inconspicuously as possible. Why he should wish to do that I shall consider later. For the moment, it's enough to note that the basic pattern for Crawley's interior view has been set. In the sentences that follow, close imitation of his mental soliloquy alternates with judicious suggestions like 'revelling' which work as a check. Crawley reveals himself through the violence of his self-justification, and Trollope's careful monitoring ensures that the point isn't lost.

Nevertheless, Trollope's intimations always retain their tact. He prefers to work by indirection rather than blur complexity by summary statement. For instance, Crawley is not said to have devoted himself to God, but to have 'determined to devote himself', as if performance may have fallen behind promise. In the next clause we are told that he also devoted himself to his wife, but towards the close of this long sentence she is all but lost in his emotional claims on their children, only to appear as a rival at the end. Again, there is a latent inconsistency between

Crawley's attempt to disregard worldly advancement at the outset of his career, and the indignation he later feels at not receiving the credit which he has come to believe that only advancement can give. Trollope leaves all this to be inferred from the succession of Crawley's memories and the way they are expressed, respecting the integrity of thoughts he presents as his character's without compromising his own moral view. To expose these contradictions by summary would be to open them to ridicule. Caught in the knots of Crawley's rhetoric, they have for us something of the force of impasse they possess for him, while at the same time embodying where he goes wrong. His continual personal pronouns and possessives, his superlatives and overstrung adjectives, build up an impassioned tide which suggests he protests too much, especially when momentarily held back by Trollope's scrupulous reminder 'as he too often told himself'. Except for this, and the word 'determined' mentioned above, the long central sentence is in coloured narrative, shading into narrated monologue towards the end where the sentimental description of the funeral service tails off into the pathos-laden cadence of 'loved their mother so much better than they loved him'.

At this point the tempo begins to alter again. The tense moves into the conditional to express Crawley's brooding over the recent trials of his poverty, and then there's a perceptible shift of direction as Trollope briefly steps back to imagine more fully what poverty means to him. This final section is concerned less with Crawley's memories than with the indignation he has masochistically provoked in himself by recalling them. The focus moves away from him into subjective narrative in lines 44-8, but only for the writing to take on a progressively deeper colouring as it closes with him again, especially in the intense narrated monologue towards the end. At first this makes itself felt largely through the self-induced rhythms of Crawley's outraged rhetoric. Conjunctions are suppressed, as in lines 41-4 and 51-2; and phrases of similar length and structure accumulate in a great welling-up of self-justification, as in lines 48-9 and 51-2. The balanced construction of lines 49-51 emphasises the argument while retaining its temper. Further on, in lines 54-7, there's a barely suppressed anger in the pointed contrasts and repetitions ('unfaithful'/'faithful', 'would have believed'/'would have believed', 'poor'/'rich'). Similarly, Crawley sarcastically reminds himself of his friend's enviable but comparatively unmerited rank by repeating it in the phrases 'the dean's carriage' and 'the dean's charity'. Hyperbole begins to take over again as he exaggerates what others think of him, what his committal means, and what its outcome may be. At its height the monologue verges on hysteria with its short sentences and exclamations, until Trollope withdraws the reader from it at the end.

For all the intensity of Crawley's resentment, the narrator's voice is always present, if only in undertone. The passage never leaves indirect discourse, however vivid it becomes. Instead there is the occasional phrase such as 'so he told himself' in line 53, neutral but telling; or a pointer like 'all that' in the same sentence, which implies that Crawley dismisses St. Paul's tribulations a little too airily. There is, too, some spiritual pride in Crawley's comparison of himself with a saint, though it's part of Trollope's meaning that St. Pauls can no longer exist in so materialistic an age. Indeed, through most of Crawley's meditation, there runs a hard seam of truth which blunts any easy moral judgement. Much of what he tells himself is correct: he has great gifts of intellect and character, and he works with all imaginable zeal in his parish, but he has miserably little to show for it, and he has suffered terrible and undeserved troubles. Where he goes wrong is to insist so much on it all, and so often. Pelican to his own starved pride, he eats out his heart by feeding it.

There is, then, a double movement in this passage, an intermingling of judgement and sympathy. It isn't difficult to score moral points off a puppet, or to allow it so much rope as to become hangman backstage. Trollope, however, sustains a sense of his character's independence, even of his autonomy. When he pauses with his typical 'I think', he acts as if Crawley were a real person whose mind isn't open to him but which he has to make some imaginative effort to read. Equally, he never comments crudely but keeps ethical measure by a judicious reminder or a weighted epithet. Then, too, Crawley's own thoughts pull two ways. While we feel his grief and desperation very strongly, our awareness of his self-indulgence never subsides for long; yet as this becomes an immolation we swing back to sympathy again. Given such a personality in such circumstances, we realise the integrity, almost the inevitability, of Crawley's response. But there is always, in the background, the narrator's tactful ethical tone, forestalling moral identification while allowing psychological immediacy. Snow almost catches this deep duality of attitude in his phrase 'at the same time brotherly and clinical',[11] but the final word is too cold. I should prefer to speak of a kind discrimination, too akin for total detachment, for total involvement too morally shrewd.

Part of the subtlety of the passage is the delicate balance maintained not only between Trollope's view and those of his characters, but between the minds of the characters themselves. The narrative filters first Mrs. Crawley's consciousness then her husband's, passing so unobtrusively between them as almost to merge them in a single continuum. Approaching the husband's reflections through those of his wife, it returns by the same route, issuing into conventional narrative and dialogue after the passage is finished by way of Mrs. Crawley's mental summary at the end. Just as the narrative envelops the minds of both characters, so Mrs. Crawley's mind seems to enclose her husband's. The structure might be compared to that of a Chinese box if the boundaries between the different consciousnesses weren't so diffuse, as if each were a semi-transparent membrane which osmosis could penetrate.

Time being a function of subjectivity, the various temporal levels of the extract are equally fluid, The narrative opens in the novel's 'present' as Mrs. Crawley sits down to consider her husband's condition – first in relation to his immediate actions, then to her previous fear of his suicide, then to what he could best do in the days to come. She remembers his idle broodings, and the self-indulgence for which she has just reproved him, but as the passage goes on the broodings themselves come into focus and her consciousness recedes. The transition takes place with the aid of a shift from the 'singulative' to the 'iterative' mode,[12] registered by the conditional 'would sit' and the past continuous 'was revelling' and 'was recalling'. No single scene is designated now, but a whole series of occasions when Crawley rehearsed the same mental arguments over and over again. In the first part of the interior view he is so remorselessly indignant as to review his whole life chronologically, pausing at each stage to bring home how much he has deserved and how unjustly he has been treated. The second part concentrates on the bitter reflections of recent memory, culminating in the disaster responsible for his desperate condition. These become so intense that it's almost surprising to be reminded by the statement 'Such were always his thoughts' that this isn't an isolated scene but a cross-section of Crawley's thinking over a period of some length. At last, however, the narrative returns to Mrs. Crawley in the novel's present where it had begun.

The two inside views have a similar structure in that each works from past to present, treating each person's memory as it influences her or his existing state of mind. The passage isn't summary, a gathering of narrative threads, but neither is it analysis, an orderly reasoned account of what each character thinks. It's closer to recreation, perhaps nowhere more so than in this constant reference from the past to current dilemmas and future possibilities. As Snow has put it, Trollope tells 'a continuous psychological history leading to a set of moral choices':[13] Crawley's past, as it determines his present state of mind, and his wife's comprehension of this, as it influences her judgement of what will be best for him. These are the reasons why Trollope introduces his interior view of Crawley not in a separate scene, as would have been the obvious choice, but through an interior view of Mrs. Crawley. The important point isn't only what he thinks and why, but what she thinks he thinks, and how this will govern her behaviour towards him. Seen in this light, the passage is extraordinary in its continuity: the undisturbed ease with which it passes from mind to mind, and the unbroken symmetry of its temporal sequence. In its structure, one interior view containing another, it seems to suggest that there's no exaggeration in Mrs. Crawley's belief that her husband's mind is entirely open to her; and for Crawley the past is intensely, almost insanely, present. Indeed it is the function of Trollope's plot to set these facts in relief. The lost cheque not only brings Crawley's worsening condition to a crisis, and in doing so calls attention to the poverty existing among some of the church's priests,[14] its crucial effect is to place Crawley's consciousness in question – and not simply his mind or his memory, but perhaps even his identity. This is so because of that interpenetrability of minds which is a running theme in

Trollope. So permeable by the opinions of others is even a rugged individualist like Crawley that he can be brought to deny his own memory and admit that he may be a thief or a madman. In Dickens the lost cheque might have been a symbol of failed social credit, in George Eliot the first collapse in a general breakdown of dependencies. Trollope explores a different order of relatedness, in which the individual mind is bathed in the vision of the community.

The style of the passage informs at every point its ease of movement and tactful lucidity. In diction it is simple, clear and unassuming. Carefully moulded to the idioms of the characters, it deviates only to reflect them, as with Crawley's unmistakable stiffness in the phrases 'derogation from the spiritual grandeur of his position' or 'veneration of the faithful'. There are no striking metaphors to conjure up the trials of consciousness, as in George Eliot, Meredith or Henry James. The passage is bare of all but the most common. Its method is not impressionistic, conveying the quality of thought by image or symbol, but mimetic in the sense that it tries to reproduce characteristic patterns of silent soliloquy. Accordingly, it relies for much of its effect on manipulation of syntax, making great play with repetition and variation of sentence structure: for instance, the circumlocutions and changes of word order when Mrs. Crawley recalls her fear of her husband's suicide; the long sentence in which Crawley looks back over his whole life, building to a climax at the end; and the rhetorical rhythms which express and fuel his indignation.

Before venturing any general remarks about Trollope's style on the basis of this single paragraph, several distinctions are necessary. First, it is an example of his mature writing. The narrator comes forward not as a showman, parading mock-heroics and hectoring his audience ironically, but as a coolly sympathetic ventriloquist. This development wasn't complete until about 1862 with *The Small House at Allington*, by which time Trollope had written most of the novels which made his early reputation. Second, the nature of the passage is itself special. The narrator's style isn't always so restrained, although it's even more closely assimilated to the characters in dialogue and letters (almost the only instances where Trollope's skill hasn't passed largely without comment).[15] A norm of decorum operates, matching less serious episodes with bathos and irony, love scenes with a sometimes indulgent, sometimes ironic, sentiment. Then, finally, there is the tone of impartial narrative or description, again often tinged with irony but on the whole plain, tolerant and unpretentious. It is a combination of this voice with the voices given to two characters that occupies the extract.

Why did Trollope, in the novels of his maturity, write so level and so plastic a style? – a style by turns so understated and so merged in its subject-matter that it has hardly seemed to exist as an entity in its own right? The *Autobiography* explains his belief that writing 'should be so pellucid that the meaning should be rendered without an effort to the reader' (201), but the given reason seems merely prudential: if reading doesn't come easily, the novel will go unread. I suggest that there is a deeper cause underlying Trollope's conscious thought about his style but influencing in different ways almost everything he wrote. He is so convinced of the need for pellucid expression because he assumes the necessity of transparent communication between one mind and another. This is of a piece with his doctrine of 'full confidence' with his reader, and with his abhorrence of mysteries.[16] At a deeper level, however, the aim of transparency is a threat, offering social harmony at the expense of synthesising the individual out of existence. As I have argued in Chapter 4, this fundamental tension probably springs from Trollope's early experiences when he fought to retain his individuality against the peer-group which despised him, but to which he wished desperately to be assimilated. It is the psychological conundrum which exercises most of his best writing, notably *The Last Chronicle of Barset*.

The interior view I have examined is a sample of Trollope's most effective and interesting writing in this form, and it is from the novel which I would contend is his best. I chose it for discussion because it illustrates very compactly the essential qualities in his presentation of inner experience, but it identifies those qualities at full stretch. Interior views in *The Last Chronicle* – particularly those that concentrate on Crawley – by and large maintain a high level of skill and insight. But that isn't true in all of the novels, as may be inferred not only from the general lack of comment on this kind of writing but from the criticisms made by some of the few who have noticed it. I have suggested in Chapter

3 that the interior view offered Trollope a convenient means of expanding his text without introducing irrelevance. It could be extended to or withheld from minor figures almost at will, and for major figures it was pliable enough to bear occasional repetition. The result was that Trollope sometimes abused it. It's difficult to defend every repetition in this sort of passage on the ground that to represent a character's state of mind the novelist had to keep showing how it developed.

Pascal advances a second criticism, claiming that Trollope didn't always sustain the style of free indirect speech consistently.[17] There is substance to this charge, but the incongruities sometimes have their motives. For instance, in the passage Pascal cites from *Is He Popenjoy?* the narrator's shifts in and out of free indirect speech humorously draw attention to the limits of Lord George Germain's knowledge of himself and the world, in his mingled stiffness, self-righteousness, and naïvety. This makes it difficult, at least on the evidence of the given passage, to endorse Pascal's further claim that at times Trollope took things too easily, slipping from moral discrimination into a facile tolerance of live and let live. Yet there's a different and a finer sense to the point which has its own validity. For one of the basic reasons why Trollope so often resorts to interior view is that his imagination was always caught by the isolated, self-conscious individual, needing to defend and justify himself under the stress of crisis or decision. His tendency to half-identify with such characters, in the peculiar equivocal form of free indirect speech, is another element in the unofficial Trollope. Yet he rarely falls into a secondhand self-pity. As his careful reminders in Crawley's interior view keep showing, there is also a conscience at work that monitors the outbursts of the ego and the extremes of its self-justification.

It remains to place Trollope's method of interior view in its historical context. Since I have emphasised the dimension of inwardness in his novels, I should end by suggesting why they foreshadow only in this and one other respect the psychological explorations of later fiction. Broadly, two developments towards the end of the Victorian period helped usher in modern psychological presentation: the attempt at rendering consciousness obliquely by metaphor or symbol, and the concept of point of view, which made possible a greater intensity. Henry James is obviously a central figure here, though similar directions may be noted in George Eliot and Meredith. More significant, however, is the fact that these writers are reflecting (and so perhaps influencing) a general change in consciousness. To put it briefly, Victorian novels are about relatedness, modern novels about fragmentation. The limited viewpoint wasn't a new invention, but it took a modern awareness to incorporate it as a method. Then, as individuals were increasingly recognised to be so far isolated from each other that the chances of unimpeded communication between them had to be questioned, there developed an awareness of that inner experience which is private to each. Trollope is modern in echoing the mental rhythms of his characters so closely, Victorian in the clarity and order of their silent soliloquies. He limits his representation of consciousness to that level on which the character talks to himself, though he sometimes goes deeper in analysis (and in this sense there is truth in the distinction between Victorian analysis of consciousness and modern representation).

The nearest Trollope comes to explaining what he intended by the kind of writing I have considered is in *Ralph the Heir*. He apologises for what he says must appear to the reader as a 'very indifferent hero', and states that his purpose was to show 'the faults of character which in life are hardly visible, but which in portraiture of life can be made to be so transparent' (II,339). He wished to convey to the reader how people talk silently to themselves in reverie, so as to allow him that full access to the mind of another which Mrs. Crawley described when she thought of reading her husband's mind as though it were a book. He does this by means of a style which tries to persuade the reader that he isn't in fact reading, that temporarily he is infiltrated into another consciousness. The reader finds both why a character should think the way he does and how he falls into error in consequence of so thinking. This is Trollope's official aim, in keeping with his often repeated emphasis on the moral value of fiction.[18] Unofficially, however, imaginative sympathy counterpoints moral insistence. And, at a further remove, the interior view suggests the same changes, the same tensions, in relations between self and others conveyed in the form of his work as a whole.

6 *Official Trollope: Land, Commerce and Class*

In the previous two chapters I have tried to show how an unofficial element informs Trollope's narratives. His interior views direct attention especially to the solitary figure, often at odds with those around him; while the whole body of his fiction reveals a repeated pattern in which the problem of identity for the self in relation to others has continually to be solved afresh. These chapters have also pointed towards what the unofficial Trollope has to tell about his society, with its stresses for the isolated figure and its pressure to conform. In the last two chapters I want to turn to Trollope's more direct and explicit views of his world. For a novelist who consistently set his work in the present, he has attracted surprisingly little criticism which approaches him on these terms.[1] That will be my aim in what follows, and I shall begin in this chapter with two novels from the earlier part of his career.

Doctor Thorne is a kind of mid-Victorian *Howards End*. The question it puts is also who should inherit England, but this finds a much blunter, a much less provisional answer than Forster proposed fifty years later. The novel is unusual among Trollope's works in drawing on a firm and deliberate reading of recent history. As with most of his fiction, the time of its setting is contemporary – it came out in 1858, and its action occurs between 1854, when Frank Gresham comes of age, and 1857, when he is married. Where *Doctor Thorne* differs is in reaching back to events in the past which not only motivate the action but help determine its meaning. These events are in part private: Dr. Thorne, the central character, adopts his brother's illegitimate child after his brother has been killed and the mother has emigrated. But more importantly they are also public, concerning the 1832 Reform Act and the changes to which it was both witness and further incentive. Trollope represents in the De Courcys, a family which plays a major part in his novel, the Whig interest which as he indicates was instrumental to the Act's passing. In another family, the Greshams, he represents the Tory squirearchy which fought Reform every step. Finally, he includes several characters who stand in various ways for the new class which had to be accommodated.

In the course of the historical summary with which he opens his novel, Trollope defines very clearly what he thought was at stake. The issue as he puts it is between 'commercial' and 'feudal' England, and it is stated with sufficient confidence to be prejudged at the outset. In *Doctor Thorne*'s second sentence the claims of Barsetshire are already being urged against those of its 'manufacturing leviathan brethren in the north'. Only a few pages later this at first guarded preference has become a hope and then practically an assurance:

> England is not yet a commercial country in the sense in which that epithet is used for her; and let us still hope that she will not soon become so. She might surely as well be called feudal England, or chivalrous England. If in western civilized Europe there does exist a nation among whom there are high signors, and with whom the owners of the land are the true aristocracy, the aristocracy that is trusted as being best and fittest to rule, that nation is the English. . . .
>
> England a commercial country! Yes; as Venice was. She may excel other nations in commerce, but yet it is not that in which she most prides herself, in which she most excels. Merchants as such are not the first men among us; though it perhaps be open, barely open, to a merchant to become one of them. Buying and selling is good and necessary; it is very necessary, and may, possibly, be very good; but it cannot be the noblest work of man; and let us hope that it may not in our time be esteemed the noblest work of an Englishman. (11–12)

Quoting the first part of this passage, Raymond Williams declares that as a description of mid-nineteenth century England it is 'ludicrous'. Objectively this is no doubt true, but a history of the period suggests a different perspective. J. F. C. Harrison calls attention to 'the mystique of landed property', whose strength, he says, 'is attested by the extent to which a social order based on land not only survived but flourished in an increasingly industrial world'.² The flummery of Trollope's language is ludicrous enough. From words such as 'chivalrous' and 'high signors' to the sub-Carlylean rhetoric of the closing sentence, the official Trollope is in full song. But it is as an expression of ideology, of conventional wisdom, that the passage has its point and even its accuracy, for Trollope revealingly hovers between objective and normative definitions, between fact and value. The 'true' aristocracy turns out to be the class that is most 'trusted'. And the priority of land over commerce is half admitted in the second paragraph to be a matter less of economics than of attitudes. In context the passage implies that Reform has changed little: whatever the source of England's wealth, the landed aristocracy is still in control. So why defend it? First, because the power of commerce and industry is increasing, as the novel in part shows. Second, because in the absence of equivalent economic power, the aristocracy's main answer is in social and moral traditions whose legitimacy needs reaffirming if their hold is to continue.

This looks like a lot to extrapolate from a passage apparently more notable for rhetoric and mystification than for political shrewdness. Yet the novel bears out the analysis I have sketched. The passage is introduced by discussion of the Gresham motto, which has two possible meanings. One is 'an address to the savages, calling on them to take care of their patron'; the other 'an advice to the people at large, especially to those inclined to rebel against the aristocracy of the county, that they should "beware the Gresham"' (11). Trollope's plot, devised for him by his brother Tom (*Autobiography*, 99), resolves the ambiguity. The novel's rebels against aristocracy are the Scatcherds, father and son. Sir Roger is an ex-stonemason who has become a millionaire contractor and a Radical member of parliament. He buys part of the Gresham property and loans large sums to the squire on the security of the remainder, but when he dies his son threatens to foreclose on the debt. This danger, however, turns into salvation from the identical quarter. Sir Roger's sister had borne an illegitimate child, who – by means of which Trollope has to work hard to persuade us – becomes the fiancée of the Gresham heir. When Sir Roger's son also dies, Mary Thorne inherits, and gives up all the property on her marriage. In this way the rebellion of the 'savages' (Trollope emphasises what he calls the 'brutality' of the Scatcherds) not only saves but advances their 'patron'.

Part of *Doctor Thorne* is as crudely ideological as this rather reduced account suggests. One contemporary reviewer noted Trollope's unfairness in making not only Sir Roger but Louis Philippe Scatcherd die of drink, and he also objected to the attempted satire conveyed in the latter's name.[3] He might further have added that as a self-made man Sir Roger Scatcherd is a wildly unlikely mixture. The mason and the millionaire we can accept, if only because Trollope is studiously vague as to how the transition could have been accomplished from a county proud not to be a hive of industry. But credulity is stretched by the murderer and the demagogue, and collapses altogether at the illiterate and at the alcoholic of over twenty years' standing. Trollope tries to motivate Sir Roger's alcoholism with a speech in which the contractor laments his inability to enjoy his success (127–8). But he has already said that Sir Roger drank heavily as a workman, and the speech indicates inaptness for a gentleman's pursuits as much as it explains Sir Roger's drinking. The same point recurs when Louis Philippe disgraces himself at the Gresham dinner-table, though the son is too obvious a caricature to be worth taking seriously. On the other side, the *Saturday Review* wittily notices the transparent device by which Trollope restores the Greshams both financially and morally: 'We will not dwell upon the trifling inconsistency of praising a man for being disinterested in the first place, and paying him 300,000*l.* for his disinterested conduct immediately afterwards'.[4] On this showing, *Doctor Thorne* could be recommended only to those who like their ideology untreated.

Luckily the story is more complex. Partly this is because Trollope lets it be seen that the Greshams are effete.[5] The squire has succumbed to pointless extravagance, harassment from his wife, and dictation from her family. The son is a standard Trollopian young gentleman, callow and conventional, but supposedly quality tested. More important, though, is Trollope's highly explicit charge against the De Courcys. Here again the novel's pre-text is significant. Following Reform, old Squire Gresham hadn't long survived 'the aspect of the men with whom he was called on to associate at St. Stephen's' (2). His son then lost most of his money fighting elections caused by Reform, and especially by his relationship through marriage with the De Courcys. This makes the De Courcys doubly guilty, for as Whigs they had helped make Reform possible. By representing their behaviour as in every way mercenary Trollope presses the charge home: they have sold out on the aristocratic values they are notable for professing, betraying their class from within. It's the De Courcys who first insist that Frank Gresham should marry money. From the same family comes a son who smugly counts on his elder brother's death and offers likely ennoblement as a bribe to matrimony, and a daughter who advises her cousin against marrying a wealthy lawyer only to wed him later herself. If Trollope caricatures the Scatcherds, he consistently satirises the De Courcys. And if the one family threatens the Greshams to save them, the other does so, as P. D. Edwards has argued, to serve as scapegoats for their inadequacies.[6]

Yet, though Trollope shows the Greshams more sympathy and tolerance than they deserve, his point of view isn't to be identified with their own. His loyalty is stated frankly enough in the title he gave to the book, and in his choice of Dr. Thorne as its hero (17). There are grounds for suspecting that Dr. Thorne is an unconscious self-portrait, half-critical, half-idealised. Like Trollope he is of old, but no longer thriving, stock. Trollope once boasted at school of an ancestor who had come over with the Conqueror;[7] Dr. Thorne, knowing his blood is among the best in England, is inordinately but quietly proud of it. Equally, Trollope like his hero 'had no right to lay claim to any position . . . other than such as he might win for himself' (18). Dr. Thorne, with family resources at an end, turns to medicine just as Trollope had to make his way as civil servant and novelist. Finally, there are similarities in character, most of all in each man's neurotic honesty and in the double identity they share of an aggressive, undeferential public self and an inner sensitivity and compassion. The question is to what extent Trollope succeeds in objectifying his hero.

One of the main qualities Trollope emphasises in Dr. Thorne is the contradiction between his pride in family and what Trollope calls his 'democratic' instincts. He is proud of his blood, yet he befriends the Scatcherds and adopts an illegitimate child. He is a thorough conservative who won't admit that anyone, lord or lady, is superior to himself. And he antagonises his medical colleagues by setting fees and mixing medicines, practices they consider 'low' and 'democratic' (30). These paradoxes his position helps explain. His prejudices in favour of rank stem from birth and upbringing. Conscious of his ancestry, he considers himself anyone's equal. At the same time, though, he knows very well that his place in the world has to be earned. About that necessity he has no false shame, but it makes him resent those placed more highly than himself as well as hate the pretenses and hypocrisies of rank. On all these points Trollope is clear, and this suggests he was honest about his own standing to himself. That probably wasn't easy for a man who had preferred to describe himself on his sons' birth certificates as a 'Gentleman' rather than an assistant postal surveyor, and who all his life held strong and well-known views on the value of 'gentlemen'.[8] There's a note of triumph in Trollope's tone, loud and clear in the exclamation marks, when he describes his hero's tincture of snobbery (26) – as if over a victory won partly against himself. But the critical question is why he made Dr. Thorne central to the novel at all.

The novel's starting point, as I have said, is the issue of land versus commerce. Trollope deliberately sets up Barsetshire in opposition to the industry and commerce of the North. Within Barsetshire he represents both internal and external threats to the landed class. What's odd at first is that he appears to find the De Courcys more dangerous than the Scatcherds. After all, the De Courcys also have much to fear from the rising power of commerce. His description of the run-down neighbouring town (181–4) rather labours this point. He attacks the De Courcys for betraying the values they professedly stand for, especially by their activities in the marriage market. But this is to avoid whatever challenge might be posed by industry and commerce. Already he had overlooked the real foundations of landed wealth. As Williams points out, he notices the poor only in a phrase that disposes of them tidily between the products of agriculture and its pleasures (1).[9] Industry he leaves a vague shadow on the horizon. Yet he defines commerce as the principal enemy, only to turn his attack upon corrupted values in the aristocracy. Dr. Thorne's importance is as a displaced squire who can not only reaffirm the principles of his class, but guide back to power those of its members who are still worth preserving. At a deeper level this is compensation for his own displacement – and perhaps, vicariously, for his author's.

Trollope's plot converts the social and political to the moral. At its climax the novel subjects Dr. Thorne's integrity to an extreme test. He is faced by a conflict of loyalties. On one side he is Squire Gresham's friend and advisor, only too well aware of the Gresham money troubles and the love affair – not at all welcome to the Greshams – between his niece and the heir. On the other side he is trustee for Sir Louis Scatcherd after his father's death, pledged to protect his interests, and if possible to help him survive his alcoholism. Sir Louis scarcely endears himself to the doctor by pressing for the Greshamsbury title deeds, courting Mary Thorne, and behaving like a boor (Trollope lays it on pretty thick here). Against all these odds Dr. Thorne is made to prove his moral worth by fulfilling scrupulously all his obligations to Sir Louis, until the heir can no longer be stopped from drinking himself to death. His reward is then to see his niece married to Frank Gresham and the Gresham fortunes restored. But so glowing a conclusion has to be earned. The happy couple have to pass a moral test as well. Mary offers to release Frank from his engagement so he can do his family's bidding and marry wealth. He neatly reciprocates by committing himself to marrying her in the nick of time before she becomes an heiress.

One way of trying to justify Trollope's plot is to argue that it provides the moral dilemmas on which the novel turns.[10] I don't think this case stands up when once it's recognised that Trollope has shifted into the moral sphere an issue he initially defined quite explicitly as social and political. Again, as the *Saturday Review* charged at the time, Trollope makes it hard to take the dilemmas seriously by rewarding their resolution with such rich and immediate prizes. But this leads to a further and more damaging point: that the basis for reward perhaps isn't moral at all. There is a revealing analogy to Frank's and Mary's dilemma when Sir Roger asks Dr. Thorne to encourage a marriage between Mary and his son. The doctor refuses, even though Sir Roger threatens to cut Mary out of his Will. This is how Trollope presents the quandary:

How far had he done right in keeping her from the sight of her uncle? How could he justify it to himself if he had thus robbed her of her inheritance, seeing that he had done so from a selfish fear lest she, who was now all his own, should be known to the world as belonging to others rather than to him? He had taken upon him in her behalf to reject wealth as valueless; and yet he had no sooner done so than he began to consume his hours with reflecting how great to her would be the value of wealth. (307)

These seem hard questions at first. We are made to appreciate how much the opportunity of wealth for his niece tells with Dr. Thorne, and especially how anxious he is not to prejudice her interests by selfishness. The passage proves him free of mercenary taint – but on grounds that have much less to do with morality than with class. The only reason he considers for bringing Mary to her uncle is her chance of a legacy in the will. The passage shuffles over his real objection to a meeting with the euphemism 'others'. It's the vulgarity of the Scatcherds that really concerns him, and it's on this account that he is prepared to sacrifice Mary's chances of wealth. Though it might be claimed that the passage represents Dr. Thorne's point of view rather than Trollope's, the author bears his character out by making the refusal count for nothing after all: despite his threat, Sir Roger doesn't alter his Will. The dilemma is simply contrived. Its result is to suggest that the Thornes are rewarded for refusing not only money, but contamination by another class.

Against this it must be remembered that Mary Thorne is half a Scatcherd by birth. Illegitimate, but brought up by the doctor, she occupies an ambiguous position which Trollope uses to explore the question of rank. Whether his inquiry goes very far may be gauged from the answer he has Mary give to the problem. Putting to herself directly the question what confers rank, she answers like this:

Absolute, intrinsic, acknowledged, individual merit must give it to its possessor, let him be whom, and what, and whence he might. So far the spirit of democracy was strong within her. Beyond this it could be had but by inheritance, received as it were second-hand, or twenty-second-hand. And so far the spirit of aristocracy was strong within her. (85)

This reply, as the narrator points out, she has learned from her uncle, and it reconciles the contradictions in her position as in his. Yet, though it seems to come with Trollope's authority, it leaves something out which the novel is alive to elsewhere. When first told by Dr. Thorne that his niece had survived, Sir Roger naturally wanted to see her. This the doctor wouldn't allow, and Sir Roger accuses him directly of snobbery: 'We are too vulgar for her' (163). Trollope here brings the issue of class prejudice right into the open, but although Dr. Thorne can manage only an evasive answer it's plain where his sympathies lie. The point of distinction isn't rank or birth but manners: 'Her life is not like your life, and her ways are not as your ways.' And it is reinforced by Sir Roger's own inability to make a gentleman of his son despite all that money can buy. Mary is a gentlewoman not at all by birth, and only partly by merit; her real advantage is her upbringing – she's lived with the Greshams as well as with Dr. Thorne.

Mary's assimilation despite her birth to gentility further strengthens the novel's underlying theme by which the gentry takes over what will benefit itself. That Trollope recognised this at some level of awareness appears from the striking fact that he made his heroine the offspring of a rape committed by a gentleman on a working girl.[11] Frank Gresham's nursing is a parallel example. Nature, says the narrator, gives women like Lady Arabella 'bosoms for show, but not for use' (28). So women in need are exploited – a supply of them is kept up at Courcy Castle 'for the family use'. Trollope gets in a further satirical flick at the De Courcys by making the nurse they provide a drunkard, and he has her replaced by none other than the then impoverished wife of Roger Scatcherd. The result isn't only that Frank Gresham is well nursed, but that the unhappy mother comes to prefer him over her own child (294, 354-5). Because Trollope heartily endorses this preference, he disables his criticism of wet-nursing. Exploitation it may be, but it has worked to laudable effect with the Gresham heir. Milk and deference are only, however, foretastes of what Frank will later absorb. Mary Thorne will give him not only herself but most of her property (562-3). And he will have learned the conduct that wins her not from his own family but from Martha Dunstable, another heiress with no claims to status on the score of birth. It's

Miss Dunstable who stops Frank being corrupted by the De Courcys with her witty forthrightness about cash, and her insistence that it shouldn't influence marriage. Her counterpart in the novel is Moffat, the tailor's son, who jilts Augusta Gresham when he sees a better chance of a bargain. Moffat's fate is a whipping at the hands of self-righteous Master Frank, who without advice from Miss Dunstable might have committed the same crime by jilting Mary Thorne. Miss Dunstable gets her reward in the next novel of the series, *Framley Parsonage*, where by a special symmetry she marries the doctor himself.

The plot of *Doctor Thorne* favours so strongly the values – in both senses – of the landed gentry that it's necessary to ask how Trollope negotiated it so well.[12] His main ploy is the narrative voice which he handles with such unassuming aplomb. There's an early example at the start of his second chapter when he affects to apologise 'for beginning a novel with two long dull chapters full of description'. He explains how alive he is to the dangers of such a course, yet pleads:

> I find that I cannot make poor Mr. Gresham hem and haw and turn himself uneasily in his arm-chair in a natural manner till I have said why he is uneasy. I cannot bring in my doctor speaking his mind freely among the bigwigs till I have explained that it is in accordance with his usual character to do so. This is unartistic on my part, and shows want of imagination as well as want of skill. Whether or not I can atone for these faults by straightforward, simple, plain story-telling – that, indeed, is very doubtful. (17–18)

Like the paragraph in Trollope's *Autobiography* in which he discusses *The Warden*,[13] this passage claims that the author has no ulterior designs. The narrator professes no higher aim than the truth – but, it should be added, no lower aim either. For all his alleged unskilfulness, the examples he cites to excuse his practice actually justify it. They also suggest that the novel's chief interest is in character, and in doing so initiate the shift away from the social and political themes that the opening chapters define. The importance of those chapters I have tried to clarify, but Trollope had to play them down if he was, without losing their benefit, to divert into ethics the contest they set up between land and commerce. Similarly, Trollope is a master at finessing conventions. For instance he declares: 'Frank Gresham was absent from Greshamsbury twelve months and a day: a day is always added to the period of such absences, as shown in the history of Lord Bateman and other noble heroes' (370). This is to admit the fairytale element in his story while still enjoying the use of it. But the best example of Trollope's slyly cavalier art is what he says about the provisions by which Mary Thorne inherits under Sir Roger Scatcherd's Will. He apologises for his ignorance of the law, and agrees with a proposal from the *Saturday Review*, which had criticised *The Three Clerks* on the same grounds, that novelists should retain a barrister to advise them.[14] Then he continues:

> But as the suggestion has not yet been carried out, and as there is at present no learned gentleman whose duty would induce him to set me right, I can only plead for mercy if I be wrong in allotting all Sir Roger's vast possessions in perpetuity to Miss Thorne, alleging also, in excuse, that the course of my narrative absolutely demands that she shall be ultimately recognized as Sir Roger's undoubted heiress.
>
> Such, after a not immoderate delay, was the opinion expressed to Dr. Thorne by his law advisers; and such, in fact, turned out to be the case. I will leave the matter so, hoping that my very absence of defence may serve to protect me from severe attack. If under such a will as that described as having been made by Sir Roger, Mary would not have been the heiress, that will must have been described wrongly. (536)

Heads I win, tails you lose. No wonder the *Saturday Review* critic renewed his objection.[15] But Trollope probably gets most readers' consent by the humorous transparency of his design. His narrator is a nineteenth-century descendant of Fielding's, in a novel which in ideology as in plot harks back to *Tom Jones*.

The bias of Trollope's plot, and his bland refusal to conceal it, should complicate any assessment of *Doctor Thorne*. As a commentary on contemporary England the novel is as much mystifying as mystified. It prefers ignorance not only about the law but about the real importance of industry and commerce, and even about the economy of the landed estate it endorses. Within its own ideology the novel may be judged very favourably.[16] Once, however, the limitations of that ideology have been recognised, the critic may be reduced to admiring technique, which has been the tendency of recent American criticism,[17] and indeed *Doctor Thorne* is technically very clever. I don't myself think that the novel's significance can be so easily detached from its period. The value of *Doctor Thorne* is to demonstrate the working out not only of a process in English society, but of the means by which it was rationalised. We see the landed gentry consolidating itself with a tenacity – decisive though apparently quite undeliberate – which in the real world long enabled it to hold on to power. And we see the justification for that retention of power in its renewed integrity and assurance. Trollope would have achieved much more in his novel had he revealed rather than reflected this development. In his inability to take full imaginative grasp of the process he presents, he resembles Defoe – that other so-called 'photographer' of his own present-day world. Yet it still has to be said that, like Defoe, Trollope had sufficient insight to convey the process. He did so with a thoroughness that sometimes prompts the question whether he wrote partly with tongue in cheek. Certainly he was committed to his themes – especially the need to keep free from both hypocrisy and self-interest in matters of rank and wealth. At the same time, his handling of plot and narrative voice can uncomfortably, too uncomfortably, recall the easy assumption of *droit de seigneur*. A condition of England novel *Doctor Thorne* obviously isn't. But though immersed in ideology it doesn't quite drown there. The strains of those realities Trollope tried to accommodate ripple, sometimes break, the smooth narrative surface. Despite itself, the novel has its honesties about what it is supporting.

After his success with *Framley Parsonage*, Trollope set out on his most ambitious fiction to date. *Orley Farm* discovers his aspirations partly in its form. At an estimated 330,000 words it is considerably longer than anything he had written before,[18] and the stylistic and other revisions to his manuscript which I discussed in Chapter 3 indicate that he took some care over it. But the novel demonstrates his ambition chiefly in mounting a triple challenge. First, as Edwards has suggested, *Orley Farm* tries for a higher aim than the works for which he had become famous.[19] The story of Lady Mason has a tragic potential absent from his fiction since *The Macdermots of Ballycloran* – both *The Bertrams* and *Castle Richmond* turn to melodrama. Second, in *Orley Farm* Trollope confronted a very recent vogue in fiction on its own ground. Again Edwards makes the connexion:

> *Orley Farm* was begun in July 1860, when *The Woman in White* had almost completed its progress through the pages of *All the Year Round*, and its subject – a lady of high rank and moral repute threatened with the exposure of a degrading secret from her past – is one that the sensationalists were soon to appropriate to themselves.[20]

But Trollope's third aim was the most important. For the first time he was attempting a panoramic novel, with the range that distinguished the major fiction of his time. Probably he hadn't felt himself ready for such a project before. Now, returned permanently to make his home in England, he could attempt what Robert Adams has called 'his first effort really to come to terms with English society as a whole'.[21] Though the range is more limited than Adams admits, it's still impressive: from landed gentry to city lawyers, commercial travellers to kitchen maids and clerks, all in the various grades of their callings, and encountered in both urban and rural localities from London and the home counties to Yorkshire.

One question is whether this crowded scene has a focus. Proposals for a central, unifying theme have varied so widely that the answer cannot be encouraging. *Orley Farm* has at different times been presented as an assault on the English legal system, a half-baked critique of 'commercial man', a vision of a fallen world in which absolute principles no longer hold, a failed tragedy, and an attack on the moral code of the Victorian middle classes.[22] Such major differences in interpretation and assessment may suggest that the novel is compromised or confused, as its two toughest critics – Adams and Edwards – have argued. There is some truth is such a view, as I shall indicate. But the point to grasp about *Orley Farm* is that despite certain of its appearances, and despite what most of its modern interpreters wish, the novel's relation to Victorian society is not essentially critical.

The novel begins from a point of view close to that of *Doctor Thorne*, except that it has no equivalents to the De Courcys.

Instead, corruption comes directly from within the commercial class. The roots again lie in the past, though not this time the historical past. Lady Mason, the main character, had become the second wife of a rich city merchant after her father had gone bankrupt. Sir Joseph, the narrator says, had taken her to his bosom 'as his portion of the assets of the estate' (I,13), but with no intention of providing specially either for her or the child she has by him. He wished to concentrate his wealth on his heir by his first marriage, being 'burdened with an ambition to establish a family as the result of his success in life' (I,14). So his elder son was to receive Orley Farm as well as the estate already bought for him at Groby Park. Lady Mason found her life in her son rather than in her husband. Wishing to establish him in the world, she forged a codicil to her husband's Will by which the child would acquire Orley Farm. This, to two of the novel's interpreters, represents her use against her husband of his own 'commercial ethic'.[23] But even Trollope didn't go so far as to equate commerce with outright fraud. His suggestion is rather that even a virtuous person from the commercial class may, in circumstances that partly extenuate it, be capable of such a crime. He drops a tell-tale clue in his opening description of Lady Mason with its code words 'sharp' and 'meanness' (I,19) – words he is to repeat in describing the successful lawyer Furnival (I, 98) as well as Dockwrath, the grasping attorney (I,48).

Trollope's two leading foils for Lady Mason heavily underline the contrast between what he sees as true gentility and as its new-made imitation. Her neighbour Sir Peregrine Orme is the soul of honour. Successor to an old estate and title, but not wealthy for such a position, he keeps up the traditional values of his class. These include denying on the score of birth any claim to gentility on the part of Joseph Mason of Groby Park. Trollope has Mason's behaviour bear Sir Peregrine out. Though a gentleman in pretensions and station, he cannot escape the values of the market. That means reducing all relationships to contracts, which he stringently fulfils to demand his 'pound of flesh' (I,63) in return. Along with Sir Joseph's other children, he had treated his father 'as a coffer from whence money might be had' (I,15), and from his own children he exacts titles of respect 'because he had a right to them' (I,64). He hates Lady Mason bitterly not so much because she enjoys the estate that should belong to him, the real motive for his malice is that she has come between him and his rights. His wife is equally unalluring, with a pathological meanness that inflicts harsh economies on family, household and guests to indulge selfishness in dress and appetite. It has often been noticed that Trollope goes out of his way to represent Lady Mason as worthy despite her crime, and her opponents as abhorrent despite their right. What isn't usually recognised is that the distinction has a social rather than a moral basis, and that it partly extends to Lady Mason as well. Her son Lucius, though a gentleman, resembles his half-brother more than the son of her neighbour Sir Peregrine Orme. As Joseph Mason checks his coffee for adulteration, so Lucius has checked his guano (I,63). The resemblance is sharpened by the incident from which Trollope has the novel's action start. Lucius, insisting on the bare rights of contract, dismisses a long-standing tenant so he can farm the land himself (I,23). As Sir Peregrine's reaction shows (I,42–3), this is an act quite opposed to the traditions of the landed estate. The result is that the tenant, originally obliged to Lady Mason, turns against her and instigates the lawsuit which leads to the loss of Orley Farm.

The details show how thoroughly Trollope imagined the circumstances of his plot. More important, they also reveal how deeply he was permeated by an ideology of class. This ideology his plot acts out, primarily through the Ormes. Faced with the threat of a trial contesting her title to Orley Farm, Lady Mason first turns to Sir Peregrine for help. What she wants isn't practical aid, which she gets from Furnival her lawyer, and still less moral support. Instead she requires what the novel calls Sir Peregrine's 'countenance', a kind of standing character-reference guaranteed by this high-minded gentleman's willingness to associate with her. But Lady Mason's ploy succeeds too well. Sir Peregrine falls for her and at first she can give no reason not to accept when he proposes marriage. The novel's turning point comes when his generosity calls out an equal generosity from her. Realising that the marriage would lose him respect, and knowing he would share her disgrace if she were found guilty, she refuses him in the only way he will accept by confessing her crime. Part of the effect of this dramatic reversal was recognised by Hutton in his commentary on Trollope's treatment of Lady Mason: 'There is certainly much art in the added vividness which her own sense of guilt takes the moment the pressure of constant concealment is removed, and she sees it reflected back from the minds of friends whom she reveres.'[24] But the relationship with the Ormes doesn't just bring Lady Mason to confession by calling from her a response to match Sir Peregrine's offer. It also identifies for the first time 'The inner, true, living woman' (II,45), and it leads her to the act of restitution by which alone she can atone for her crime. The Ormes are the agents of her penitence. After the acquittal, Mrs. Orme ensures the property's surrender by telling Lucius Mason what his mother cannot bear to tell him herself – that she has been guilty all the while.

Trollope's development of the Ormes places them at the novel's moral centre, reflecting his conviction that proper feeling as well as principle lay with the old landed gentry. The Ormes don't try to excuse Lady Mason's crime, but they forgive her; and this is the attitude the novel itself recommends. The language Trollope uses of the crime doesn't suggest any attempt at justifying it. He calls it 'a rascally deed, an hideous cut-throat deed' (II,355), 'one of the vilest crimes known to man' (II,342); and speaks even of Lady Mason's effort at helping her son as 'the worst cause that a woman could well have' (II,45). At other times he applies to her pretty freely words such as 'criminal', 'felon', and 'thief' (II,53, 159–62). The crudity of these expressions is sometimes designed to heighten other characters' responses to the crime – especially Sir Peregrine's and Lucius Mason's – but Trollope hardly dissociates himself from the basic view they imply. It has been argued that he had the outcome of the trial express what he really thought of Lady Mason's guilt.[25] This is far from clear. The trial reinforces what the novel has to criticise in the courts, exemplifying three kinds of forensic dishonesty: browbeating witnesses, pleading falsely, and playing on public prejudice. This last point is forcibly put by Moulder the commercial traveller: 'When such a low scoundrel as Dockwrath is pitted against a handsome woman like Lady Mason he'll not find a jury in England to give a verdict in his favour' (II,374). But Trollope hardly shares Moulder's satisfaction. His point is much more likely to have been that the crime was a crime whatever its circumstances, whatever the motives of the trial. It isn't necessarily reassuring that the verdict is influenced not only by the repulsiveness of Lady Mason's accusers but by the countenance of those who support her. The young defence counsel Felix Graham probably comes closest to expressing Trollope's own view:

> He felt as though he were engaged to fight a battle in which truth and justice, nay heaven itself must be against him. How can a man put his heart to the proof of an assertion in the truth of which he himself has no belief? That though guilty this lady should be treated with the utmost mercy compatible with the law; – for so much, had her guilt stood forward as acknowledged, he could have pleaded with all the eloquence that was in him. He could still pity her, sympathize with her, fight for her on such ground as that; but was it possible that he, believing her to be false, should stand up before the crowd assembled in that court, and use such intellect as God had given him in making others think that the false and the guilty one was true and innocent, and that those accusers were false and guilty whom he knew to be true and innocent? (II,290–1)

What Graham is made to think here is fully in keeping with what the narrator says elsewhere both about the wrongness of false pleading and about the need for mercy as well as justice (II,357). On the first score he is quite categorical: 'I cannot understand how any gentleman can be willing to use his intellect for the propagation of untruth, and to be paid for so using it' (II,165). This view coincides not only with Felix Graham's but with that of the Ormes. Even Mrs. Orme, who could forgive her friend immediately when she confessed, is brought almost to wish she would be convicted after witnessing the dishonesty of the lawyers' defence (II,332–3).

There are two further signs of Trollope's attitude to Lady Mason. One is built into his plot, which has the novel work out a natural justice – Lady Mason is punished for her crime by alienation not only from her friends but her son, the very person for whom she had performed it. Secondly there is his treatment of her as a heroine. Edwards claims that with Lady Mason Trollope was unable to find a language for expressing powerful feeling.[26] I think that he bears this out, but that the root failure is one of sympathy. Trollope's interior views of Lady Mason on the whole lack conviction and intensity because he couldn't bring himself to identify with her sufficiently. This is part of his protest against sensational fiction. He will have nothing to do with Furnival's idea that the wonderful cleverness of the crime should almost excuse it (I,130-1), or with the public's tendency to regard Lady Mason as a heroine the more it senses she might be guilty (II,309-10), or with satisfaction in the mystery among readers of the sensational press (II,382-3). He refused to glamourise Lady Mason because he felt, conventionally, that to do so would make her crime look acceptable. For the same reason he refused to exploit as he might have done the pathos of her condition, though he shows how far her circumstances and her suffering plead for mitigation. Instead, he preserves a tactful reticence even after she has confessed, and at the novel's end he goes so far as to offer an apology for asking his readers to sympathise with 'a woman who had so sinned as to have placed her beyond the general sympathy of the world at large' (II,404). I find no sign that this apology is ironic, though to modern readers it may look just as unnecessary as his question in the title *Can You Forgive Her?*[27] Rather than attempt to draw from his readers a degree of sympathy he thought wrong for a criminal, Trollope exploited her relation to the Ormes. This enabled him both to work out what he saw as a proper moral and human response from members of the class he most favoured, and to diffuse acceptably the tragic potential of his novel. He would not end the novel tragically because he had no wish to paint Lady Mason in the colours of sentiment any more than of sensation. Yet, though *Orley Farm* leaves neither her nor Sir Peregrine utterly broken and hopeless, it asks the reader to feel as much or more for the gentleman as for the criminal.

If Trollope's presentation of Lady Mason stays firmly, if tolerantly, within conventional morality, he provides explicit reinforcement with his sub-plots. First, he draws a sharp contrast between two of the lawyers and their families. Thomas Furnival is a barrister whose ability to intimidate witnesses, among other talents, has brought him wealth and status (I,96). He lives in London and is at odds with his wife, chiefly because his success has raised him above her socially. Judge Stavely has also advanced in life, but in such a way as to have become 'revered on the bench, and loved by all men' (I,174). He has avoided 'Parliament, politics, and dirt' (I,183), unlike the more pushing Furnival, and lives in a new country house which has all the merits of a gentleman's, except those which only age can supply (I,215). These differences are plain enough, but Trollope concentrates them into a running comparison between each man's unmarried daughter. Madeline Staveley is the novel's conventional heroine. As such she gets a set-piece introduction in the manner of Fielding's description of Sophia Western in *Tom Jones* – except that Trollope is more fulsome ('a woman's happy heart and a woman's happy beauty') and less complicated by irony (I,184–5). Madeline provides an object lesson in how young ladies should behave to their lovers. True to the code, she doesn't become aware she's in love with Felix Graham till it's obvious to everyone around her – even though her mother and married sister have telegraphed the fact by warning her, and even though she has twice had to refuse someone else. This is a convention Trollope was later to question, notably in *The Eustace Diamonds*, but in *Orley Farm* it's offered at face value. But with Sophia Furnival feelings unacknowledged or otherwise hardly enter into it – she's out for the best marriage deal she can make through her own unaided policy. Trollope has her play her two suitors very carefully, but in the event she gets neither, and his disapproval is only less explicit than Lady Staveley's. In the two families he has contrasted point by point versions of what he conceived as commercial and gentlemanly attitudes to life. Though he's too skilful a novelist to paint these black and white, the distinctions he builds in are plain: between wisdom and calculation, warmth and harshness, unpretentious principle and elastic worldly honesty. It's Furnival who bullies his clerk, and – though at Lady Mason's instigation – tries to buy off Dockwrath.

I've said that *Orley Farm* isn't essentially critical of the society it represents, yet this seems inconsistent with the evidence of Trollope's attack on commercialism. Put another way, the same contradiction is what Robert Adams finds in the vigorous discussion of the novel I have mentioned. Adams argues that *Orley Farm* launches a wide-ranging critique of the commercial principle, especially in the institution of law. He finds the theme dramatised brilliantly in the early scenes when Dockwrath the attorney calls himself 'a commercial lawyer' (I,92) and announces: 'In this enterprising country all men are more or less commercial' (I,54). Dockwrath's word certainly fits those lawyers who, to Trollope, sell out on general moral principles in the exercise of their profession – like Chaffanbrass, whom he compares to a 'hired bravo' (II,359), or, more suavely, Furnival. But Trollope doesn't follow his attack through, and Adams can only conclude that he compromised it. My query is whether the attack was ever so central as Adams argues, or so critical; and whether the compromise wasn't within Trollope's aim from the start. If, as I've been maintaining, the novel is governed not by an attack on commercialism but by an ideology of class, then its approval of society as established becomes explicable.

The commercial characters play an important role in the rhetoric of *Orley Farm*. How this works may be seen in a single, tightly constructed number of the original serial issue (Chapters 21–4). Here several contrasts interweave themselves as Trollope describes the different ways his characters spend Christmas. The celebrations are joyless enough at Groby Park, frozen by Mrs. Mason's parsimony, and hardly better for Mrs. Furnival, who in the absence of husband and daughter has the company only of her unladylike confidante. In between these two scenes Trollope places Christmas with the Staveleys. Noningsby represents his domestic ideal, and here he achieves a sense of shared open-hearted enjoyment which at times seems not far short of Tolstoyan. What partly vitiates his account, however, is its persuasive bias. He spends, for instance, a paragraph on why a country church is to be preferred to a city church at Christmas; the latter, he says, 'has none of the grace of association' (I,219). This might be true, but the point – which is at least arguable – would have come less obtrusively from what his characters do and say. Fortunately that's the method he adopts in the scene's principal action, in which the idealist Felix Graham protests that Christmas has become 'essentially a material festival' (I,219), but is drawn in despite his objections to participate in and approve of the way it's celebrated at Noningsby. Graham's strictures are followed directly by the passage on Christmas in a country church, and the chapter later has him entering fully into snap-dragon and blind man's buff. Two chapters later, though, Trollope's description of Christmas with the commercial travellers bears Graham out. Their celebrations at least have a

generous spirit, set in relief by the account in the chapter before
of Christmas at Groby Park. The host, Moulder, invites others
to share in the feast, including, 'out of sheer good nature', a man
he doesn't much like (I,240). But the result is precisely a
'material' Christmas – just what Noningsby, in Trollope's
presentation, had avoided. Moulder snorts contemptuously
when church is mentioned, and has no thought of a future
spiritual life. His way of living is shown by his relation to his wife,
which simply duplicates his employers' relation to himself – a
bargain in which material indulgence rewards performance of
duty. Trollope makes Moulder a glutton and later a drunkard.
He drives home his message in a summary sentence at the
chapter's end: 'Such is the modern philosophy of the Moulders,
pigs out of the sty of Epicurus' (I,246). His portrayal of the
commercial characters reflects his assumptions about trade. In
Doctor Thorne he had declared that buying and selling could not
be the noblest work of an Englishman. The reason, he suggests,
is that the bargainer is too intent on profit to have other than
material interests. So he has Moulder boast about the size of his
turkey and its low price, rather as he had shown both Mrs.
Mason and Dockwrath wrangling for tasteless furniture because
they thought they were getting it cheap. At least the turkey is
worth eating – and Moulder carves it with scrupulous fairness.

Trollope rivets the link between salesmen and lawyers in a
later scene when Moulder defends sharp practice in the courts
by analogy:

> They're paid for it; it's their duties; just as it's my duty to sell
> Hubbles and Grease's sugar. It's not for me to say the sugar's
> bad, or the sample's not equal to the last. My duty is to sell,
> and I sell; – and it's their duty to get a verdict. . . . I say it's
> justice. You can have it if you choose to pay for it, and so can
> I. (II,213)

This is a forthright defence of the cash nexus, a theme Adams has
recognised,[28] and it goes along with the novel's other examples
of self-interest withering ties of nature, morality and tradition.
But Trollope prefers to draw out only a class view of the issue.
Moulder had earlier appeared as a spokesman for the opposite
case. The same scene in which Dockwrath calls all Englishmen
commercial turns on a dispute about customary rights. Dockwrath

insists on using a room reserved at the inn for commercial travellers, but without conforming to its rules. He considers himself governed 'by the law of the land, and not by the laws of any special room in which he might chance to find himself' (I,88). These infringements Moulder fights as 'a stickler for the rights and privileges of his class' (I,52). He also objects to Kantwise using the room to sell furniture – and even to private as distinct from wholesale dealings. Yet Trollope develops the scene's potential for genre comedy rather than for thematic interest. Moulder's support for the cash nexus contradicts his respect for tradition, but though Trollope presented the contradiction there's no sign he noticed it. His official view wouldn't let him register, let alone explore, where his fascination with custom had led.

One of the distinctions of the unofficial Trollope is just such an ability to explore the basis and implications of conventional behaviour. The kind of direction his mind often took is indicated by a comment in his next book after *Orley Farm*, *North America*. He observes that in America it isn't considered proper as it is in England to talk in railway carriages with unknown ladies. 'We soon learn the rules on these subjects,' he says, 'but who makes the rules?'[29] It's a trivial example, but this is the type of question he fails to ask in *Orley Farm*. His account of the legal congress at Birmingham shows that there are as many different kinds of legal procedure as there are nations – all defended with equal vigour. But there his curiosity stops, just as his view of the English legal system stops short at the question of an advocate's honesty. The defence of the English Bar falls to Judge Staveley, and it's a sign of the vagueness of Trollope's position that he passes this by for a further dig at Furnival (I,181). Having attacked what he sees as dishonesty in the courts, he goes on to imply that the system can absorb it fairly happily. He makes Staveley a judge, removing him from forensic dirt, without a word of how he could have reached such a position without compromise. And he has the judge defend the conduct of the two lawyers most notorious for exactly the practices his narrative so indignantly deplores (II,122).

Trollope wanted to have his say about commercial dishonesty, especially in the law. But he also wanted to show that what he regarded as the good life could be led with principle by a lawyer.

He tries to solve the problem by having Judge Staveley prove himself free of mercenary taint in allowing his daughter to marry the impecunious Felix Graham. The result is to shift the issue into private life, and to foster the tendentious distinction he has already created between gentleman and commercial lawyers. No one would mistake Chaffanbrass for a gentleman despite his fame in the law courts. Outwardly, he's just a 'dirty little man' (I,342). Then there is Solomon Aram, a Jewish lawyer from the East End at whom even Furnival blinks (I,346). These men defend Lady Mason for their fee, knowing she's guilty. Trollope presents Furnival's motives as more mixed, and in some ways more creditable. But he leaves no doubt that a man who will effectively lie in his client's defence amounts to less than his idea of a gentleman.

Only Felix Graham among the counsel for the defence shows enough scruple to fit Trollope's prescription. Yet Trollope's attitude to Graham often seems confusing. Though the character seems to speak with the same voice as the narrator in criticising the system of advocacy, he is at other times presented less sympathetically as an eccentric idealist. Adams and Edwards accordingly conclude that Graham is the figure through whom Trollope compromised his attack on the law, but the truth may be more complex. Graham certainly plays a central part in the story, but in another way - as an indirect contrast to Lady Mason. While she is brought to exile herself from gentle society for her crime, Graham is assimilated to it thanks to an accident in the sport which most characterises that society. His ignorance about fox hunting is part of his impatience with all 'conventional rules' (I,175), and the accident provides a means, almost literally, of breaking down his resistance to them. Imprisoned at Noningsby by his injuries, he succumbs not only to Madeline Staveley but to the way of life the house stands for. Again, where Lady Mason had contracted a loveless marriage with a man much older than herself, Graham avoids a loveless marriage with the young girl whose upbringing he had supervised. The Mary Snow episode isn't there simply to question Graham's idealism, and to issue a standard Trollopian warning against marriage without love, it is also a cautionary tale against marriages that cross class lines - the case in *Lady Anna* where a countess' daughter marries a tailor is exceptional in Trollope's fiction. Graham's story, and its contrast with Lady Mason's, suggests that *Orley Farm*, like *Doctor Thorne*, is really about recruiting the gentry. But the emphasis differs: instead of money, here it is talent that's needed. This Graham is supposed to supply, in the form of gentlemanly principle as well as energy – an article Trollope leaves to be taken pretty much on trust. The reason for what looks like confusion in Trollope's attitude to Graham is double. He wanted the character to demonstrate gentlemanly conscience, but at the same time he needed to show that being a successful lawyer was still compatible with being a gentleman. So Graham has to drop some of his views as impractical, and learn to tolerate the ways of the world if he's to succeed in it.

Comparison of the four young gentlemen in the novel suggests that Trollope had firmly in mind a model of how the gentry renews itself. The Ormes are a fine old family, but all Peregrine the heir will achieve will be trophies from hunting big game – the adult equivalent of his youthful rat-catching. The Staveleys are a fine new family, but here effeteness has set in. Augustus Staveley has a gentleman's taste and manners, but that's all. Trollope says that the judge 'had begun the world with little or nothing, and had therefore succeeded; but his son was already possessed of almost everything that he could want, and therefore his success seemed doubtful' (I,174). For if the novel has its straw men – Joseph Mason, the commercial characters – it also has its stuffed shirts. Augustus Staveley has little to recommend him, except his appreciation for Felix Graham (I,217), yet Trollope can compare him very much to his own advantage with Lucius Mason. As the comparison springs from Sophia Furnival's choice between her two suitors, it's also a way of reflecting on her when she plays coy with Staveley. Trollope weights the point with a heavily commercial metaphor: 'There are ladies who prefer Worcester ware to real china; and, moreover, the order for the Worcester ware had already been given' (II,269). The distinctions between the four men are all too neat. Orme attracts most of the narrator's sympathy, but he's from an old stock which is dying out. Staveley, from a family newly advanced, has no incentive to better himself. Graham, with few means, has such an incentive, and by 'birth, education,and tastes' he comes from the right class (II,124). He and not Orme gets the girl, and the suggestion is that he and not his friend will follow in Judge Staveley's footsteps. Measured by the same criteria as Graham, Lucius Mason isn't a pattern gentleman, though high-principled. He is accordingly despatched to make a new life in Australia after the surrender of Orley Farm.

It's a sign of Trollope's bias that he doesn't see the emptiness of such a figure as Augustus Staveley. Perhaps any gentleman who hunts is all right, but apart from this almost all Staveley does in the novel is flirt with Sophia Furnival and pour cold water on Graham's interest in his sister (Graham being acceptable as a friend, but not necessarily as a member of the family). Yet Trollope has this conventional gentleman administer a lesson to the idealist: 'A man, as I take it, must through life allow himself to be governed by the united wisdom of others around him' (II,352). Such a statement from a figure with so little apparent authority cannot pass without comment, so Trollope adds that Staveley's 'words of worldly wisdom' are spoken 'from the depth of his life's experience'. But the tone of his irony is mild, and the novel scarcely challenges this oracle of conformism. The son probably learned it from his father, who also advises Graham to forget his utopian dreams (II,258), and whose moral instructions to his daughter are strictly of the cracker-motto variety: 'Money and rank are only good, if every step by which they are gained be good also' (II,184).

Where *Orley Farm* offers criticism, its source is a latent fear that the others around a man whose united wisdom should guide him might not always be gentlemen. The danger is that commercial attitudes – and perhaps not only attitudes – are infiltrating the gentry as they have done the law. The motive of Trollope's plot is to prevent both the danger and the fear from being realised. This is done by showing the gentry renew and consolidate itself, and by endorsing its traditional role as moral guardian. But I also mean the other sense of 'realised', for the novel never defines directly the true nature of the fear. Its insistence on honesty and integrity is worthy but mystified, and for two basic reasons. First, Trollope never acknowledges the steps lower down in the social process through which money and rank are supplied. Money is presented simply as an abstract – the product of activities which, except in the case of the commercial characters, are taken for granted. This exception

suggests the second reason, which is that the morality the novel
recommends is difficult to separate from what it assumes in the
form of ideology. *Orley Farm* comes very near to implying that
disinterested conduct is possible only for the gentry. Its confidence in the continued strength and scruple of this class
provides the grounds for its affirmation in what it shows us of
English society. Abuses, Trollope suggests, certainly exist –
especially in the law – but they may be lived with, and gradually
reformed. Felix Graham's only fault is in wanting to change
things too fast. So powerful is the charmed circle of ladies and
gentlemen that even commerce may be rendered tame, as it is in
the shape of a children's game at Noningsby. But to keep the
power ladies and gentlemen have to join hands and close ranks;
and this, the novel would have it believed, is England's best
chance.

Orley Farm illustrates at their most perplexing some of the
difficulties in assessing Trollope. Its sheer length is a formidable
obstacle. A novel in which each part interlocks can only be
considered as a whole. As *Orley Farm* is this kind of novel, the
view it represents of Trollope's society can only be measured by
absorbing and understanding what can sometimes be tedious
detail. I hope I haven't offended too much here, but even in
what I've tried to make a fairly full account of the novel, I've left
out such minor interests as the marriage of John Kenneby and
Mrs. Smiley, which crudely contrasts, in its emphasis on money
dealings, with the smoother arrangements of the gentry. This of
course points to another problem in evaluating *Orley Farm*. If,
with Adams, we approach the novel as a panorama of English
society, we shall be disappointed because it has too little of the
range and intelligence we find in the best work of Dickens,
George Eliot, even Thackeray. The novel takes too much on
trust. It doesn't just wear its ideology on its sleeve, like
conventional fiction of the period, but in its whole dress and
fashion. This might provide a way at least of admiring
Trollope's art, for within its limits the novel is imagined and
constructed with skill and insight. *Orley Farm* without doubt is a
much more considerable work than the sensational fiction it
implicitly criticises. But to say this is only to raise a related
problem: that the novel seems as much a response to a vogue in
literature as to what was happening in English society. If this

question can be dealt with, there remains the difficulty that Trollope's art cannot be fully understood or appreciated in dissociation from the way of seeing that informs it – precisely because the novel is so deeply saturated in ideology. It is possible to value Trollope's technique, but this gets problematic once the uses it serves are recognised.

Another possibility is to redefine the novel's aims, to find its vision less class-bound, more humane, than I've argued. But that could only be done either by silently editing out, or by rationalising much that is discordant. This has been the method of those who have hailed *Orley Farm* as a type case for Trollope's so-called 'Situation Ethics'.[30] The kind of editing I mean shows up in the omission, by the critic who first developed this notion, of an essential qualifying clause from a remark Trollope made elsewhere. Ruth apRoberts quotes from a discussion of American courtship customs, in which she has Trollope state: 'These practices are right or wrong, not in accordance with a fixed rule of morality prevailing over all the earth . . . but right or wrong according to the usages of the country in which they are practised.'[31] The words left out are: '– such a rule, for instance, as that which orders men not to steal' – an exception that seriously inconveniences the case for Trollope's moral relativism. This is an exact parallel to *Orley Farm* where Trollope has been represented as justifying an act which he thought absolutely wrong whatever the circumstances. Editing out or rationalising come naturally enough if the novel is detached from the society in which it was written. Yet taking Trollope seriously doesn't only mean reading his works as completed wholes. It also means reading them against their period, against what they meant in their time. This is as vital an element in their coherence as their rhetoric, their structure, or – at a further remove – the imaginative psychology of their writer. And, to change the metaphor, it is the arena in which Trollope entered a deliberate challenge by setting his novels so persistently in the present.

What *Orley Farm* has to offer is, like *Doctor Thorne*, official Trollope. Trollope here expresses, as he does in various other novels, a working out of the thinking by which the dominant class in Victorian society justified its leadership. The limitation of such novels is their tolerance for that ideology, reproducing it altogether too comfortably (*Orley Farm* offends more than *Doctor*

Thorne in this respect). But also, perversely, this is one of those novels' achievements. For if they show Trollope accepting ideological assumptions too easily, they also show him reflecting them with unimpeachable fidelity. No one else is so truthful a witness to what people of his class were thinking and feeling in the 1860s, when he was at the height of his popularity – or so skilful a witness, in the art of his representations. If *Orley Farm* is content to rethread the pattern of conventional assumptions, one reason probably lies in Trollope's personal history. His family had lost Julians, their country house, and Julians Hill, the model for Orley Farm (*Autobiography*, 2–3, 21–3). For this he had now compensated through his success as a professional gentleman: it was in late 1859 that he had moved into Waltham House, which in turn represents the ideal he described in Noningsby. Yet, if *Orley Farm* doesn't alter the pattern of conventional assumptions, or work its threads differently, the thoroughness with which Trollope had absorbed it and lived it would later allow more varied and more critical representations. This, rather than A. O. J. Cockshut's theory of a 'Progress to Pessimism',[32] is how to account for the development that takes place in his thinking, and which my final chapter will examine.

One step by which the unofficial Trollope emerges from the official is the recognition that the codes which shape social life have their formal and arbitrary element. To take this step it is necessary not only to learn the codes but to inhabit them, which is largely what Trollope was doing both in his fiction and in his life at this period. *Orley Farm* can manage such a recognition only in observing the customs respected by Moulder, and in Trollope's extended study of institutional thinking in the law. Here Cockshut is quite right – Trollope does show that the real function of legal traditions is to 'enable all connected with the law to think in two separate and inconsistent ways without discomfort'.[33] But it doesn't follow, as he affirms, that Trollope somehow thought those traditions justified.

The novel's other sign of the unofficial Trollope is the unquestioned deference it assumes to the power of public opinion. It is that power which prevents Sir Peregrine from marrying Lady Mason, and which drives her so stubbornly to vindicate herself despite her guilt. This tells something more essential about Victorian society than anything in the novel's official message, but Trollope never fully draws it out – perhaps, as I've argued, because he couldn't sympathise with Lady Mason in the way he would later sympathise with Josiah Crawley or Phineas Finn. In later, better, novels the unofficial Trollope would come more into his own, though his freedom always remained qualified. My next and final chapter will discuss three novels which show him developing a more critical perspective on his society as his career unfolded. It is this kind of novel, if any, that might entitle him to the name of a realist, and that will be the line of my inquiry.

7   Realism and Ideology

Does it make sense to call Trollope a realist? Most of his reviewers thought so – in Donald Smalley's index to his anthology of contemporary criticism this topic attracts more references than any other.[1] Recent critics have agreed, but there remain problems in defining exactly what Trollope's realism consists in. One of these problems is that the concept of realism has itself fallen into distress. It is argued that language, as an autonomous signifying system, can in no sense re-present reality; and that reality is in no sense a neutral, indifferent 'given', but is produced by human activity. Fiction, the reminder constantly goes, is always and only fiction; and so, some add, is history.[2] No wonder, in such a climate of opinion, if explorations of Trollope's 'realism' have generally entered little into the relations between his novels and the life they are supposed to represent. Instead, most recent inquiry has preoccupied itself with what might be called realism as rhetoric. The point in this is not to demonstrate what Trollope has to tell about the nature or substance of his world, but to indicate the narrative strategies by which he attempts to persuade his readers that his version of that world is a true one. Examples of this approach may be found in the recent books by James Kincaid, R. C. Terry, P. D. Edwards, and Joan Mandel Cohen. The latter supplies an especially plain instance in her distinction between what she calls 'the *essence* of realism' and 'the appearance of realism, which is a matter of the identification of specific techniques'.[3]

It's possible that realism as rhetoric is attractive at such a time of cultural disorientation as the present, when it's difficult to be sure about one's sense of the world, let alone one's ability to influence things. Yet it isn't clear that definitions of realism which emphasise content rather than form are any more helpful

with Trollope, even if the epistemological and linguistic objections I have mentioned can be negotiated. Georg Lukács, for
example, declares that the truly great realists 'present social
institutions as human relationships and social objects as the
vehicles of such relationships'.[4] This could only be said to be true
of Trollope in a limited sense. The relations between, say, people
connected with the Church in *The Last Chronicle of Barset*, or with
the law in *Orley Farm*, are nothing like as dense and concrete as
they are in Dickens' Chancery (*Bleak House*) or Tolstoy's army
(*War and Peace*). Another possible test to apply from Lukács is the
notion of the type, which he describes as 'the central category
and criterion of realist literature' and defines like this:

> What makes a type a type is not its average quality, not its
> mere individual being, however profoundly conceived; what
> makes it a type is that in it all the humanly and socially
> essential determinants are present on their highest level of
> development, in the ultimate unfolding of the possibilities
> latent in them, in extreme presentation of their extremes,
> rendering concrete the peaks and limits of men and epochs.[5]

I do not think there is a single character in Trollope who fits this
definition. Trollope repeatedly describes his characters as
typical in just the sense that Lukács is so concerned to repudiate:
as ordinary, average, commonplace. Even when he introduces
extraordinary figures, he either cuts them down to size – Lady
Mason in *Orley Farm* is no tragic heroine; Josiah Crawley in *The
Last Chronicle* is no saint – or suggests, as with Louis Trevelyan in
He Knew He Was Right, that they are strange eccentrics.[6] Perhaps
the answer is that there are degrees of realism, and that Trollope
locates himself in the humdrum rather than in the epic.

This is certainly the meaning of what must be the most often
quoted and most influential definition of Trollope's peculiar
territory: Henry James' paradox that 'His great, his inestimable
merit was a complete appreciation of the usual'. Yet paradoxes
don't always make very good touchstones, and this one contains
more than a whiff of damnation by faint praise. That becomes
unmistakable in the words of critics less careful than James. It's
not much recommendation to be told by J. H. Wildman that
Trollope 'rediscovered the banal'. Then, too, it's easy to
sentimentalise what Trollope achieved by calling him, in

Terry's phrase, 'the laureate of the commonplace'.[7] But there
are several ways out of this critical *cul de sac*. apRoberts has
discovered a special kind of moral realism in Trollope's
handling of the cases of conscience which she sees as central to
his work; and Edwards has argued convincingly that Trollope's
best novels convey the sense 'at once of the strangeness of
common life and of the naturalness, the inherent ordinariness of
seemingly out-of-the-way experience'.[8]

Yet, persuasively as apRoberts and Edwards have written in
support of these claims, they do not fully establish Trollope's
entitlement to be considered as a realist. For it is the realist's
distinction to reveal the nature of his society, what, fundament-
ally, it means to live in such a society. The realist is the historian
of the present, and though apRoberts and (especially) Edwards
comment interestingly on the relation between Trollope's
fiction and his times, this element in their work often seems more
incidental than essential. apRoberts, for instance, describes
ways of thinking about morality and politics at the period that
are akin to Trollope's; and Edwards has much to say about
Trollope's novels in relation to trends in the serious and popular
fiction of the day, as well as contributing appendices on the links
between the Barsetshire and the Palliser novels and history. But
neither of these approaches can take us all that far into
Trollope's versions of the present. R.M. Polhemus notes the
importance of the word 'chronicle' that Trollope applied to his
stories. Yet, in assessing the relations between history and
Trollope's fiction, he gets little further than sweeping generality
(for example: 'his novels from the "hungry forties" deal with the
tragic power of historical determinism, and his comedies of the
mid-fifties tend to express the expansive, boom-time psychology
of those years').[9] Perhaps, as John Vincent has remarked, there
is history on the one hand and 'Eng Lit history' on the other.[10]
Whether or not it's true, as he says, that 'the latter genre . . .
exists in a world all its own', the anomaly cannot be denied that
critics have made little of the very qualities in Trollope that
interest the historian or sociologist. The term 'chronicle'
suggests a reason why his novels should be difficult for the critic
to approach in this way. According to the *Oxford English
Dictionary*, a chronicle is 'a detailed and continuous register
of events in order of time; a historical record, *esp.* one in

which the facts are narrated without philosophic treatment, or any attempt at literary style'. So Trollope's own word isn't very flattering if taken literally. Yet it's not without its accuracy. The first part of the definition catches very well the surface topicality, almost in the sense of a journalist, shared by many Trollope novels – as with *The Warden* and clerical scandal, or the social and political ephemera that occupy the foreground in the Palliser series. In earlier parts of this book I have suggested that it's only at a deeper level than they acknowledge that Trollope's novels take on their true representativeness – through their structure, and through their interior views of persons who are alone but can never be separate. But this still leaves the problem. Does the immediate to-and-fro of life in his work have to be left on a par with the *Annual Register*, or (for the more sophisticated) as embalmed ideology? Perhaps this was simply a tale of a tub, diverting his mind while his imagination escaped.

There is, though, still another reason why Trollope's 'realism' has been relatively little explored. This is the apparent inclusiveness and self-containment of the world he created. Nathaniel Hawthorne's image of a chunk of earth in a glass case, quoted approvingly by Trollope in his *Autobiography* (125), has defined the scope of much recent Trollope criticism. If the novels' world is autonomous, then why refer it to the real world? The sheer weight and volume of Trollope's complete works, not to mention the piles of criticism and 'Trollopology',[11] perhaps become a labyrinth from which the pioneer critic can emerge, only to blink at what he sees outside. Yet confinement within limits seemingly so ample can bring comfort, especially as the world Trollope constructs is one almost calculated to appeal to the disillusioned liberal, the averagely decent conservative. No doubt the increasing professionalism of literary study has also contributed to this narrowing of range, not least at a time when there has been no lack of critic-philosophers to de-construct fiction, or history; to call in question the very possibility of 'realism'.

Such reservations have their reasons. If it's claimed that realism in literature offers something like objective knowledge of reality, then this has not only to be denied, but declared not worth proposing. The denial isn't out of any hostility to science.

It should go without saying that reality is so unimaginably complex that to attempt even objective description of, say, a flower would only start at numbering the streaks of its petals. Second, following from this, what literature does not or cannot know, literature must imagine. So what it offers is an image, or a vision, of reality. The truth of this image is in no sense privileged, any more than is the truth of a scientific observation or theory. Instead that truth, just as in science, has to be measured against the phenomena to which it refers and the procedures by which it has been produced. Yet, because literature depends more extensively than science on the constructive power of an individual mind, what the mind works with must also come into play. Literature doesn't offer only an image of reality; it also demonstrates, inscribed within itself, the assumptions and imaginative projections which serve to construct its image of reality. To give an example: we should not read Balzac or Stendhal for objective knowledge of French history in the aftermath of Napoleon. What they created were imaginative versions, from two different points of view, of what each thought and felt was happening at that period – and, at the same time, demonstrations of how each point of view put together the reality it claimed to reflect. Stendhal's famous image of a novel as a mirror carried along the road suggests the paradoxes in this.[12] The authenticity in his representations and Balzac's springs not only from the verve and grasp with which they relay their sense of the present, it also comes from the force, always powerful – even, sometimes, in contradictions – with which they directed points of view that themselves stemmed from the history in which they were embedded. Not that the character of that history can be taken for granted either. But it is possible to have confidence in this kind of knowledge, so long as it's remembered that all knowledge is always produced, and produced by particular people at particular times in particular places. That at least will be the footing on which the following account will move forward.

In trying to assess Trollope's realism, then, it may help to start from a clue to what he thought was real. In a letter to George Eliot he wrote this of the novel he was sending her: 'In *Rachel Ray* I have attempted to confine myself absolutely to the commonest details of commonplace life among the most ordinary people, allowing myself no incident that would be even remarkable in everyday life. I have shorn my fiction of all romance' (*Letters*, 18 October 1863, p. 138). This statement suggests that *Rachel Ray* might be regarded as 'realistic' in three ways: in its opposition to the sensational or romantic, in its verisimilitude (no improbabilities), and in its subject matter (ordinary people and events). Trollope emphasises the last of these most firmly, and in doing so implies a definition of what he considered ordinary. On the novel's evidence, 'ordinary people' are middle-class. The heroine and her mother live on a small private income left by her father, who had been an ecclesiastical lawyer. The hero works at improving his inheritance of a share in a brewery, having given up his position as an articled clerk. 'Ordinary incidents' include attempts to frustrate marriage between hero and heroine, but also an election as well as the small change of daily life in a country town. Accepting *Rachel Ray* as 'realistic' means agreeing to a class-based definition of what is real; or, perhaps more accurately, to a definition based on what the specific audience Trollope was aiming for might be expected to see as real. If this is so, the novel's 'realism' is a matter of ideology – by which I mean, here, the conventions that inform the author's and readers' sense of what is real.[13] Those conventions are social and religious, as well as formal. The hero and heroine of *Rachel Ray* negotiate ultimate happiness against inferiors both social (the brewing family) and doctrinal (the influence of the Low Church). It is only those inferiors who receive comic-strip names (Tappitt and Prong respectively). Neither is of a class likely to read Trollope; ironically, this novel was rejected by the Evangelical magazine, *Good Words*, because it would have offended its readers.[14] The novel's formal conventions could also be traced back in part to its readership – probably largely female, and dependent on the lending libraries. These conventions include the commonsense, avuncular tone, and the plot – romantic in subject if not in treatment – of love and marriage.

Three other novels of the 1860s which conform to Trollope's statement in his letter to George Eliot are *Miss Mackenzie*, *The Claverings*, and *The Belton Estate*. Of these the first keeps closest to the plain level of middle-class life. It even defines the 'ordinary

Englishman' whom it assumes for its readership: he 'has eight hundred a year; he lives in London; and he has a wife and three or four children' (*Miss Mackenzie*, 106). But the best of the three novels is *The Claverings*. Like the others, it has a plot in which almost nothing happens out of the ordinary – in the sense defined above. As the *Saturday Review* recognised, 'The author reproduces the world very much in those aspects which it wears in the eyes of most of us'.[15] What makes *The Claverings* interesting is largely that those aspects agreed on as real by the kind of people likely to read both novel and review are themselves part of the novel's subject.

The action of *The Claverings* springs from uncertainties in the standings of its three main characters. Julia Brabazon is the only unmarried daughter from an old aristocratic family whose money has run out. She marries Lord Ongar deliberately for his rank and wealth, only to find that they can't bring her happiness even after his death has set her free. Harry Clavering is the presumably talented son of a clergyman who lacks the means to provide for him. He holds a fellowship, but has no mind for the Church. After teaching for two years, and after being rejected by Julia Brabazon, he sets out to train as a civil engineer. The partner of the firm in which Harry goes to learn his job is a self-made man with an attractive daughter, to whom Harry becomes engaged. The uncertainty of Florence Burton's position is a result of the slowness with which change in social standing follows change in economic standing in a class society. Socially the Burtons are at a disadvantage to the Claverings, and the question is whether Harry will keep his word. Other characters are more exotic. Lord Ongar is a pale shadow of *Vanity Fair*'s Lord Steyne, presented at the end of his life, exclusively from the outside, and with no Thackerayan checks to a response of complacent middle-class righteousness. Sir Hugh Clavering and his family represent an equally sterile life of landed leisure. Sir Hugh is cold and tyrannical, his wife waterily dependent. His younger brother, Archie, empty-headed and purposeless, belongs to the world of clubs and seedy enjoyments, where his friend Captain Boodle makes a precarious living from bets and games of chance. Finally there is Sophie Gordeloup, the so-called Russian spy, whose dress is never of the cleanest; and her brother the devious epicure Count Pateroff. Both are on the make, having followed Lady Ongar home after her husband's death in that most un-British of countries, Italy.

The novel's plot is to rectify the varying social imbalances between its principal characters. None of the imbalances is striking, and the end is attained with a minimum of event. Harry Clavering faces a bourgeois choice of Hercules, but his mind is made up for him in a manner most unherculean – by a convenient illness and the efforts of a few determined women. Illness in Victorian fiction means nervous breakdown; here, the hero buckles under conflict, and gains time to reach the right decision. In this he is guided not only by his mother but by his prospective sister-in-law; not only by Florence, sturdy in her innocent Virtue, but by Florence's rival, an unusually forthright and self-aware version of Pleasure. All leads to what is apparently a conventional ending, with Lady Ongar punished by losing Harry and finding no joy in her riches, and Harry rewarded by Florence and future succession to his uncle's title and property. The novel seems meant, as the *Saturday Review* wittily put it, 'to vindicate the ways of society to women'.[16] But it has to be asked what the ways of society are, and in what manner the novel might be thought to vindicate them.

Central here is Julia Ongar's punishment. *The Claverings* emphasises, as do other works by Trollope, the priority of romantic love. Those who betray their love have to suffer, those who stay true, no matter what the material difficulties, will be saved. In case the message is lost, there are counter-examples to Julia Ongar: Harry's sister, who accepts a penniless curate; Florence's sister, happy and prosperous after an impecunious beginning; and the advice to Florence herself not to delay marrying Harry for reasons of material prudence. The moral is only too clear, as in Chapter 12 describing Julia at her estate, with its heavy refrain 'she had the price in her hands'. But as a moral it's reductive and sentimental – a matter of ideology rather than of 'realism'. Yet underneath the broad schematic design is another suggestion.

This develops when it is questioned just how Julia gets punished. She suffers, first, from ostracism: the penalty of those guilty – or thought to be guilty – of sin against marriage. Not that Julia actually is anything but innocent, except of marrying without love. Rumours are spread by Count Pateroff, a hanger-on in whose interest it is that she not remarry; and her brother-in-law determines her unacceptability in society by harshly refusing to meet her on her return. This is why Julia cannot enjoy her new possessions – she has no one but the disreputable Sophie Gordeloup with whom she might appreciate them, no one to share her thoughts and feelings with. It might be considered that this kind of punishment, arbitrary as it is, works as the outcome of a natural law: this is what a woman lets herself in for if she marries a *roué* for ambition. But to have the ways of society vindicated through the activities of Count Pateroff on the one hand, and of the sadistic Sir Hugh on the other, isn't likely to let anyone who thinks about it feel comfortable with them.

Secondly, Julia is punished by being denied Harry Clavering. The trouble here is that it's difficult to think of Harry personally as anything but a poor prospect either for Julia or Florence. His role in the novel is almost wholly passive, and when he does exert himself the spectacle can be unpleasant – as when he argues against the curate Saul that, as a curate, Saul has no right to propose to his sister. Trollope intimates that Harry is physically attractive, though he hardly specifies how. Intellectually, the hero's fibre is suggested less by his fellowship than by his reply to the question whether he has any doubts about Christianity; 'I might have them if I came to think much about it' (17). Morally he is well-intentioned but vacillating and short on self-awareness. So unimpressive a figure calls for apology, as when the narrator admits Harry's faults and asks for tolerance on the grounds that most young men are imperfect, and that this one is being scrutinised 'almost unfairly' (98). Yet Harry possesses one paradoxical asset. Julia recognises it when she asks herself: 'Was it not manifest that Harry Clavering was a gentleman, qualified to shine among men of rank and fashion, but not qualified to make his way by his own diligence?' (381–2). The narrator adds: 'In saying this of him, she did not know how heavy was the accusation that she brought against him; but what woman within her own breast, accuses the man she loves?' The paradox springs from conflict between upper-class and middle-class values: a gentleman doesn't soil his hands with getting money, but a man worth his salt can succeed by enterprise and industry. It's a question here whether Trollope hasn't given way to confusion or compromise. The same doubt occurs earlier when Mrs. Clavering realises that her son 'would never excel greatly in any drudgery that would be necessary for the making of money' (363). Though we're told that this is a matter of regret more than pride, the word 'drudgery' registers equivocation. Trollope perhaps tries to have it both ways, in order to appeal to a readership in which both kinds of value were active. Harry's limited ability to earn his keep seems obscurely related to his inability to 'sell himself for wealth' in marriage (131). That, in turn, provides a convincing psychological explanation of why he should be loved by a woman who feels guilty for having done just that. But his main qualification turns out to be simply that he makes a good heir to a title and an estate: 'No man had ever been born fitter for the position which he was now called upon to fill' (475). Though that may not say much for such a position.

It is, however, 'the world's opinion' (98) that the reader is encouraged to adopt about Harry, even if the narrator later has to admit that 'the man . . . was not worth the passion' felt for him by Julia (394). Harry is certainly flattered by comparison with the other men Julia knows, but scarcely by comparison with Julia herself. If the main part of her punishment is the loss of this mediocre lover, it is necessary to ask again whether Trollope is vindicating the ways of society – especially to women. For what sharpens the barb is the double standard of conduct that always favours men. While Julia is stigmatised for having contracted an unworthy marriage, Harry could betray Florence with impunity. As Theodore Burton recognises, 'He might proclaim the offender to the world as false, and the world would laugh at the proclaimer, and shake hands with the offender' (291). Harry could marry Julia Ongar with every advantage, including his father's keen approval. Again Burton speaks the truth: 'You would forgive a man anything, and a woman nothing' (329). This is said to his wife, for it is women themselves who enforce the double standard so rigidly: 'When men went astray in matters of love it was within the power of Cecilia Burton's heart to forgive them; but she could not pardon women that so sinned' (295). Again, it's psychologically apt that a person whose own happiness is built on acceptance of inequity should demand that others undergo the consequences of that inequity. But the double standard applies to class as well as to sex, as Mrs. Burton underlines in expressing her anger that Harry Clavering 'is allowed to be dishonest' to Florence 'because he is a gentleman' (332).

If 'the respectable god of social justice' – to take another phrase from the *Saturday*'s review of *The Claverings* – turns out to undermine by his own working part of what he stands for, the same might be said of the natural providence which Trollope enlists to round out his story. The sailing accident in which callous Sir Hugh and feckless Archie Clavering perish seems an unusually dramatic, and also an unusually arbitrary, event in Trollope's fiction. Yet, though the accident allows Harry to occupy the position for which he's best fitted, it doesn't change anything crucial. Harry has already proved that he is in one way fit to become the heir by ceasing to think of this as a possibility. An early scene has Florence disapproving of his smug calculation that he is well placed to succeed his uncle (106), but when the news of the accident reaches him it takes him some time to grasp its implications for himself (460). This is despite the decision he has already taken to marry Florence, and it shows that Julia's wealth hadn't tempted him much. So the accident is set up to provide a test like those in *Doctor Thorne* to show Harry's improved moral worth. But there's a key difference. Much more than what happens in *Doctor Thorne*, the accident calls attention to itself as an extraordinary piece of luck – for Harry, of course. Whether not wishing for title and property in itself qualifies him to inherit them remains pretty doubtful. It may seem part of the natural fitness that he should become the heir, and be freed from the necessity – onerous to him – of making his own way in life. Yet it isn't possible to claim that what he gets is what he deserves. The arbitrariness of the god from the machine is Trollope's ironic point.

Nevertheless, determining Trollope's point of view in the novel isn't easy. On the one hand, as the *Saturday Review* critic saw clearly, the reader is invited to take the world's opinion, to assess the novel's characters and events with the same standards that he takes for granted in everyday life. On the other hand, the novel points to shallowness and inconsistency in those standards – though it could hardly be called a work of sustained social criticism or satire. If Trollope plays the role of man of the world, initiate in all the 'ordinary social rules' (133), he also suggests the view, not quite of the underground man, but at least of the disillusioned inhabitant of the surface. It's Harry Clavering who declares in callow complacency: 'No man has a right to be peculiar. Every man is bound to accept such usage as is customary in the world' (232). Trollope makes possible a different kind of perception by seeming to endorse the ideology of the readership he wrote for, and then quietly allowing its shortcomings to appear.

'The author reproduces the world very much in those aspects which it wears in the eyes of most of us' – what the writer in the *Saturday Review* reveals is the basis in ideology of Trollope's realism. I've suggested that one of the apparent inconsistencies in *The Claverings* may be explained by Trollope's need to gratify middle-class as well as upper-class expectations. (I don't mean that all middle-class or upper-class readers would have shared the same respective expectations, since moral and social values – though originating in different classes – often cut across class lines.) An interesting example is the presentation of Florence's brother. Theodore Burton is a hard-working office manager whom Harry has to consider under-bred because he dusts his boots with his handkerchief. Yet it's Burton who is the better man, as his firm common sense over Harry's difficulties makes clear. Again, though, the book comes much more from a point of view like Harry's than from one like Burton's. Despite all Harry's studies, we get no idea of what life in the office entails: it's as if Trollope is writing for those with gentlemanly aspirations – at least in conduct and values – who respect the middle-class virtues of solidity and self-help. Florence is an unexceptionable girl in her own right, but it's still felt that she gets an extra polish from mixing with the Claverings (165–6). These questions become all the more interesting when Trollope's own position is remembered. Like Burton he worked in an office, and had succeeded in his profession. Yet he was also by birth and upbringing a gentleman. His divided attitude to class corresponds to another ambiguity in the novel: what it makes of its foreigners. These it presents largely as targets for prejudice, figures of somewhat seamy fun. But Trollope also allows them the power to jar self-satisfaction, as when Sophie Gordeloup attacks English stupidity and heartlessness (483–4). If most Victorian novels imply a complacent but potentially sympathetic reader, *The Claverings* appears to echo the normal consciousness of its readers closely enough so as not to disturb their contentment. But this is very much a matter of how the novel is read. Anyone who thought about the world the novel represents would come to some unsettling conclusions about what it took for granted, what it valued, and what it hated.

Trollope's realism, then, is his ability to articulate in fiction the ways of behaving, feeling and thinking that characterised the dominant social class to which he belonged. This he did in three main ways. First, he dealt again and again with such typical but essential events in the life of that class as courtship and marriage, making a career or settling into an inheritance. Second, he voiced the conventional wisdom of his day, the opinion of what so often in his fiction he calls 'the world'. Third, and most important, he raised questions about ordinary thought and conduct, both through the structure of his stories and increasingly through narrative comments. *The Claverings*, like some of his other novels of the 1860s, takes for its sphere what he described in his letter to George Eliot as 'commonplace life'. In another group of novels, written in the 1870s, Trollope turned his attention from provincial life to metropolitan, from commonplace life to the life of power and fashion. This shift, connected to and parallel with the movement from the Barsetshire to the Palliser series, also reflects a more explicitly critical emphasis. In *The Way We Live Now* the result was the closest Trollope comes to satire, but a similar colouring marks *Phineas Redux*, *The Prime Minister*, *Is He Popenjoy?* and *The American Senator*. A good example of this type of novel – and one which is half in and half out of the Palliser series – is *The Eustace Diamonds*. Here it's possible to test what I have been arguing about Trollope's realism by considering a novel with a different setting and with an element of satire in its intention.

Trollope's satirical target in *The Eustace Diamonds* is dishonesty. As we have seen, this was not an unfamiliar theme for him, and in the novel he makes it very obvious. The novel's structure is based on a central contrast between one woman whose life is a tissue of deceit and another who tells the truth at risk of losing all she holds valuable. *The Eustace Diamonds* includes hardly an event which doesn't concern one form or another of lie, from conscious and deliberate untruth to pretence, evasion, and self-deception. But this isn't a novel of incident. Trollope is interested less in the theft of the diamonds than in the dishonesty which that theft makes possible and throws into relief. As in *Orley Farm*, his plot comes from literature rather than life: from Wilkie Collins' *The Moonstone*, and from another novel that hinges on a contrast between two women, Thackeray's *Vanity Fair*. What matters, though, is what the plot has to show about what was for him normal consciousness.

It must be admitted at the start that Trollope to some extent remains within that consciousness. The plainest example is a minor but nasty example of anti-Semitism. The novel's plot is set in motion by the Jewish jeweller and moneylender whose speculative financial aid allows Lizzie to entrap Sir Florian Eustace. The same figure instigates the schemes to steal the Eustace diamonds, and, when the second attempt succeeds, he disposes of them profitably – if at the expense of a long term in jail. Much more prominent than Mr. Benjamin, however, is a character whose role in the plot is slight. Joseph Emilius is Lizzie's least prepossessing lover, who has nothing to do but present his lap till she falls into it as her temporary nemesis (he's later to be exposed as a bigamist). Explicitly, she marries him because no one else will have her and because she doesn't have the taste to know better (713–15). Both the function of Emilius in the novel and his characterisation are quite indefensible (see, for instance, the crudity of Trollope's words in Chapter 73). Emilius isn't an epitome of the lying and dishonesty which the novel says are epidemic in fashionable life, but a bogy, a projection of phobias. He represents an example of Trollope's either unthinking or cynical acceptance of conventional prejudice, which is the more difficult to forgive because of his ability to penetrate beyond it elsewhere.

Whether or not the figure of Emilius shows Trollope compromising deliberately with a prejudice likely to be shared by many of his readers, the novel's narrator often presents himself as a knowing spokesman for 'the world' and its ways. The novel's angle of vision seems an insider's, compounded of shrewd observation, digested experience, and unillusioned but tolerant wisdom. It's on that level that the narrator appeals to the reader, as if putting into words what people of a certain class know without articulating it, or perhaps without even knowing that they know it. Phrases such as 'we all know', or 's/he was the kind of person who . . .' testify, as so often in Trollope, to a community of opinion, one which likes to think of itself as standing for good-humoured common sense, worldly-wise but not cynical. Trollope deftly indicates the choice of life open to Frank Greystock by drawing on his readers' sense of how different parts of London register socially: 'There was the Belgrave-cum-Pimlico life, the scene of which might extend itself to South Kensington, enveloping the parks and coming round over Park Lane, and through Grosvenor Square and Berkeley Square back to Piccadilly. . . . And then there was that other outlook, the scene of which was laid somewhere north of Oxford Street' (118). The same viewpoint is assumed when, after Frank Greystock has spoken in parliament as a good party man, the narrator says: 'We all know the meaning of such speeches' (60); or when he declares that newspaper censure, 'as we all know, is very common, and in nine cases out of ten it is unjust' (444). This is the official voice, the voice of the Establishment, reassuring us of security and rightness – not least the security and rightness of its own sense of the world.

Again, then, Trollope's realism, his 'complete appreciation of the usual', is centrally a matter of ideology. But the genial ease with which he expresses what is taken for granted can be deceptive. We are told, for instance, that Frank Greystock's mother is, 'as we are so wont to say of many women, the best woman in the world' (267) – the cliché, characteristically, being at once accepted and questioned. Greystock's father is 'the dear dean, who really had a conscience about money'. Yet the attitudes these people demonstrate in their behaviour – attitudes which are presented as normal and natural – are anything but agreeable. Both parents seek to rationalise the contradictions into which their worldliness leads them: 'Mrs. Greystock declared to her daughter that no one in the whole world had a higher respect for governesses than had she. But a governess is a governess; – and for a man in Frank's position such a marriage would be simply suicide' (268). Similarly, the dean 'would not for the world have hinted to his son that it might be well to marry money; but he thought that it was a good thing that his son should go where money was'. Both these sentences illustrate what H. S. Davies has called Trollope's special cadence, identifying the gap between profession and practice.[17] Another example a few pages later contains a phrase which finely reveals the true nature of Mrs. Greystock's wishes, whatever her reluctance to admit them: 'She did not declare to herself that it would be a good thing that her son should be false to Lucy Morris, in order that he might marry his rich cousin; but she did feel it to be an advantage that he should be on terms of intimacy with so large an income as that belonging to Lady Eustace' (270). That wish for intimacy with an income leads to a shabby arrangement in which Greystock's fiancée is practically shelved with his own consent, on the chance that he may drop her for Lizzie Eustace. An inevitable protest from Greystock's father is escaped by the simple expedient of not telling him: 'The dean was so short-sighted and imprudent, that he would have professed delight at the idea of having Lucy Morris as a resident at the deanery' (275). Here the persuasive definition – 'short-sighted and imprudent' for 'impulsive and generous' – nicely complements the euphemism of 'intimacy with so large an income', which reveals so much more than it covers up.

Still, admitting Trollope's skill at conveying such self-deceptions, as well as the verbal shuffling that enables them, it has to be asked whether the critique goes very far. He gives his readers an evaluation they can agree with, despite his suggestion that in practice their response might be closer to the Greystocks' than they'd like to think. In just the same way, the choice between Lizzie and Lucy is never exactly made difficult. There's none of Thackeray's taxing ambivalence about Becky Sharp and Amelia Sedley. Trollope apparently does little to extend or call in question his readers' sense of what is right and wrong.

To an extent this is true, yet there are occasions when Trollope steps beyond the ordinary morality – whether practised or not – of his readers. Early in the novel, for instance, he repudiates what he calls 'the common theory' on love. According to this, no woman should entertain feelings of love for a man until a man has approached her in that spirit. Trollope argues on the contrary that it's generally the woman who has scope and occasion 'to think closely and decide sharply on such a matter' (30), while the man drifts thoughtlessly. Habit-blindness, suggests the comfortably dispassionate tone of the narrative, comes so naturally that a man's misconduct to a woman seems almost excusable. The discussion is very Trollopian not only in that tone, but in the gradual shift from the slight fault, the unthinking attention, to the suffering caused when the man leaves the woman whose affections he has allowed himself to engage. Trollope's most brilliant example of how slowly, but how inexorably, a tiny slip can lead to tragedy is his account of a marriage breaking up in *He Knew He Was Right*. Here, however, the gradualness of the shift might make it easy to miss the force with which the 'common theory' is being questioned. But Trollope develops the problem in equally careful steps, so that as he returns to it his inquiry goes steadily deeper.

One of those steps is the commentary discussed above on how the Greystocks feel about marriage between a man and a woman without a large unearned income. A later example concerns the much more sympathetic figure Lady Fawn, who nevertheless thinks likewise: 'Woman-like, she regarded the man as being so much more important than the woman, that she could not think that Frank Greystock would devote himself simply to such a one as Lucy Morris' (414). Now Trollope pushes further into the contrarieties of the double standard, emphasising that Lady Fawn thinks this way despite holding a much lower opinion of Frank than of Lucy, for there is a connexion: 'It may seem to be a paradox to assert that such bad opinion sprung [sic] from the high idea which she entertained of the importance of men in general; – but it was so' (415). The same paradox is borne out in the favoured treatment Lady Fawn extends to her son, whom she knows to be less worthy than her daughters, especially when he is allowed to act unreasonably to Lucy, who is supposed to have no right of reply. Lady Fawn almost expects, and indeed half-excuses, misconduct in men: 'According to her view of things, a man out in the world had so many things to think of, and was so very important, that he could hardly be expected to act at all times with truth and sincerity' (415). Such a view is confirmed when Frank receives a prodigal's welcome on finally returning to Lucy, despite what the narrator minces no words in describing as 'his gross misconduct' (701).

This apparently casual demonstration of unexamined assumptions, of intellectual and moral inertia, also reaches beyond private life to public. Frank Greystock spends no more time in considering which party he should join than about the difference between Lucy and Lizzie; and the point is enforced when discussion of his politics directly follows discussion of how unthinkingly he treats Lucy. Again, nothing could seem more natural. Trollope explains how a barrister 'finds that his own progress towards success demands from him that he shall become a politician', and how opportunity may dictate whether he becomes Whig or Tory, since as an advocate he is 'peculiarly conversant with the fact that every question has two sides' (34). He goes out of his way to declare that such an absence of decided principle implies no slur on the profession. Yet it's difficult not to feel that the unvarnished account of an attitude so taken for granted doesn't carry its own criticism. Trollope, while seeming to formulate conventional wisdom, probably has his tongue in his cheek. What makes this likely is not only his own political principle – evident in his candidature at Beverley and his subsequent disillusion – and his critical view of lawyers generally. There is also his description, in the same passage, of what the traditional member of the party joined by Greystock actually believes. Once more Trollope's tone is indulgent, man-of-the-worldly, but what he says amounts to an indictment of complacency:

> These people are ready to grumble at every boon conferred on them, and yet to enjoy every boon. They know too their privileges, and, after a fashion, understand their position. It is picturesque, and it pleases them. To have been always in the right and yet always on the losing side; always being ruined, always under persecution from a wild spirit of republican-demagogism, – and yet never to lose anything, not even position or public esteem, is pleasant enough. A huge, living, daily increasing grievance that does one no palpable harm, is the happiest possession that a man can have. (33)

That Greystock, who holds no fixed political views, should join a party so rich in prejudice isn't just ironic. The combination sharply expresses the essential paradox of the Tory party at this period, composed of backwoodsmen and opportunists who really had little in common. What guaranteed their alliance was that the opportunists could accomplish reforms which backwoodsmen could accept, because they came from their own side and could be relied upon not to destroy their privileges.[18]

The novel's main representative of Whig attitudes illustrates another kind of institutional thinking. Lord Fawn is a dull if well-meaning administrator. The institution he stands for is the aristocracy, which managed to hang on to power by diplomacy and default during the nineteenth century. Trollope presents Lord Fawn's characteristic way of thinking as he agonises over the question of marriage:

> And yet what was such a one as he to do? It was of course necessary for the maintenance of the very constitution of his country that there should be future Lord Fawns. There could be no future Lord Fawns unless he married; – and how could he marry without money? 'A peasant can marry whom he pleases,' said Lord Fawn, pressing his hand to his brow, and dropping one flap of his coat, as he thought of his own high and perilous destiny, standing with his back to the fireplace, while a huge pile of letters lay there before him waiting to be signed. (101)

The juxtaposition of 'high and perilous destiny' with Fawn's actual task of signing letters is as telling as his ridiculous self-pity in comparing himself to his own disadvantage with a peasant. The maintenance of the *status quo* may require that such men as Lord Fawn be under-secretaries, but the passage doesn't suggest it's for the good of the country.

Yet Trollope only prompts that recognition after first making Lord Fawn's dilemma seem natural and inescapable. He is an Irish peer, whose estate doesn't bring in what he thinks it should and he supports his mother, several unmarried sisters, and the family house:

> Being a poor man, filling a place fit only for rich men, he had been driven to think of money, and had become self-denying and parsimonious, – perhaps we may say hungry and close-fisted. Such a condition of character is the natural consequence of such a position. There is, probably, no man who becomes naturally so hard in regard to money as he who is bound to live among rich men, who is not rich himself, and who is yet honest. (74)

This is a view of Lord Fawn's life from the standpoint of conventional wisdom. But in his case conventional wisdom turns out to resemble the hollowed-out coconuts used to catch monkeys.[19] The monkey can no more unclasp his grip on the bait in order to release his hand from the coconut than Fawn can relinquish the assumption that his position calls for a way of life which is really beyond his means. Once again Trollope suggests how gradually a person may become habituated to a manner of thinking that becomes increasingly dubious: 'Such a man almost naturally looks to marriage as an assistance in the dreary fight. It soon becomes clear to him that he cannot marry without money, and he learns to think that heiresses have been invented exactly to suit his case' (75). So it is that by slow degrees Fawn brings himself to the absurdity of proposing to Lizzie Eustace, whom he doesn't know, with whom he has nothing in common, and whose only attraction is her social position and her money. Trollope's relaxed, easy-paced narrative is perfect for conveying the slow blurrings of rationalisation, the steady deliquescence of principle, under the influence of what everyone says or does. To use one of his own repeated words, it all seems so natural – until the meaning of what's been taken for granted stands revealed in its results.

Lord Fawn's difficulties are presented as typical: 'Such a condition of character', 'such a position', 'such a man'. The same is true of Frank Greystock, who is described as belonging to 'a middle class of men . . . who literally cannot marry for love, because their earnings will do no more than support themselves' (681). That word 'literally' conceals another coconut trap, another case of value rigidity. The very next sentence indicates that Greystock should be able to support a wife and family, and he finally marries Lucy Morris without expecting to starve. Ironically, he bears out his own argument earlier that what keeps men from marrying isn't the prospect of poverty but of what passes for poverty in the world (222). As so often in Trollope, though, a person won't necessarily act on what he thinks or knows, and Greystock's conversation with his friend about marriage tails off into facetiousness and inconsequence. The examples of Greystock and Fawn illustrate that Trollope's notion of a type is very different from the definition by Lukács which I have quoted. It can't be said that in them 'all the humanly and socially essential determinants are present on their highest level of development'.[20] On the contrary, Trollope places both as pretty average specimens. His sense of the type depends on social and economic position but also, and crucially, on the character's acceptance of the way of life conventionally associated with his social and economic position. In other words, the typical in Trollope is bound up with the institutional. His characters rarely become larger than life because they remain, on the whole, willing prisoners of institutional thinking. It is Trollope's ability to explore that kind of thinking, at the level of its own practice, and to display what it entails, that constitutes his own kind of realism.

Those who suffer most from conventional thinking are women. Frank Greystock self-confidently rejects the argument that women are disadvantaged in marriage because they are more numerous than men: 'As one of the legislators of the country I am prepared to state that statistics are always false' (221). But the novel unobtrusively proves him wrong in its bleak demonstration of what life is like for the spinster Miss Macnulty, dependent on the whims of Lizzie Eustace or the harshness of Lady Linlithgow. Miss Macnulty's fate shows the life Lucy Morris can expect if Greystock deserts her, but it's arguable whether remaining unmarried within one's own family is much better. Trollope marks with uncomfortable precision the difference in status conferred by marriage when Lady Fawn has to hear her married daughter denounce Lizzie Eustace, and then prevent her unmarried daughter from visiting Lizzie with her. Augusta Fawn is naturally disappointed: 'As, however, her position was that of a girl, she was bound to be obedient, – though over thirty years old, – and she obeyed' (82). The same episode also demonstrates the vexations of a widow's position. Lady Fawn has to defer both to her only son and to her only married daughter, while looking after the seven girls who remain unmarried. Even Lady Linlithgow, a much sterner figure, keeps her best bedroom for the exclusive use of her son although he only spends five nights in town each year (4). In detail after detail Trollope conveys how such people – and especially how such women – are ruled by the assumptions that their class entails upon them. Lady Linlithgow is a striking example in her dogged insistence on performing duties in

which, outside their due execution, she has no belief whatever.

Again, it's above all their own acceptance of what the
ideology of their class prescribes that limits these characters.
Lizzie Eustace, another widow, works on the assumption that 'a
woman by herself in the world can do nothing, and that an
unmarried woman's strength lies only in the expectation that
she may soon be married' (714). It follows that she will devote
herself to securing the most advantageous match possible, using
the diamonds as a badge of wealth and a magnifier of beauty, as
she had done with the jewels allowed to her by Mr. Benjamin so
that she could ensnare Sir Florian Eustace. The enterprise fails
not through any unsoundness in itself, but in her title to the
diamonds. Lizzie is no Becky Sharp but an innocent who tries to
succeed in society with only a superficial knowledge of the rules
of the game. It's the men who hold all the cards, as appears from
the genial but cynical talk in which Lizzie's brother-in-law asks
Frank Greystock to take the embarrassment off his hands by
marrying her: 'She's worth nearly £5000 a year as long as she
lives, and I really don't think that she's much amiss' (35). In such
a setting it's scarcely surprising that Lady Glencora Palliser
should attempt to defend Lizzie from 'a feeling that any woman
in society who was capable of doing anything extraordinary
ought to be defended' (423).

But Lady Glencora can no more think beyond this half-
articulate protest than any other woman in the novel. The only
instance of outright rebellion is Lucinda Roanoke's refusal at
the last moment to go through with her marriage. This,
however, isn't at all a principled or a reasoned act, but
instinctive repulsion from the sadist chosen for her as a good
match. What makes the incident all the more odd is that Mrs.
Carbuncle, who has arranged the marriage, knows the would-
be husband's character, and yet believes she has her niece's
interests at heart. She has nothing to gain from the marriage for
herself except the satisfaction of having 'married the girl who
was in her charge' (636). Her only other discoverable motive is
an obscure wish to enlist Lucinda in the melancholy regiment of
married women: 'Had not other girls done the same thing, and
lived through it all, and become fat, indifferent, and fond of the
world? It is only the first step that signifies' (627). Trollope

catches here the note of weary acceptance in this sharp but undemonstrative vignette of how it's possible to enter and gradually adapt to a life of tedium and unfulfilment. There's even a wish on Mrs. Carbuncle's part that her niece be subdued to the same dissatisfaction she herself has had to endure: 'Mrs. Carbuncle hardened her heart by remembering that her own married life had not been peculiarly happy' (628). As in *The Claverings*, it's perversely apt that a woman who has had to school herself to accept disadvantage should require that others too should submit.

One central question the novel raises is whether it's possible to break out of such conventional thinking, especially when it produces impasse, unhappiness or inequity. It's a question proposed in the story of Lucy Morris, who is doubly disadvantaged as a woman and as an orphan with education but no money. Lucy's penalty for these deficiencies is that she has to remain almost totally passive in relation to the man who offers what appears to be her only chance of fulfilment. All she can do is to wait and see whether he will return and marry her. When she writes a letter to bring him as gently as she can to a decision, she ends by burning it. This isn't because she's shy or submissive by nature, but because she feels that nothing she can say or do can alter the quality of his commitment to her. On that alone she depends, and if she so depends wrongly she will take the consequences. Where she can and does assert herself is in her relations with her employers. She stands up to the termagant Lady Linlithgow and earns her respect. Most of all, she refuses to be browbeaten by Lord Fawn and in so refusing calls in question one of the rules by which her class lives. The rule is that 'under no circumstances could a lady be justified in telling a gentleman that he had spoken an untruth' (245), and it applies with special force to Lucy as an inferior. To lie is defined as ungentlemanly, so no gentleman can bear to be accused of lying. As in Trollope at his best, a trivial incident shakes into visibility a whole network of practices and entailments which are normally assumed in behaviour. For the very rule by which Lucy is wrong to speak out against Lord Fawn permits Lizzie Eustace all the freedom of her unsystematic dishonesty. The solicitor employed to recover the diamonds is simply unable to deny a statement he knows to be false when Lizzie claims that her husband gave her the necklace, and that they were within his disposal (149).

What this might lead to is a recognition that the gentlemanly code, which determines what is unsayable or unthinkable, is itself responsible for much pretence and deception. The point is glanced at repeatedly in all the euphemisms that offer to disarm the terrible accusation of lying – from 'untruth' (discussed by the narrator at the beginning of Chapter 29), to so soothing a phrase as 'incorrect versions' (617). But Trollope, explicitly at least, stays within the bounds of the thinkable. He pinpoints the hypocrisy which the gentlemanly code is allowed to generate, without questioning whether the code is itself wholly valid. So too with conventional wisdom. Trollope, who had read Charlotte Brontë's *Villette* (*Autobiography*, 217–18), permits no suggestion that Lucy might have imagined another life for herself than that of a wife and mother or that of companion or governess. He stays within the bounds of what I have called normal consciousness. The limitations of such an approach emerge clearly when *The Eustace Diamonds* is compared not only with *Villette* but with *Middlemarch*, a novel which is its almost exact contemporary. George Eliot's characters have much more to tell about human and social possibility, because her imagination can push to the limits of normal consciousness, though even she doesn't quite get beyond them (was there no chance for Dorothea to find fulfilment outside marriage?). The questions that Dorothea, Lydgate, and even Casaubon ask themselves go deeper than anything that occurs to people in Trollope: not 'How do I maintain myself in the world with integrity?', but 'What should be my object in life?', or 'What is it in life that is absolute and fundamental?'. Trollope's narrower scope defines him as the lesser novelist. But although he doesn't, on the whole, ask radical questions about what it means to live in the world he portrays, he does at his best prompt such questions. This I've tried to demonstrate, but as a final test the strengths and limitations of his temper may be gauged from his attitude to the diamonds of the novel's title.

Trollope's treatment of the diamonds has often been admired. Cockshut suggests that it was a satirical masterstroke to reveal, through the opinion of Mr. Dove the legal expert, that the jewels which had excited controversy and crime were 'fictitious' property which was best 'annihilated' (651).[21] This sounds like a kind of ironic nihilism in which, Cockshut implies, Trollope suddenly lays bare the baselessness of his characters' behaviour. But in this part of his story Trollope is much more straightforward, even obvious. Not everyone is bemused by the diamonds, least of all Lucy Morris. She, like the novelist, commands a position from which what the diamonds stand for can be seen as a sham. Trollope telegraphs the point with typical bluntness in comparing Lucy's real tears, more than once, to diamonds (24, 174). If diamonds are unreal compared to unaffected feeling, they are also 'fictitious' in the sense that their value depends not at all on what they can produce but on opinion and the use to be made of it. Diamonds are to real tears as they are to property – that is, land. In other words, the basis of Trollope's satire is none other than that in *The Way We Live Now* and the earlier *Struggles of Brown, Jones and Robinson*. It is the ideology of the landed estate, which we've also seen governing *Doctor Thorne* and *Orley Farm*, with its frank hostility to speculation. The diamonds, marks of distinction, ensure that Lizzie Eustace will be noticed. If she had taken more care, and had kept herself on the right side of notoriety, they would have raised her stock as surely as did the jewels which she borrowed to attract Sir Florian. Trollope's plain contention is that this is fraud, and that the scandalous interest the diamonds generate only reveals shallowness. He underlines their actual emptiness not only by having the thieves first steal an empty box, but by having the necklace broken up at the end – to use Mr. Dove's word, 'annihilated'.

It is partly on such grounds as these that Edwards has argued that *The Eustace Diamonds* is an attack on 'sensationalism as a habit of mind, the habit of mind, seemingly, of a whole society'. But persuasive as this view is, it's only a part of the truth. Edwards comes near to contradicting himself when he says that the novel 'is at once sensational in itself and highly critical of sensationalism'.[22] How could it be both? The only way to sustain the point is to stretch the meaning of the term, as Edwards does. However, though Trollope doesn't entirely disdain a certain kind of suspense, his novel can hardly be described as sensational. The plot is very ordinary, concerned as it is, like Thackeray's plot in *Vanity Fair*, with the attempts of two young ladies of very

different backgrounds and temperaments to establish themselves in life, through marriage. In the working out of this plot,
the diamonds become first an embarrassment, then an anxiety,
and finally an irrelevance. Just as Trollope emphasises that
their social value is empty and arbitrary, so he undermines their
value in his fiction. Their role is far from the power and mystery
of Wilkie Collins' Moonstone. They are passive, inert, interesting
not in themselves but only as reflectors of social attitudes and
behaviour. Yet what the novel has to show on this explicit level
of its meaning is much less telling than what it reveals in its
asides, its subtle account of ordinary assumptions and their
entailments. It's as if Trollope constructed a well-made novel on
a firm central theme – the relations between the plots could
hardly be clearer, the moral message scarcely less direct – but in
doing so freed himself for more tentative, exploratory questioning. Again the quiet, unofficial self proves a better guide than
the conscious, directing moralist.

No character in *The Eustace Diamonds* is capable of thinking
beyond conventional assumptions. Even the most intelligent
and spirited person among them, Lucy Morris, is confined to
passivity not just by economic dependence but by a code which
is as much social as it is moral. Lucy's outburst against Lord
Fawn implicitly calls in question both the double standard and
the code of the gentleman. But it's quite spontaneous, and it
doesn't, for her, reach beyond its occasion. Its lack of connexion
with her quiet tolerance of Frank Greystock's much greater
unfairness is ironic and telling. That Lucy accepts Greystock
wholeheartedly after he has almost betrayed her underlines her
acquiescence in the very standards that have permitted his
misbehaviour.

But in *Mr. Scarborough's Family*, a novel written at the end of
his life and published posthumously, Trollope does seem to
present a character who enjoys the power of thinking beyond
normal consciousness. Mr. Scarborough is like other central
figures in Trollope, such as Alice Vavasor in *Can You Forgive
Her?*, Josiah Crawley in *The Last Chronicle*, or Louis Trevelyan
in *He Knew He Was Right*, in his eccentricity, his refusal to
conform to convention. What distinguishes him is that he gains
from the novel an authority denied to the others. He is no typical

figure in the way that Harry Clavering or Frank Greystock are, enmeshed in and accepting the ways of the world. The novel contains such a character in Harry Annesley, but Mr. Scarborough's point of view unsettles any ready identification with a standard young gentleman's complacent certainties. More than that, Mr. Scarborough is set against a model of a social world which even for Trollope is highly elaborate. The novel's large cast of characters and complicated sub-plots have found few defenders at a time when claiming structural coherence for the longest of Trollope's novels has become, as I have said, commonplace.[23] Whether or not all of the subordinate matter can be justified, its extensiveness allows for the representation of those expectations and presuppositions that make up the normal, working conventions of Mr. Scarborough's world. It is against that background that he requires to be measured. Like other novels by Trollope, *Mr. Scarborough's Family* concerns itself not with the best that is thought and said in the world, but with what is ordinarily thought and said and done. But for once this isn't an exclusive interest. The novel's special value is largely that it permits an extraordinary figure to put so much of the ordinary in question.

This is clear from a change in Trollope's intentions about Mr. Scarborough. The novel's manuscript shows that he initially set out to present Mr. Sandover (as Mr. Scarborough was at first called) in a strictly qualified light.[24] For instance, the sentence 'He had lived with his wife, off and on as people say' was followed in the manuscript by a sentence later deleted: 'and had done the same with other people's wives' (1.4/3). A few pages later another cancelled passage, concerning Mr. Scarborough's feelings for his niece, states categorically: 'Of anything like true love his heart was incapable. He was a goodnatured, brave, but utterly selfish man, as to whom the ultimate fate in life of this poor girl was a matter of utter indifference.' This Trollope revised as follows, to reverse completely the emphasis: 'And of true love for such a girl his heart was quite capable. He was a goodnatured, fearless, but not a selfish man, to whom the fate in life of this poor girl was a matter of real concern' (1.18/15). Again, Trollope first wrote that the fraud by which Mr. Scarborough disinherits his elder son 'had taken place in the first instance almost from accident, the false fact of Mr. Sandover's marriage having been in the first instance received in England, and then the true fact of the subsequent marriage having been at the moment concealed' (I.13/11). These lines, which he later deleted, would have suggested a self-serving opportunist. But the impression Trollope chose to create was of an eccentric principle and benevolence, clear-sighted and essentially honest to itself. Even at a later stage in the manuscript, when his view of the character had matured, he cancelled another passage which might have produced an unfavourable impression, when Mr. Scarborough casts doubt on the doctrine of the Trinity (6.8/194). Trollope enlists sympathy and respect for his hero by presenting his bravery and good humour in the face of serious illness and surgery. Mr. Scarborough's doctor, who despite his disapproval for the old man's schemes comes to admire and even love him, both represents and guides the reader's viewpoint. The manuscript revisions unmistakably work in the same direction. They show that Trollope wasn't disposed, after considering the matter carefully, to permit his readers any direct or easy challenge to this remarkable figure. Although Peter K. Garrett has convincingly argued that Trollope often distances his central characters from his readers' sympathies,[25] Mr. Scarborough seems an exception.

This is the more striking in that by normal standards Mr. Scarborough's behaviour is scandalous. He refuses to observe the codes of the three institutions, each linked with the others, by which landed society perpetuates itself; marriage, entail and primogeniture. What connects these institutions is the need to hand down property securely, and what shocks everyone about Mr. Scarborough's way of doing this is its utter and unabashed pragmatism. Marriage has no sanctity for him, it is simply 'a mode of enabling men and women to live together comfortably' (5), all the more convenient because it gives him a way to dispose of his property as he prefers. He gets round the strict entail on his estate, which requires inheritance according to primogeniture, by marrying his wife twice, secretly and abroad. He may then suppress the first marriage if he decides that his elder son should not be his heir, or publish it to confirm him as heir or to reinstate him. Events bring him to the outrageous performance of both acts. When Mountjoy, his elder son, incurs debts that threaten the whole property, Mr. Scarborough disinherits him by declaring him illegitimate. Then, when the moneylenders have been paid their bare capital, without any of the exorbitant interest they would have demanded from Mountjoy as heir, Mr. Scarborough rehabilitates him, having discovered in the meantime his younger son's worthlessness. These manoeuvres, which are properly Machiavellian in setting ends over means consistently, depend on Mr. Scarborough's violation of another convention; that no gentleman is supposed ever to tell lies. He is able to turn his society's written and unwritten rules to his own ends by virtue of the unthinking rigidity with which others observe them.

This is borne out again and again. First, Mr. Scarborough depends for the success of his schemes upon his highminded lawyer, Grey. What makes Grey so suitable isn't just his reputation, but the fact that he himself cannot believe that a gentleman such as Mr. Scarborough could perpetrate what appears to him as a series of moral and legal atrocities. Secondly, Mr. Scarborough depends on the acquiescence of his younger son, Augustus, to the paying off of Mountjoy's creditors. This he obtains partly through Augustus' suspiciousness, which won't quite allow him to believe that he could receive the estate unencumbered. More important, though, is Augustus' dependence on the letter of the law for guaranteeing his claim to the estate; he simply can't imagine that Mountjoy could be reinstated. Thirdly, Mr. Scarborough needs the creditors' agreement. He gets it through his success with Grey and Augustus, through the moneylenders' natural wish to regain at least their capital, and through both law and public opinion which allow no redress for a kind of speculation which finds little sympathy. To revert to the analogy of the monkey trap, Mr. Scarborough wins by the inability of his dupes to think their way out of all that they assume unnecessarily.

Trollope gives many examples in the novel of thinking limited by its own assumptions. The moneylenders advance £40,000 to the irresponsible Mountjoy at 250 per cent interest, on the understanding that his father's awaited death will enable him to pay up. Yet, cherishing their own code of conduct, they are scandalised when the old man outwits them: 'It was pleasant to see how these commercial gentleman, all engaged in the natural course of trade, expressed their violent indignation, not so much

as to their personal losses, but at the commercial dishonesty
generally of which the Scarboroughs, father and son, had been
and were about to be guilty' (584–5). The moneylenders are so
habituated to their own practices that they can't see what's
wrong with them. It isn't that they're quite without ethics, as
one of their number draws the line at dealing with a gentleman
who is drunk. Nor does Trollope suggest that their attachment
to a code is mere protective rationalisation – within its own
terms, it is sincere. This is, in other words, a further case of
institutional thinking. But he shows himself much less perceptive, much more subject to the assumptions of his class, in
representing the moneylenders as stereotype Jews. One of them
in particular, Samuel Hart, is an offensive caricature (see
especially Chapter 11). Trollope's own experience of having to
pay over £200 for an original bill of £12 plus £4 in cash must
account for some of his acrimony – though he doesn't suggest
that his persecutor was a Jew (*Autobiography*, 41–2).

The professional gamblers who fleece Mountjoy also abide by
their own peculiar and limited code. Captain Vignolles finds
that by obeying certain little rules – such as knowing his game
thoroughly, remembering every card, never giving himself
away or flustering himself with drink – he can win almost as
consistently, and much more safely, than he could by cheating.
When Mountjoy, having lost over £200, is reduced to offering
him a promissory note, the Captain is as righteously indignant
as a justly aggrieved public servant:

> To him it was a fact that he had been cruelly used in having
> such a bit of paper thrust upon him instead of being paid by a
> cheque which on the morning would be honoured. And as he
> thought of his own career; his ready-money payments; his
> obedience to certain rules of the game, – rules, I mean,
> against cheating; – as he thought of his hands, which in his
> own estimation were beautifully clean; his diligence in his
> profession, which to him was honourable; his hard work; his
> late hours; his devotion to a task which was often tedious;
> his many periods of heartrending loss, which when they
> occurred would drive him nearly mad; his small customary
> gains; his inability to put by anything for old age; of the
> narrow edge by which he himself was occasionally divided

from defalcation, he spoke to himself of himself as of an honest hard-working professional man upon whom the world was peculiarly hard. (407–08)

What is unusual here is the degree of inwardness allowed by Trollope's irony. There's nothing attractive about Vignolles or his life, but Trollope shows how the gambler has adapted himself so thoroughly to the rules by which he survives that only they have importance. The comparison to a hard-working professional man is subversively right, for it's also characteristic of the official mind to attend more to the rules of the game than to what the game is played for. Trollope, in part despite and in part because he had been a civil servant, could see this; and he could also see how the man could not only justify but respect himself. Yet his own standards were very different, as appears from the autobiographical passage in which he tells how he felt dishonest because he had enjoyed the facilities at Monte Carlo without permitting himself to gamble (95–7).

The novel, then, concerns itself with the rules by which people live, the conflicts between different codes and within individual codes, and the difficult task of adjusting relations between convention, feeling and interest. Mr. Scarborough's role isn't only to set the plot in motion, though he also influences the principal sub-plot both directly and indirectly. More important, he calls in question the ways accepted by almost everyone unthinkingly. To him law, like religion, is an absurdity:

It consisted of a perplexed entanglement of rules got together so that the few might live in comfort at the expense of the many. Robbery, if you could get to the bottom of it, was bad, as was all violence; but taxation was robbery, rent was robbery, prices fixed according to the desire of the seller and not in obedience to justice, were robbery. (194)

What makes these views interesting is Mr. Scarborough's recognition that law is essentially the bulwark of property. This the novel shows again and again, despite the belief expressed by the lawyer Grey and his daughter that there's such a thing as abstract honesty, and that law may be reconciled with justice. In one part of his mind Trollope shared such convictions, yet he couldn't prevent himself from taking that other, unofficial view put by his hero. This comes out in his presentation of the lawyer. Grey's sense of 'abstract honesty' (141) amounts to little more than an belief in the value of tradition. His motto is '*Stare super vias antiquas*' (153), whether refusing to alter his nominal dinner-hour to a time which would fit his habits, or to accommodate his professional code to changing social practices. But not even Grey is as strict as his daughter, and this shows how little abstract his honesty really is. Dolly Grey opposes all departures from truth whatever, even when he advises a client to ask for a more favourable marriage settlement than he means to accept in order to counter the inflated demands of the lady's solicitors. This is a typically Trollopian dilemma. In tolerating accepted professional practice Grey is compromising with principle, but principle as firm as his daughter's would prevent him from practising altogether. Before the end of the novel he has decided to retire, and this is as much because he feels his profession is losing its integrity as it is because of his sense of injury over the Scarborough case.

The novel's deep preoccupation with law, especially property law, also motivates its main sub-plot. Here there are two central figures. One is a superannuated squire, Peter Prosper, the other Harry Annesley, his nephew and heir. Annesley resembles his predecessor in *The Claverings* in several ways beyond sharing the same first name: both are clergymen's sons, court girls called Florence, hold Cambridge fellowships, and are generally well-advantaged – except that the position of both is at issue. In Annesley's case this is because he seems to his stuffy, stiff-necked uncle to show too little respect. A telling metaphor expresses what is at the basis of this relationship when Annesley's father enlightens him that 'there was a contract understood, if not made. . . . That you should be to him as a son' (220–1). It is because, as Annesley expresses it to himself, 'he had declined to accept his share of the contract' (234) that he is threatened with disinheritance. This is a pretty explicit way of noting what underpins the fabric of gentility: property follows deference. The point is emphasised in the deliberately crude episode which crushes Prosper's plan to oust his nephew. Prosper has to capitulate because the wife he proposes to solve his problem of childlessness is robustly under-bred and refuses to take his self-importance seriously. More galling still, Prosper in pursuit of his

scheme is led to compromise his own sense of being a gentleman.
Miss Thoroughbung pushes directly to those economic facts of life
that the gentlemanly code prefers to censor. 'You know about my
property?', she asks – and he evasively denies it: 'He was a
gentleman, whereas Miss Thoroughbung was hardly a lady.
Matter of consideration her money of course had been. How
should he not consider it?' (247). Gentlemen have lawyers to do
their bargaining for them, but in observing this item of the code
Prosper infringes that other item that requires honesty and
straightforwardness. Trollope reminds us a few pages afterwards
that according to the servants, infallible judges in such matters,
Prosper really is a gentleman, and Miss Thoroughbung really
isn't quite a lady (252). This reinforces the arbitrariness of the
distinction as well as its strength, because humanly Prosper is a
rather inconsiderable figure. There's a more positive note in
Grey's point that Prosper is implicitly a gentleman because he
'wants nothing but what is or ought to be his own' (259), until,
that is, one thinks what 'his own' might mean, a fact which the
novel doesn't neglect in showing the negotiations between the
parties. We even find that it would have been 'gentlemanlike'
for Prosper to have demanded Miss Thoroughbung's whole
income, leaving her little or no jointure (425); what isn't
gentlemanly is prevaricating over trifles in order to get out of a
marriage which he increasingly finds unthinkable. Finally,
Prosper is tempted to offer money in reparation, but that too 'he
thought would not be gentlemanlike' (462), and the lady lets
him off the hook at last with a dose of humiliation.

   This sustained quizzical exhibition of what the code of the
gentleman can mean is central to Trollope's kind of realism, and
bears witness to the curiously abstract quality of his imagination.
Realistic but abstract – the link sounds contradictory. What
justifies it is the thoroughness with which Trollope reflects what
codes of conduct involve in operation, a thoroughness not only
in giving human and social embodiment to the conflicts that are
generated, but also in envisaging a range of applications for the
rules in each case. Trollope's world is after all comparatively
insubstantial. It shows nothing like the respect for material fact
with which Balzac appalled and fascinated Henry James.[26]
Instead Trollope focuses almost exclusively on interpersonal
relations. There is little sense of an individual's physical, let

alone visceral, feelings, and almost no sense of relationship with the natural world – except in a few transparently allegorical scenes.[27] Even the phrase 'interpersonal relations' is possibly misleading, because Trollope is interested not just in the immediate give-and-take (sometimes give-or-take) of social encounters; he's more deeply preoccupied with the assumptions that inform those encounters, ranging from an individual's awareness of what others are thinking to his or her degree of consciousness about the rules that guide behaviour. But getting the rules and their applications right would hardly be enough to qualify Trollope as a realist. For one thing, it's not simply a question of rules but of the ideology implied by them – as in the code of the gentleman. To this deeper level, as we have seen, Trollope also penetrates. Secondly, and crucially, Trollope's sense of the rules, of the ideology, isn't one of inertia and passive acceptance. Through the intricate patterns of his stories he allows, and in his later work perhaps necessitates, a critical appraisal. The sociologist, J. A. Banks, identifies a vital part of the novelist's achievement when he observes that Trollope sometimes 'set out consciously to get his readers to stand back and look with him at the norms and to consider whether there was any justification for them save their very existence'.[28]

Such a question is repeatedly raised in *Mr. Scarborough's Family*. To take a further example, Trollope emphasises the moral absurdity that Mountjoy Scarborough is banned from his club not because he is suspected of having conspired to defraud his creditors, but because he fails to pay a gambling debt (30). A gentleman may apparently cheat moneylenders, but not his gaming partners. Again, Harry Annesley gets into trouble because he is led into a defensive lie by Augustus Scarborough. The lie can be justified according to the ways of the world, though Harry prefers the gentler term 'untruth' (231). But anyone with a grievance against Harry can call this ungentlemanly and repudiate him – as his uncle Prosper tries to do, and also the relatives of the girl he wants to marry. What sort of a norm is it whose rigidity leads to such a distortion? Conversely, one of Mr. Scarborough's merits is an almost defiant straightforwardness about his actions once performed. He, alone of all the characters, perhaps of all people in Trollope, acknowledges in so many words that he has lied. He says to Harry Annesley:

'You haven't that kind of ingenuity which enables a man to tell a lie and stick to it. I have. It's a very great gift, if a man be enabled to restrain his appetite for lying' (73). This admission contrasts strongly with Annesley's evasiveness a moment before in saying he knows nothing of Mountjoy – he wants, naturally enough, to keep quiet about having knocked Mountjoy down in defending himself. Yet the novel is to show that, outrageously, Mr. Scarborough is himself lying when he declares that he has lied about Mountjoy, whom he will later prove legitimate after all. No wonder Annesley calls Mr. Scarborough 'the meanest fellow I ever met' (554). Yet this reflects more on speaker than subject, for it's a stock response from a stuffed-shirt hero about a man whose motives and peculiar morality he is too limited to grasp. Not only is Mr. Scarborough a generous man, as his own actions to Annesley show. He is also a man of good feeling, who 'hated most those suspected by him of mean or dirty conduct' (195). Mr. Scarborough may spend his life devising schemes for defeating the laws of property, but he can't be called grasping or crooked, however unconventional his own kind of honesty.

The main general code of behaviour explored by this novel is that of the gentleman; the main specific codes are those of family obligation (especially concerning inheritance) and courtship. In addition there are subsidiary codes, such as those of money-lending and gambling. Trollope's multiple plot has often been criticised for its apparent over-elaborateness and redundancy, as I have said. Yet by setting up repeated similarities and differences in circumstances and conduct, it subtly demonstrates the ritual character of much that passes for ordinary behaviour. A case in point is how Dolly Grey and her father treat their feckless relatives. Mr. Grey has undertaken to support his sister and her family, although the Carrolls have no formal claims on him, and are offensive both to him and his daughter. In principle this is admirable, in practice somewhat different. For the work of actually helping the Carrolls falls on Dolly, who bleakly persists against the grain in what she assumes to be a duty. Her other motive is respect for her father's wishes, but this is compromised by her loyalty to him in the face of what he sees as the Carrolls' ingratitude and greed. It's not surprising that she should be unable to hide her resentment when an obligation she takes for granted forces her to look after people she can only regard with contempt. Though she gestures towards 'what Christianity demands' (167), charity for her has become virtually emptied of meaning. The Greys' obligations to the Carrolls compare and contrast with Prosper's obligations to his nephew and Mr. Scarborough's to his sons. At an even further remove is the relation between Harry Annesley's fiancée, Florence Mountjoy, and her aunt. Florence is taken to stay with her uncle in Brussels to get her away from Annesley, but again responsibility falls on the woman. Lady Mountjoy's duty is to persuade Florence into marrying someone who might be thought more suitable. She does all she overbearingly can, yet she can only contradict herself in replying to the question whether it matters to her at all who her sister-in-law's daughter marries (291). Trollope's multiple plot runs the gamut of family obligations from the near to the distant, showing their greater or lesser dependence on codes of behaviour and convention.

Similarly with courtship. A series of marriage proposals and negotiations threads in and out of the novel's action. Partly, as with Prosper and Miss Thoroughbung, it is questions of property and class that are emphasised: for instance in the proposals of Grey's partner, Barry, to Dolly Grey, and in Juniper's to Amelia Carroll. But Trollope is also interested in the elements of the courtship ritual as such, especially in the woman's enforced passivity. For one basic rule in the ritual is that a woman has no right to refuse to listen to a man's addresses, however repugnant to her personally, so long as he has leave to approach her. In this way Florence Mountjoy has to submit to double proposals from a trio of unwelcome suitors; and Dolly Grey, inveterate spinster, has to hear out her father's partner. Both women are in effect confined by a web of custom and interest. Florence has long been designed for Mountjoy, who at the time of his proposal has the richest of prospects; Hugh Anderson is well connected, and besides her uncle owes him money; and Dolly Grey's marriage to Barry would be almost a business arrangement. No wonder each rebels, and with increasing vehemence. The source of the woman's powerlessness in considerations of property and status stands out plainly. Yet the effect of the sustained parallels by which Trollope reinforces this point seems less a criticism of such behaviour for its callous manipulativeness, than a demonstration, through repetition, of its sheer formality. Though Grey has his daughter's welfare at heart, the convention of giving the suitor at least two chances takes precedence over her wishes.

To consider social life as directed by rules, the character of which is to a greater or lesser extent formal or arbitrary, is to treat it as a kind of game, and this is a basic metaphor of *Mr. Scarborough's Family*, as of other novels by Trollope. The metaphor occurs most explicitly in one of the foxhunting scenes which Trollope, who loved the sport, so often worked into his fiction. Games, by definition, are self-justifying, having no end beyond themselves. It follows that the object of fox hunting is 'not so much to run a fox as to kill him in obedience to certain rules of the game' (264). The priority of the rules is demonstrated in the scene where two hunts fall into conflict over a single covert. Significantly, the source of conflict is again a question of property. The covert is part of one hunt's territory, but by convention it is open to the other hunt if led to it by a fox to which they have acquired a right by hunting it continuously. The point at issue is delicate, the whole matter is intrinsically trivial, yet it's only by luck that no blood is shed. Meanwhile the fox, which one might naïvely suppose to be the common enemy, is gone; he is of minor importance compared with the rules which each hunt thinks the other has violated.

The metaphor of the game is highly apt for a novel whose characters so often appear mentally or morally trapped by the institutions to which they belong and pay deference. Such institutions – like the laws about property, the code of the gentleman, or the conventions of courtship – are larger and more complex than the sport of fox hunting, but they also operate according to rules which tend to take over their initial practical aims. Some of the novel's characters themselves employ the game metaphor, but in different ways. Both Mr. Scarborough (199) and his son Augustus (186) describe the contest between them as a game, and the moneylender Hart speaks of his game with Mountjoy, which puts gambling in the shade (100). With Hart the word means no more than the cunning exercise of his profession; with Augustus no more than the sharp self-interest of a narrow legalism. Mr. Scarborough's sense of the game ranges more widely and more deeply. Only he can exploit the written and unwritten laws of the society in which he lives to reach what he considers to be a just end. Yet it's ironic, to say the least, that Mr. Scarborough finishes by playing the game on behalf of a person who will not only waste his whole estate, but waste it at cards through his 'apparent forgetfulness of all rules and ignorance of the peculiarities of the game he was playing' (406). In other words, Mr. Scarborough plays out his game for very little benefit. He knows before his death what will happen to his estate (477), for he has little hope of reforming his son. But he dies in apparent peace.

What this suggests is that playing the game has its own value, irrespective of the end achieved. Society is a kind of perpetual-motion machine which maintains its own equilibrium and minimises change. Just as Mr. Scarborough has to go back to 'the correct order of things' (522), so Prosper must 'reconcile himself to what the entail had done for him' (546), Mrs. Mountjoy and her family have to accept Florence's marriage, and Dolly Grey will stay with her father, continuing to help the Carrolls. All that has happened by the end is that Mr. Scarborough has died, Grey has retired, the moneylenders have been outwitted, and there have been three marriages. Things will muddle on much as they have done in the past, just as Sir Magnus Mountjoy, for all his incompetence, has always been found a diplomatic post by his friends (88–9). Customs tend to stick, not so much because they are shared as, paradoxically, because they are in a measure arbitrary. This is a point that arises from the Brussels episodes, where Trollope suggests how relative conventions may be by showing how difficult it is for foreigners to penetrate them. On the one hand there is a striking display of mind-reading between Sir Magnus Mountjoy, his butler and his wife in Chapter 32; while, on the other hand, Florence's Belgian suitor utterly fails to understand her reply to his proposal. Grascour, who 'spoke English so well that he would only be known to be a foreigner by the correctness of his language' (440), cannot grasp Florence's categorical rejection, whereas her countryman Hugh Anderson, whose speech is slangy and ungrammatical, has no difficulty whatever. Comprehension of language doesn't depend as much as might be expected on grammatical competence. However full his knowledge of linguistic rules, Grascour knows too little of the social rules that modify them, which can only come through prolonged familiarity with the society from within. The trouble is that familiarity usually means acceptance, and too often acceptance without thinking.

This isn't a charge that can be made good against Trollope, if only because it's the novelist who places before us the workings of convention. But the element of acceptance in Trollope's attitude is implied by the need to employ so neutral a phrase as 'places before us'. Trollope cannot be said to criticise the ways of the world; rather he offers them to us with ironic amusement as the fruits of his observation. We may use his observation to construct a critical perspective, but the novel's own tenor doesn't recommend it. Its own conventionality is sufficient token of this. *Mr. Scarborough's Family* is a standard Victorian three-decker, with intricate plots involving such routine topics as love and inheritance, filled out by a worldly-wise narrator and rounded off with an anodyne ending. However subversively the novel may glance at conventions of social behaviour, and with whatever skill it enlivens its own use of fictional conventions, the fact remains that the form itself is emphatically an established one, indeed almost outmoded at the time of publication (1883), and without the ability to change people's ways of seeing. Worse, parts of the novel read as though Trollope were only going through the motions. This accounts, I think, for the criticism attracted by the subordinate material.

I've tried to show the relevance of these episodes to the novel as a whole, and necessarily at some length as the links are complex. But it remains difficult to feel concern for Prosper and Miss Thoroughbung, for Florence Mountjoy's suitors, the Greys' family problems, or even for the well-being of Harry Annesley – that obligatory hero whom the novel can't take very seriously. There's a kind of dry distance in Trollope's relation to such characters. It isn't just that so much of the comedy they produce is uncomfortable, based in social embarrassment – witness Miss Thoroughbung and the Carrolls – it is also that the characters too often seem to function abstractly, either as average social or fictional types, or as carriers of the novel's themes.

There is more than a suspicion that Trollope is aware of this. One of the reasons for what I've described as the abstractness of *Mr. Scarborough's Family* is that the novel, as well as the society it represents, is treated in part as a game. In itself this is nothing new. Trollope is almost notorious for, as Henry James put it, 'reminding the reader that the story he was telling was only, after all, a make-believe'.[29] The difference is that in this case Trollope carries his self-reflexiveness as author much further. To begin with, the words 'tale' and 'story' occur well over a hundred times – we are reminded again and again that the term 'plot' has a double application. Characters are made to think in metaphors from drama and fiction, so that Augustus Scarborough, in telling the story of Mountjoy's encounter with Annesley, considers that 'there was no need to mention himself, – no necessity for such a character in making up the tragedy of that night' (117). Mr. Scarborough's plot is variously described as a 'farce' and as a 'romance', and Annesley tells Augustus that Mountjoy's career 'has been what the novel readers would call romantic' (43). Again, after Mr. Scarborough has claimed that Mountjoy is illegitimate, the creditors believe 'that the story was a fiction' (11); and finally, when Mountjoy is reinstated, Grey declares that Mr. Scarborough's 'present tale is a made-up fable' (519).

Trollope's repetition of metaphors from drama and story-telling calls the reader's attention to the fact that what he is reading is itself a 'fiction' or 'made-up fable'. And his own plot parallels that of its hero in its effect on the reader, who is just as ignorant as the people in the novel about what Mr. Scarborough will do next. There is a sense in which Trollope is just as unscrupulous as his hero in not telling the truth about Mountjoy's legitimacy, especially as this violates his boasted policy of 'full confidence' with his readers.[30] Like his hero, Trollope plays less than fair when he states quite explicitly that for Mr. Scarborough to reinstate Mountjoy 'would be impossible' (364). So, just as Mr. Scarborough's role in the novel is parodied by Prosper's, at the same time it parallels the author's role outside the novel. But this is a strange, almost self-destructive, playfulness. Edwards has argued that the Prosper sub-plot 'compromises the moral and emotional impact of the main plot'. I believe this is so, but that it may have been what Trollope meant – bearing in mind the novel's self-reflexiveness. Cockshut is probably nearer the mark when he observes: 'If the Scarborough story criticises society, the Prosper story criticises the criticisms. In one sense it is satire turned against the author himself.'[31]

The realism of *Mr. Scarborough's Family* does not, then, consist in any direct relation between Trollope's story and the world he lived in. As Bradford Booth suggested, the novel's sources are much less topical than literary, in the Jacobean drama that fascinated him (Booth instances, among other plays, Massinger's *A New Way to Pay Old Debts* and Jonson's *Volpone*) and in the stock eighteenth-century trio of good-natured patriarch, prodigal and hypocrite. (Edwards compares Mr. Scarborough's two sons to Tom Jones and Blifil; they might also be related to Charles and Joseph Surface in Sheridan's *School for Scandal*.[32]) What the novel does impressively reflect is the pressure of ideology in the sense I have defined – that of the codes and conventions by which people live – and this includes what might be called the ideology of novel writing. As a producer of fiction, Trollope had long found a series of formulae on which he could play almost innumerable variations. So practised had he become that he could write to order, turning out remarkably well-engineered fictions with production-line regularity. It's difficult not to link this way of writing with the persistent metaphor of the game. Beyond this, I would suggest that the metaphor represents Trollope's own sense of alienation from what he produced so mechanically. The game is always accepted on its own terms as worth playing. This means that Trollope always acquiesces, finally, in the given social system as in the practice of writing three-decker novels. Like his character Mountjoy, Trollope enjoyed too much the 'sense of his own equality with others' (401) in the society of the club, the world from which in earlier life he had been excluded. He said he loved fox hunting with an affection he could not himself 'fathom or understand' (*Autobiography*, 54), and this testifies to his need to belong. Yet, as well as sharing Mountjoy's unthinking need to participate, he had some of Mr. Scarborough's detachment about the institutions to which he belonged. The result is a novel that appraises those institutions ironically, wryly reflects upon its own conventions, and in the end offers a disenchanted affirmation. To go further would have required a framework other than that of the Victorian novel. But Trollope's presentation of normal consciousness, of institutional thinking, has its own merit. And there

is much to admire in the human warmth which seems his final
resource. Edwards perhaps makes too much of Mr. Scarborough's
good nature, if we allow for the effects of the old man's schemes
on those around him (notably on his sons and his lawyer). But
Mr. Scarborough's death takes place in a surprisingly gentle
atmosphere of respect and even love, the unchristian leaving the
world as peacefully as an Addison (568).

To stand back from *Mr. Scarborough's Family* is to confront a
paradox. The aim of the novel's plot, considered analytically, is
to prevent a gentleman's estate from being taken over by the
moneylenders. This design belongs to the prejudiced, Establishment Trollope: preserve the land from Jews and adventurers.
Yet that plot is worked through by undermining the very
institutions that secure landed property – marriage, entail and
primogeniture. At the end, a wastrel is to be allowed to gamble
the estate away rather than let a Jewish creditor become its
owner. It is a curiously equivocal conclusion, reflecting the
tension between the unofficial and the ideological in Trollope's
imagination.

Notes

Chapter 1

[1] See, for instance, Terry, R. C. (1977), *Anthony Trollope: The Artist in Hiding*, London, Macmillan; Totowa, New Jersey, Rowman and Littlefield; Tracy, R. C. (1978), *Trollope's Later Novels*, Berkeley, Los Angeles and London, University of California Press; Harvey, G. (1980), *The Art of Anthony Trollope*, London, Weidenfeld and Nicolson; New York, St. Martin's Press; and Hall, N. (ed.) (1980), *The Trollope Critics*, London, Macmillan; New York, Barnes and Noble.

[2] *Criticism and Ideology: A Study in Marxist Literary Theory* (1976), London, New Left Books; New York, Schocken Books, p. 181.

[3] See, for example, the remarks of R. H. Hutton and Henry James collected in Smalley, D. (ed.) (1969), *Trollope: The Critical Heritage*, London, Routledge & Kegan Paul; New York, Barnes and Noble. These on the whole are balanced estimates, like that in the best recent book on Trollope; Edwards, P. D., *Anthony Trollope: His Art and Scope*. Others dismiss Trollope as roundly as Eagleton does, for instance Leavis, F. R. (1948), *The Great Tradition*, London, Chatto & Windus, pp. 1-2, p. 21; Williams, R. (1970), *The English Novel: From Dickens to Lawrence*, London and New York, Oxford University Press, pp. 84-6; and Myers, W. (1971) 'George Eliot: Politics and Personality', in Lucas, J. (ed.), *Literature and Politics in the Nineteenth Century*, London, Methuen, pp. 105-07.

[4] *The Victorian Multiplot Novel: Studies in Dialogical Form* (New Haven, Connecticut, and London: Yale University Press, 1980), p. 184.

[5] Hall, N. J. (ed.) (1972), Oxford and New York, Oxford University Press. See Chapter 2, below. References to this work are given in parentheses in my text.

[6] Several such plans survive in the three volumes of Trollope's working papers in the Bodleian Library at Oxford, Ms. Don. c.9, c.10, c.10*.

[7] *Trollope: The Critical Heritage*, p. 543. James's essay was first published in the New York *Century Magazine*, n.s.4 (July 1883), 385-95.

[8] *Anthony Trollope: His Art and Scope*, pp. 108-09.

[9] See *An Autobiography*, pp. 205-06, and *Thackeray* (1879), London, Macmillan; New York, Harpers, pp. 184-91.

[10] Anthony Trollope, *Four Lectures*, Parrish, M. L. (ed.) (1938), London, Folcroft Press, p. 73; *North America*, 2 vols. (1862), London, Chapman & Hall, Dawsons of Pall Mall, 1968, vol. I, p, 325.

[11] Vol. I, p. 326. For Trollope's relationship with Kate Field, see Michael Sadleir, *Trollope: A Commentary*, especially pp. 218–22, 226–38, and 283–95.

[12] *Trollope's Palliser Novels: Theme and Pattern* (1979), London, Macmillan; New York, Oxford University Press, p. 174.

[13] See below, Chapter 7.

[14] Introduction to *Phineas Finn* (1972), Harmondsworth, Penguin Books, pp. 23–6.

[15] See especially Kincaid, J. R. (1977), *The Novels of Anthony Trollope*, Oxford and New York, Oxford University Press.

[16] See Lukács, G. (1962), *The Historical Novel*, trans. H. and S. Mitchell, London, Merlin Press, p. 54ff; and *Studies in European Realism*, trans Bone, E. (1972), London, Merlin Press, pp. 10–13.

[17] 'Alien Intruders: Trollope's vision of the Jew', *Jewish Chronicle Supplement*, 8 April 1966, p. vii.

[18] Tracy, R., *Trollope's Later Novels*, pp. 100–01, and Polhemus, R. M. (1968), *The Changing World of Anthony Trollope*, Berkeley and Los Angeles, University of California Press, pp. 128–9, 194–5. Polhemus cites Bradford A. Booth's discussion of *Nina Balatka* in *Anthony Trollope: Aspects of His Life and Art* (1958), Bloomington, Indiana University Press; London, Edward Hulton, pp. 30–1. He is also the only Trollope critic to mention Rosenberg's study (see below).

[19] McMaster, J., *Trollope's Palliser Novels*, pp. 103–28, and Harvey, G., *The Art of Anthony Trollope*, pp. 33–7, 153–9.

[20] *Anthony Trollope: The Artist in Hiding*, p. 4. The quotation, which is hardly conclusive evidence, is from *South Africa*, 2 vols. (1878), London, Chapman & Hall, Dawsons of Pall Mall, 1968, vol.I, p. 4.

[21] *From Shylock to Svengali: Jewish Stereotypes in English Fiction* (1960), Stanford, California, Stanford University Press; London, Peter Owen, 1961.

[22] *Ibid.*, p. 362. As Rosenberg indicates, Trollope's plan is reproduced in Sadleir's *Commentary*, pp. 426–8.

[23] See Edwards, P. D., *Anthony Trollope: His Art and Scope*, pp. 182–9.

[24] See Edwards, p. 208. There is a selection of contemporary reviews in *Trollope: The Critical Heritage*, pp. 394–416.

[25] *Autobiography*, pp. 90–4; *Letters*, p. 100, 1 January 1862, and pp. 500–01, undated.

[26] Sadleir, *Commentary*, p. 206, refers the story to the memoirs of Yates (1884), *Edmund Yates: his recollections and experiences*, London, Bentley; Terry, R. C., *Artist in Hiding*, p. 265, refers it to Sir Algernon West, *Contemporary Portraits* (1920), London, T. Fisher Unwin.

[27] *Anthony Trollope: His Art and Scope*, pp. 9–56.

[28] See especially Terry, *Artist in Hiding*, and Kincaid, *The Novels of Anthony Trollope, passim*.

Chapter 2

[1] *Victorian Novelists and Publishers* (1976) London, Athlone Press, pp. 44–9, 133–51.

² See Edwards, R. D. and Williams, T. D. (eds.) (1956), *The Great Famine: Studies in Irish History 1845–52*, Dublin, Browne and Nolan; New York, New York University Press, 1957); and Woodham-Smith, C. B. (1962), *The Great Hunger: Ireland, 1845–9*, London: Hamish Hamilton; New York, Harper and Row, 1963.

³ Clark, J. W. (1975) *The Language and Style of Anthony Trollope*, London: André Deutsch; New York, Academic Press, pp. 100–18.

⁴ See Terry, R. C. (1972), 'Three Lost Chapters of Trollope's First Novel', *Nineteenth-Century Fiction*, 27, 71–80; and Wittig, E. W. (1973), 'Significant Revisions in Trollope's "The Macdermots of Ballycloran" ', *Notes and Queries*, n.s.20, 90–91.

⁵ *Victorian Novelists and Publishers*, p. 134.

⁶ See Curtis, L. P., Jr. (1971), *Apes and Angels: The Irishman in Victorian Caricature*, Washington, D.C., Smithsonian Institution Press; and Newton Abbot, David and Charles.

⁷ *Trollope: The Critical Heritage*, pp. 547, 548, and 549–52 respectively.

⁸ According to T. H. S. Escott, who knew Trollope and wrote his first biography, Carleton was the most important influence. See *Anthony Trollope: His Public Services, Private Friends, and Literary Originals* (1913), London, John Lane; Port Washington, N.Y., Kennikat Press, 1967, pp. 53–4. Sadleir gives further information on Trollope's Irish reading in his *Commentary*, pp. 143–4.

⁹ *Critical Heritage*, p. 553.

¹⁰ Trollope's Irish Fiction' (1973), *Eire: A Journal of Irish Studies*, 9, 97–118 (p. 104).

¹¹ Irwin, M. L. (1926), *Anthony Trollope: A Bibliography*, New York, H. W. Wilson, pp. 24–5.

¹² Nowlan, K. B. (1965), *The Politics of Repeal: A Study in the Relations between Great Britain and Ireland, 1841–50*, London, Routledge & Kegan Paul; Toronto, University of Toronto Press, p. 218. O'Connell's campaign for Repeal of the Union between England and Ireland led to his arrest in 1843 on charges amounting to sedition. He was found guilty in 1844, but although this judgment was later reversed, the Repeal movement never afterwards regained its momentum.

¹³ King, H. G. (1965), 'Trollope's Letters to the *Examiner*', *Princeton University Library Chronicle*, 26, 71–101. Page references to these letters are given in parentheses in my text.

¹⁴ Trollope says that 'the deaths from absolute famine were, comparatively speaking, few', and that deaths from disease 'far outnumbered, probably quadrupled, those which were attributable to starvation' (82). The numbers of deaths attributed to famine were in fact 6058 in 1847 and 21,770 in 1846–51, but there were hundreds of thousands of deaths from disease, and over a million emigrations. See O'Neill, T. P., 'The Administration of Relief', in Edwards and Williams (eds.), *The Great Famine*, pp. 254–5.

¹⁵ *The Irish Crisis* (1848), London, Longman. Trollope was later to take issue with Trevelyan on the subject of competitive examinations for the Civil Service, caricaturing him as 'Sir Gregory Hardlines'. Later still, as his career advanced, Trevelyan became his friend (*Autobiography*, 96).

¹⁶ *The Changing World of Anthony Trollope*, p. 65.

[17] The best account of *The Landleaguers* is by Wittig, E. W., in 'Trollope's Irish Fiction', 109–15.

[18] 10 volumes (1833–42), Edinburgh, William Blackwood; London, T. Cadell, and Edinburgh, n.p., 1816. These sources Trollope acknowledges in his Preface to *La Vendée*, pp. iii–iv. There is a modern edition and translation of the *Memoirs* (1933) by Cecil Biggane, London, Routledge.

[19] Sadleir, M. (ed.) (1923), London, Constable.

[20] 'Merivale's History of the Romans', *Dublin University Magazine*, 37, May 1851, 611–24, and 48, July 1856, 30–47. Both articles were unsigned.

[21] *Victorian Novelists and Publishers*, p. 136.

[22] 'The Civil Service', *Dublin University Magazine*, 46, October 1855, 409–26.

[23] See Arnold, R. (1961), *The Whiston Matter*, London, Hart-Davis, to which I am indebted in what follows.

[24] See Robert Martin's account, to which I am indebted, in *Enter Rumour: Four Victorian Scandals* (1962), New York, Norton; London, Faber, Chapter 3.

[25] 'The Road to Hiram's Hospital: A Byway of Early Victorian History', *Victorian Studies*, 5, 1961, 135–50 (p. 147).

[26] 'Dickens and the Origin of *The Warden*', *The Trollopian*, 2, 1947, 83–9.

[27] See Martin, pp. 182–3, and Best, p. 148.

[28] 'The *Times* Correspondent and *The Warden*', *Nineteenth-Century Fiction*, 21, 1967, 325–6.

[29] *The Victorian Church, Part I* (1966), London: A. & C. Black; New York, Oxford University Press, p. 127.

[30] 'The Road to Hiram's Hospital', 136ff.

[31] I thank John Lucas for drawing the importance of the religious census to my attention.

[32] The Scottish census report was published separately in 1854: it was even more discouraging. See Chadwick, p. 369.

[33] *1851 Census Great Britain: Report and Tables on Religious Worship, England and Wales*, vol. 89 of *Parliamentary Papers, 1852–53*, p. clviii.

[34] *The Victorian Church, Part I*, p. 369.

[35] Sadleir, *Commentary*, pp. 165ff. Trollope's correspondence with Longman was destroyed in the Blitz, but Sadleir's transcripts survive. See *Letters*, p. 24.

[36] *The Victorian Church, Part I*, p. 265.

[37] See Sharp, R. L., 'Trollope's Mathematics in *The Warden*', *Nineteenth-Century Fiction*, 17, 1962, 288–9; and Milne, A., 'The Great Trollope Mystery', *Punch*, 9 July 1980, pp. 56–8.

[38] See Hawkins, S., 'Mr. Harding's Church Music', *ELH: A Journal of English Literary History*, 29, 1962, 202–23; and apRoberts, R. (1971), *Trollope: Artist and Moralist*, London, Chatto & Windus, pp. 34–42; published in America as *The Moral Trollope*, Athens, Ohio, Ohio University Press, 1971. Neither critic, of course, accepts Trollope's claim to artlessness, but both commend his 'realism'.

[39] *Clergymen of the Church of England* (1866), London, Chapman & Hall, p. 28. This work has been published in a modern edition by apRoberts, R. (1974), Leicester, Leicester University Press; New York, Humanities Press.

[40] As P. D. Edwards has recognised in a tough-minded reading of the novel. See *Anthony Trollope: His Art and Scope*, pp. 11–16.

[41] One of the novel's first reviews noted this. See *Critical Heritage*, p. 31.

[42] 'Mr. Harding's Church Music.'

[43] *Critical Heritage*, pp. 534-5.

[44] See Houston, M. 'Structure and Plot in *The Warden*', *University of Texas Studies in English*, 34, 1955, 107-13.

[45] *Victorian Novelists and Publishers*, p. 134.

[46] *Critical Heritage*, p. 534.

[47] See Vincent, J. (1966), *The Formation of the British Liberal Party 1857-1868*, London, Constable, 1966; New York, Charles Scribner's Sons, 1967, pp. 39-47.

[48] *Enter Rumour*, p. 181.

[49] 'Mr. Harding's Church Music', 210.

[50] *Commentary*, pp. 168-9, and *Letters*, p. 24. See note 35, above.

[51] See Hall, N. J. (ed.), *The New Zealander*, pp. xii and xlii.

[52] Hall suggests that 'The Civil Service' was inserted in *The Three Clerks* as the chapter of the same title dropped from all editions after the first, and that the material in 'Trade' may have been used in *The Struggles of Brown, Jones and Robinson*. See *The New Zealander*, pp. xx-xxi.

[53] *Ibid.*

[54] De Tocqueville's *Democracy in America* was first published in an English translation between 1835-40, 4 vols. Trollope's library catalogue, compiled in 1874 and now in the Forster Collection of the Victoria and Albert Museum, indicates that he owned a copy of a one-volume edition.

[55] The *Daily Telegraph*, founded while Trollope was still working on *The New Zealander* on 20 June 1855, made the running for the cheap daily press. See Williams, R. (1961), *The Long Revolution*, London, Chatto & Windus; New York, New York University Press, 1961; Harmondsworth, Penguin Books, 1965, pp. 217-20.

[56] See, for instance, an expression he uses in *The Way We Live Now*, 'we think that we have thought' (II,406), and repeats in *The Prime Minister*, 'he thought that he thought' (I,17).

[57] Sadleir, *Commentary*, p. 169.

[58] Hall (ed.), *The New Zealander*, pp. xii-xiv.

[59] See Hall, p. xxxvii.

Chapter 3

[1] *The New Zealander*, Appendix II, p. 216, and Bodleian Ms. Don. c.9.

[2] *Victorian Novelists and Publishers*, pp. 135-42.

[3] *Letters*, p. 21, 28 June 1854; and Sadleir, *Commentary*, p. 203.

[4] *Critical Heritage*, pp. 103-04.

[5] The best account is in Sutherland, pp. 142-51.

[6] Sadleir, p. 205.

[7] *Victorian Novelists and Publishers*, pp. 148-51.

[8] *Anthony Trollope and His Contemporaries: A Study in the Theory and Conventions of*

Mid-Victorian Fiction (1972), London, Longman; New York: St. Martin's Press, p. 9.

[9] 'The Three Clerks', *Saturday Review*, 4, 1857, 517–18. The review is excerpted in *Critical Heritage*, pp. 55–8.

[10] *Critical Heritage*, p. 98.

[11] Sadleir, *Commentary*, p. 417; Bodleian Ms. Don. c. 10*.

[12] *Critical Heritage*, pp. 56–8.

[13] Bodleian Ms. Don. c.9.

[14] 'Number-length and its Significance in the Novels of Anthony Trollope', *Yearbook of English Studies*, 5, 1975, 178–89 (p. 180).

[15] *Ibid.*, 180–1, 188–9.

[16] *Ibid.*, 186–7.

[17] See Sutherland, *Victorian Novelists and Publishers*, pp. 171–2.

[18] *Is He Popenjoy?* was written in sixteen parts and published in forty; *The Duke's Children* in twenty and published in thirty; and *Mr. Scarborough's Family* in sixteen and published in fifty-six. See Hamer, M. 'Number-length and its Significance', 185, and note 41, below.

[19] The books were *Lotta Schmidt: And Other Stories* (1867), London, Strahan; and *Sir Harry Hotspur of Humblethwaite* (1871), London, Hurst & Blackett. See *Letters*, pp. 196–7, 10 March 1867, p. 277, 18 October 1870; and Sadleir, M. (1928), *Trollope: A Bibliography*, London, Constable; Dawsons of Pall Mall, 1964, pp. 119, 288–9. On an earlier occasion, as he records in his *Autobiography* (p. 289), Trollope had failed to stop publication in three volumes of a novel intended only for two. Sadleir identifies the novel as *The Belton Estate* (*Bibliography*, p. 282), and this is confirmed by Trollope's list of his works in the Bodleian Library (Ms. Don. c.10*), and by the separate list printed by Ray, G. N., 'Trollope at Full Length', *Huntington Library Quarterly*, 31, 1968, 313–40.

[20] *Boswell's Life of Johnson*, Hill, G. B. (ed.) revised and enlarged by Powell, L. F. (1934), 6 vols., Oxford, Oxford University Press, vol. I, p. 72.

[21] See Hall, N. J., 'An Unpublished Trollope Manuscript on a Proposed History of World Literature', *Nineteenth-Century Fiction*, 29, 1974, 206–10. Hall also illustrates the importance to Trollope of order and method in 'Trollope's Commonplace Book, 1835–40', *Nineteenth-Century Fiction*, 31, 1976, 15–25. Geoffrey Harvey has explored Trollope's readings in drama and their influence on his fiction in *The Art of Anthony Trollope*, pp. 17–38.

[22] *Victorian Novelists and Publishers*, p. 149.

[23] What follows is extrapolated from the novel and from Trollope's sketch map of Barsetshire which he drew while writing *Framley Parsonage*, and which is reproduced on the front inside cover of the World's Classics edition of *Barchester Towers*. There is an improved version of the map, with commentary, in Tingay, L. O., 'Mapmaking in Barsetshire', *Trollopian*, 3, 1948, 19–32.

[24] See Hamer, M., '*Framley Parsonage*: Trollope's First Serial', *Review of English Studies*, 26, 1975, 154–70.

[25] 'A Walk in a Wood', *Good Words*, 20, September, 1879, 595–600.

[26] See 'The Civil Service', and the two reviews of Merivale's *History of the Romans*, all in the *Dublin University Magazine* (see notes 20 and 22, Chapter 2, above).

[27] The index of *Trollope: The Critical Heritage*, p. 566, illustrates how frequent this charge was among Trollope's contemporaries. Henry James perhaps puts it best (pp. 525-9, 537-8). Few Trollopians will nowadays concede that Trollope wrote too much, but see Booth, B., *Anthony Trollope: His Life and Art*, pp. 121, 161-4.

[28] 'Three Lost Chapters of Trollope's First Novel.'

[29] 'The Nineteenth Century Three-Volume Novel', *Papers of the Bibliographical Society of America*, 51, 1957, 263-302.

[30] Sadleir, *Commentary*, p. 170.

[31] '*Framley Parsonage:* Trollope's First Serial.'

[32] Bodleian Ms. Don. c.9.

[33] 'Three Lost Chapters of Trollope's First Novel', 79. See also Wittig, E. W. 'Significant Revisions in Trollope's "The Macdermots of Ballycloran"', 90.

[34] I consulted the manuscript and refer to it in what follows by permission of the Carl H. Pforzheimer Library. References to the manuscript are given in my text in the order: manuscript part and page numbers; World's Classics edition volume and page numbers.

[35] See *Autobiography*, pp. 104-05, and *Letters*, p. 57, 13 April 1860. John Sutherland comments interestingly on the image in *Victorian Novelists and Publishers*, pp. 149-51.

[36] Trollope wrote this before he began dictating his novels to his niece, Florence Bland. His only other helper seems to have been John Tilley, his Post Office colleague and brother-in-law. Tilley was his agent with Longman over the corrections to *Barchester Towers* (*Letters*, pp. 25-6, 20 December 1856), and for the proof-reading of *The Bertrams* (pp. 43-5, 2 December 1858, 11 January 1859). Sadleir, *Commentary*, p. 316, records that the manuscript of *The Life of Cicero* is entirely in Rose Trollope's hand. See also note 44, below.

[37] *An Editor's Tales* (1870), London, Strahan, p. 359.

[38] *Anthony Trollope: His Art and Scope*, pp. 57, 107-08.

[39] Ray, G. N., in 'Trollope at Full Length', pp. 339-40, lists thirty-three manuscripts. apRoberts, R., 'Anthony Trollope', in Ford, G. H. (ed.) (1978), *Victorian Fiction: A Second Guide to Research*, New York, Modern Language Association, pp. 143-71, adds that the manuscript of *The Way We Live Now* 'is known to be extant but in limbo', p. 146.

[40] These are *The Claverings*, *The Duke's Children*, *The Eustace Diamonds*, *The Last Chronicle of Barset*, *Miss Mackenzie*, *Mr. Scarborough's Family*, and *Orley Farm*.

[41] The working diary is headed '1056 pages at 250 words', the revised manuscript 'There are 834 pages and 260 words a page'. The latter figures must represent equivalents, as Trollope did not recopy his manuscript and its page numbering is as given in the diary. The manuscript is in the possession of Yale University at the Beinecke Rare Book and Manuscript Library, through whose kind permission I was able to consult it. In what follows references to the manuscript are given in the same way as to that of *Orley Farm* (see note 34, above). Although *The Duke's Children* was published in thirty parts, the manuscript is divided into only eight. This is because Trollope wrote the novel for serial publication either in eight parts or in twenty numbers (later reduced to sixteen). See Bodleian Ms. Don. c.10.

[42] Juliet McMaster argues for the importance of some of the material Trollope

cut, but I think this can be true only in a few instances. See *The Palliser Novels: Theme and Pattern*, pp. 206–07, 229–30.

[43] *Trollope* (1975), London, Macmillan; New York, Charles Scribner's Sons, p. 142.

[44] Sadleir, *Commentary*, p. 316, indicates that the manuscripts of the following novels are partially in the hand of Florence Bland: *Cousin Henry, Kept in the Dark, Dr. Wortle's School, An Old Man's Love, The Fixed Period, Marion Fay, Mr. Scarborough's Family*. Ray, G., 'Trollope at Full Length', 339–40, adds that parts of *Ayala's Angel* and of *Miss Mackenzie*, and also eight pages of *John Caldigate*, are not in Trollope's hand. In the case of *Miss Mackenzie*, the only one of these I have studied, the part in question (MS vol. II, pp. 153–97) looks like a fair copy produced after the novel had been printed. It is a single continuous section, written with few corrections on different paper from the rest of the manuscript, but spliced in directly to the middle of a sentence at the beginning and of a paragraph at the end; and it has no printers' marks.

[45] *Critical Heritage*, p. 471.

[46] *Anthony Trollope: Aspects of His Life and Art*, p. 159.

[47] Sadleir, *Commentary*, p. 428.

[48] As Frank O'Connor says, this is 'an extraordinary example of the way in which Trollope brooded over his creations'. *The Mirror in the Roadway* (1956), New York, Knopf; London, Hamish Hamilton, 1957, p. 179.

Chapter 4

[1] Carroll, D. (ed.) (1971), *George Eliot: The Critical Heritage*, London, Routledge & Kegan Paul: New York, Barnes & Noble, p. 353; Orwell, S. and Angus, I. (1968), *The Collected Essays, Journalism, and Letters of George Orwell*, London, Secker & Warburg; New York, Harcourt, Brace & World, vol. I, p. 454.

[2] Tracy, R. *Trollope's Later Novels*, p. 97, quoting Frith, W. P. (1887–8), *My Autobiography and Reminiscences*, 3 vols., London, Bentley; New York, Harper, vol. I, p. 441. At least one contemporary review compared Trollope and Frith; see *Trollope: The Critical Heritage*, p. 152.

[3] 'The Problem of Structure in Trollope', *Nineteenth-Century Fiction*, 15, 1960, 147–57.

[4] 'Preface to *The Tragic Muse*', in Blackmur, R. P. (ed.) (1934), *The Art of the Novel*, New York and London, Charles Scribner's Sons, p. 84.

[5] See, for instance, Hennedy, H. L. (1971), *Unity in Barsetshire*, The Hague, Mouton; Cohen, J. M. (1976), *Form and Realism in Six Novels of Anthony Trollope*, The Hague, Mouton; McMaster, J., *The Palliser Novels: Theme and Pattern;* Tracy, R., *Trollope's Later Novels*; and Harvey, G., *The Art of Anthony Trollope*.

[6] Samples of Hutton's work on Trollope may be found in *Trollope; The Critical Heritage*. See also the bibliography in Skilton, D., *Anthony Trollope and his Contemporaries*, pp. 160–2, which includes some further attributions.

[7] Review of *Phineas Finn*, Critical Heritage, p. 311.

[8] *Anthony Trollope and his Contemporaries*, pp. 100–25, 140–3.
[9] Review of *The Golden Lion of Granpère, Critical Heritage*, p. 358.
[10] *The Form of Victorian Fiction* (1968), Notre Dame, Indiana, University of Notre Dame Press, p. 123.
[11] Cabinet edition (1877–80), Blackwood, Edinburgh and London, vol. I, ch. 27, p. 403.
[12] Acton, H. B. (ed.) (1972), *Utilitarianism, On Liberty, and Considerations on Representative Government*, London, Dent, 1972; New York, Dutton, 1976, p. 120.
[13] *Collected Essays* (1969), London, Bodley Head; New York, Viking Press, p. 108.
[14] Sadleir, *Commentary*, p. 390. See also Dustin, J. E., 'Thematic Alternation in Trollope', *PMLA*, 77, 1962, 283. Trollope's development of his prototypes is, however, more creative than Dustin allows.
[15] The three short stories were first published in magazines in 1860 and 1861 and reprinted in *Tales of All Countries*, first and second series. 'The Courtship of Susan Bell' is from the first collection, London, Chapman & Hall, 1861; World's Classics series, 1931; 'The Parson's Daughter' and 'The Mistletoe Bough' from the second, London, Chapman & Hall, 1863. Donald D. Stone has commented on Trollope's short stories and some of their links with his novels in 'Trollope as a Short Story Writer', *Nineteenth-Century Fiction*, 31, 1976, 26–47.
[16] See Hagan, J. H., '*The Duke's Children*: Trollope's Psychological Masterpiece', *Nineteenth-Century Fiction*, 13, 1958, 1–21.
[17] See especially *Knots* (1970), London, Tavistock; New York, Pantheon Books.
[18] Cabinet edition, vol. I, ch. 18, p. 274.
[19] *Ibid.*, vol. III, pp. 464–5 ('Finale').
[20] *Critical Heritage*, pp. 131–2.
[21] 'Can You Forgive Him? Trollope's *Can You Forgive Her?* and the Myth of Realism', *Victorian Studies*, 18, 1974, 5–30.
[22] *Ibid.*, 8.
[23] *Critical Heritage*, p. 510. Tony Tanner has commented on this review in '*The Way We Live Now*: Its Modern Significance', *Critical Quarterly*, 9, 1967, 256–71.
[24] 'Can You Forgive Him?', 27.
[25] John Vincent goes so far as to declare: 'The nostalgic idea of great noblemen undertaking office in a spirit of *noblesse oblige* is quite without foundation, for probably at least half the Liberal Cabinet ministers earned more from their official incomes than from their private ones.' (*The Formation of the British Liberal Party*, p. 128.)

Chapter 5

[1] *Robinson Crusoe*, Crowley, J. D. (ed.) (1972), London and New York, Oxford University Press, pp. 46–7, 69, 70 respectively.
[2] *The Rise of the Novel* (1957), London, Chatto & Windus; Berkeley, University of California Press, pp. 296–9.

[3] See, for instance, Edel, L. (1955), *The Psychological Novel, 1900–1950*, London, Hart-Davis; Philadelphia, Lippincott, pp. 19–22. Edel is very well aware, however, that consciousness can only be rendered by means of conventions.

[4] See 'Narrated Monologue: Definition of a Fictional Style', *Comparative Literature*, 18, 1966, 97–112. There is a bibliography in Cohn's extended study, *Transparent Minds: Narrative Modes for Presenting Consciousness in Fiction* (1978), Princeton, Princeton University Press; see also Pascal, R. (1977), *The Dual Voice: Free indirect speech and its functioning in the nineteenth-century European novel*, Manchester, Manchester University Press; Totowa, New Jersey, Rowman & Littlefield, pp. vii–viii. 'Narrated monologue' is the term Cohn prefers to 'free indirect speech'; for reasons given below, I agree. The latter may be defined most simply as a character's speech or thoughts conveyed in his or her own words but in the same tense and person as those of the narrative.

[5] *Die erlebte Rede im englischen Roman des 19. Jahrhunderts*, Schweizer anglistische Arbeiten, 20, Berne, A. Franke, 1948.

[6] *Anthony Trollope and his Contemporaries*, pp. 140–3. John W. Clark also has some remarks on what he calls Trollope's passages of 'psychological analysis'. See *The Language and Style of Anthony Trollope*, pp. 197–201.

[7] *The Dual Voice*, pp. 88–97 (p. 89).

[8] 'Trollope: The Psychological Stream', *On the Novel*, Benedikz, B.S. (ed.) (1971), London, Dent, pp. 3–16.

[9] I thank Professor J. Hillis Miller for calling this passage to my attention. The text is from the first edition, 2 vols., London, Smith, Elder, 1867, I, 99–100. The manuscript, which I have checked through the courtesy of the Beinecke Rare Book and Manuscript Library of Yale University, shows that Trollope introduced corrections which clarify what was probably a passage written straight through in first draft.

[10] Narrative and Dialogue in Jane Austen', *Critical Quarterly*, 12, 1970, 201–29.

[11] 'Trollope: The Psychological Stream', p. 3.

[12] I borrow the terms from Genette, G., 'Time and Narrative in *A la recherche du temps perdu*', in Miller, J. H. (ed.) (1971), *Aspects of Narrative*, New York, Columbia University Press, pp. 93–118.

[13] 'Trollope: The Psychological Stream', p. 16.

[14] Shortly before beginning the novel, Trollope had raised this abuse in *Clergymen of the Church of England*, pp. 97–104. He replied to the attack which greeted his remarks in a letter to the *Pall Mall Gazette* of 24 July 1866, pp. 3–4. This is reprinted in the introduction to Ruth apRoberts' edition of *Clergymen*, pp. 45–8.

[15] The only two substantial discussions of Trollope's style are still Davies, H. S., 'Trollope and His Style', *Review of English Literature*, 1, 1960, 73–85; and Aitken, D., '"A Kind of Felicity": Some Notes About Trollope's Style', *Nineteenth-Century Fiction*, 20, 1966, 337–53.

[16] See, respectively, *Barchester Towers*, pp. 129–30; and *The Bertrams*, vol. 1, p. 279.

[17] *The Dual Voice*, pp. 89–97.

[18] See, for instance, 'On English Prose Fiction as a Rational Amusement', 1870, in *Four Lectures*, pp. 94–124; *An Autobiography*, pp. 184–94; and *Thackeray*, pp. 202–06.

Chapter 6

[1] The two main exceptions are Polhemus, R. M., *The Changing World of Anthony Trollope*, and Halperin, J. (1977), *Trollope's Politics: A Study of the Pallisers and Others*, London, Macmillan; New York, Oxford University Press. Unfortunately Polhemus takes too broad a view to avoid superficiality, while Halperin follows Trollope too far into the trivialities of Society and party politics.

[2] *The English Novel: From Dickens to Lawrence*, p. 86; *The Early Victorians, 1832-1851* (1971), London, Weidenfeld & Nicolson; New York, Praeger, p. 89.

[3] *Trollope: The Critical Heritage*, pp. 69-70.

[4] *Ibid.*, p. 77.

[5] As P. D. Edwards has argued in *Anthony Trollope: His Art and Scope*, pp. 31-2.

[6] *Ibid.*, pp. 35-6.

[7] See Escott, T. H. S., *Anthony Trollope: His Public Services, Private Friends, and Literary Originals*, pp. 3-4.

[8] See Hennessy, J. P. (1971), *Anthony Trollope*, London, Jonathan Cape; Boston, Little, Brown, p. 191; and *An Autobiography*, p. 34.

[9] *The English Novel: From Dickens to Lawrence*, p. 85.

[10] As Arthur Pollard does in *Anthony Trollope* (1978), London and Boston, Routledge & Kegan Paul, pp. 63-4.

[11] James Kincaid, who notices this and other elements of disturbance in *Doctor Thorne* (*The Novels of Anthony Trollope*, pp. 113-20), accepts them rather blandly.

[12] P. D. Edwards notes that *Doctor Thorne* was reissued no fewer than twenty-nine times in Trollope's lifetime – more than twice as many as its nearest rival, *Framley Parsonage* (*Anthony Trollope: His Art and Scope*, p. 55).

[13] See pp. 32-4, above.

[14] *Critical Heritage*, pp. 57-8.

[15] *Ibid.*, p. 77.

[16] Sadleir speaks of the novel's 'sensational perfection' (*Commentary*, p. 375), and P. D. Edwards also rates it highly (*Anthony Trollope: His Art and Scope*, p. 36).

[17] See, for instance, James Kincaid, *The Novels of Anthony Trollope*, and J. M. Cohen, *Form and Realism in Six Novels of Anthony Trollope*.

[18] The estimate is Gordon Ray's, in 'Trollope at Full-Length', 338.

[19] Edwards interestingly suggests that Trollope may have been responding to criticism that had found his emotional range limited. See *Anthony Trollope: His Art and Scope*, p. 107.

[20] *Ibid.*

[21] '"Orley Farm" and Real Fiction', *Nineteenth-Century Fiction*, 8, 1953, 27-41.

[22] See, respectively, Newbolt, Sir Francis (1925), *Out of Court*, London, Philip Allan, pp. 1-73; Adams, '"Orley Farm" and Real Fiction'; Polhemus, *The Changing World of Anthony Trollope*, pp. 76-88; Booth, B.A., 'Trollope's *Orley Farm*: Artistry *Manqué*', in Rathburn, R. C., and Steinmann, M., Jr. (eds.) (1958), *From Jane Austen to Joseph Conrad*, Minneapolis: University of Minnesota Press; London, Oxford University Press, pp. 146-59: Edwards, *Anthony Trollope: His Art and Scope*, pp. 107-13; and Harvey, G., *The Art of Anthony Trollope*, pp. 89-108.

[23] Polhemus, *The Changing World of Anthony Trollope*, p. 84; and Harvey, *The Art of Anthony Trollope*, p. 98.

[24] *Critical Heritage*, p. 149.

[25] See, for example Cockshut, A. O. J., (1955), *Anthony Trollope: A Critical Study*, London, Collins; New York, New York University Press, 1968, p. 168.

[26] *Anthony Trollope: His Art and Scope*, pp. 111-13.

[27] Geoffrey Harvey assumes the apology is ironic (*The Art of Anthony Trollope*, p. 97).

[28] '"Orley Farm" and Real Fiction', 33.

[29] *North America*, vol. I, p. 198.

[30] See especially apRoberts, R., *Trollope: Artist and Moralist*, pp. 45, 52-53, 77.

[31] *Ibid.*, p. 125. The quotation is from *Lotta Schmidt: And Other Stories* (1867), London, Strahan, pp. 324-5. apRoberts also misses out the words 'they are' between 'but' and 'right'.

[32] This is the title of Part II of *Anthony Trollope: A Critical Study*, and it is Cockshut's underlying theme.

[33] *Ibid.*, p. 167.

Chapter 7

[1] *Trollope: The Critical Heritage*, pp. 567-8.

[2] See Roland Barthes, *S/Z*, trans. Miller, R. (1975), London, Jonathan Cape, New York, Hill & Wang, and 'Historical Discourse', in Lane, M. (ed.) (1970), *Structuralism: A Reader*, London, Jonathan Cape; published in America as *Structuralism: An Introduction*, New York. Basic Books, 1970, pp. 145-55; and Miller, J. H., 'The Fiction of Realism: *Sketches by Boz, Oliver Twist*, and Cruikshank's Illustrations', in *Charles Dickens and George Cruikshank* (1971), Los Angeles, California, William Andrews Clark Memorial Library, pp. 1-69; and 'Narrative and History', *ELH: A Journal of English Literary History*, 41, 1974. 455-73.

[3] *Form and Realism in Six Novels of Anthony Trollope*, p. 100. The other books are, respectively, *The Novels of Anthony Trollope, Anthony Trollope: The Artist in Hiding*, and *Anthony Trollope: His Art and Scope*.

[4] *Studies in European Realism*, pp. 92-3.

[5] *Ibid.*, p. 6.

[6] See Garrett, P. K., *The Victorian Multiplot Novel*, pp. 180-220. I would argue, however, that Trollope's interior views express a countervailing sympathy.

[7] 'Anthony Trollope', in *Critical Heritage*, p. 527; *Anthony Trollope's England* (1940), Providence, Rhode Island, Brown University, p. 16; and *Anthony Trollope: The Artist in Hiding*, p. 5.

[8] See, respectively, *Trollope: Artist and Moralist*, and *Anthony Trollope: His Art and Scope* (p. 6).

[9] *The Changing World of Anthony Trollope*, p. 3.

[10] 'Literary Victorians', *Listener*, 89, 22 March 1973, p. 384, from a review of Watson, G., *The English Ideology*.

[11] The word is David Skilton's, in *Anthony Trollope and his Contemporaries*, p. 138.

[12] Epigraph to *Le Rouge et le Noir*, Book I, ch. 13. Stendhal repeats the phrase with slightly different wording in Book 2, ch. 19.

[13] I am indebted to Tony Bennett for his explanation of the concept of ideology in the work of the Russian theorist, Valentin Vološinov. See *Formalism and Marxism* (1979), London and New York, Methuen, pp. 78-9.

[14] Michael Sadleir tells the story in *Trollope: A Commentary*, pp. 242-52. See also *Autobiography*, pp. 160-2.

[15] *Critical Heritage*, p. 280.

[16] *Ibid.*, p. 281.

[17] 'Trollope and His Style.'

[18] See Cooke, A. B. and Vincent, J. (1974), *The Governing Passion: Cabinet Government and Party Politics in Britain, 1885-86*, Brighton, Sussex, Harvester Press; New York, Barnes & Noble, pp. 65, 82-3.

[19] See Pirsig, R. M., *Zen and the Art of Motorcycle Maintenance: An Inquiry into Values* (1974), New York, Morrow; London, Bodley Head, pp. 312-13.

[20] See note 5, above.

[21] *Anthony Trollope: A Critical Study*, pp. 183-5.

[22] *Anthony Trollope: His Art and Scope*, pp. 171 and 169 respectively.

[23] See p. 84, above. The novel's one defender in this respect has been Gordon Ray in 'Trollope at Full Length', 323-5.

[24] I have examined the manuscript, which is in the Taylor Collection at the Firestone Library of Princeton University, through the kindness of Mr. Robert H. Taylor. References in what follows to manuscript and World's Classics text are given in the same form as for *Orley Farm* and *The Duke's Children*, i.e. by the part and page numbers of the manuscript followed by the World's Classics edition page number. It is of interest to note that *Mr. Scarborough's Family* underwent a further revision - or more accurately bowdlerisation - when it first appeared in *All the Year Round*. This was apparently not supervised by Trollope. See Edwards, P. D., 'Trollope and "All the Year Round"', *Notes and Queries*, n.s.23, 1976, 403-05.

[25] *The Victorian Multiplot Novel*, pp. 180-220.

[26] See 'The Lesson of Balzac' in Edel, L. (ed.) (1957), *The House of Fiction*, London, Hart-Davis, pp. 60-85; and 'Honoré de Balzac', in *Notes on Novelists* (1914), London, Dent; New York, Charles Scribner's Sons, pp. 24-43.

[27] E.g. the swimmers in the river at Basle whose freedom contrasts with Lady Glencora's sense of constraint (*Can You Forgive Her?*, ch. 69), or the act of a character balancing on stepping stones to stand for the difficulties of decision (*He Knew He Was Right*, ch. 24).

[28] 'The Way They Lived Then: Anthony Trollope and the 1870s', *Victorian Studies*, 12, 1968, 137-200, p. 188.

[29] *Critical Heritage*, p. 535.

[30] See above, p. 120. Edwards makes this point in *Anthony Trollope: His Art and Scope*, pp. 200-01.

[31] *Ibid.*, p. 202; *Anthony Trollope: A Critical Study*, p. 151.

[32] *Anthony Trollope: Aspects of His Life and Art*, p. 131; *Anthony Trollope: His Art and Scope*, p. 204.

Index